PRAISE FOR *MUSING APPALACHIA*

"Harvey Hughett's books bring back humorous memories of life growing up in Appalachia."

--- *Garland "Buddy" Teague, Brentwood, TN*

"Finally, a book that speaks to the comical side of country folks."

--- *David Britton, Bean Station, TN*

"Harvey Hughett provides a gift to the reader as he looks back on his growing up in an Appalachian culture...The stories and tales of family and friends are enriched by his skilled use of the vernacular tongue, providing humor that molded and shaped family values and traditions and certainly memories to be shared with family and friends!"

--- *"Dr. Glenn Wilde, faculty member in English/American Studies and Dean of Libraries, Utah State University, initiated/directed the Western Writers' Conference and The Fife Conference on Western American Folklore. The Fife Folklore Archives in the Merrill-Cazier Library has become a national treasure for American Folklore and Folk Culture."*

MUSING APPALACHIA
VOLUME 4

LOVE HUNTIN' AND OTHER CRAZY HILLBILLY STORIES

MUSING APPALACHIA
VOLUME 4

Copyright © 2025 by Harvey L Hughett, Jr

All rights reserved.

The scanning, uploading, and distribution of this book without permission is a theft of the author's intellectual property. If you would like permission to use material from the book (other than for review purposes), please contact pioneer45700@gmail.com.

NO AI TRAINING: Without in any way limiting the author's exclusive rights under copyright, any use of this publication to "train" generative artificial intelligence (AI) technologies to generate text is expressly prohibited. The author reserves all rights to license uses of this work for generative AI training and development of machine learning language models.

Cover Design | Book Design and Typesetting
Enchanted Ink Publishing

The text type was set in Times New Roman

ISBN: (E-book)
ISBN: (Paperback)

Thank you for your support of the author's rights.

Author Website

This book is dedicated to Cousin Imogene, Uncle Andrew, Uncle Bryant, Uncle Nathan, Mamaw, and my father for sharing family photos and stories about old-timers and the bizarre things they experienced.

OTHER TITLES BY HARVEY HUGHETT

Whimsical Observations about Hillbillies
Wrestling with Life in the Flatlands
Field Diamonds, Granny Women, and Yondering
Love Huntin' and Other Crazy Hillbilly Stories
Stories of Mischief, Moonshiners, and Hot Rods

Contents

CRAZY RELATIVES AND WHERE MY STORIES COME FROM ... 1
THE JAY BIRD BOYS TALK TRASH ... 4
THE SNUGGLE INN HALF-STAR HOTEL ... 13
A CHRISTMAS VISION THE PREACHER COULDN'T UNSEE ... 22
THE JAY BIRD BOYS GIT DRUNKER THAN SKUNKS ... 26
APPALACHIAN BOYS WHIZZING GAME ... 34
A STRANGE HILLBILLY LOVE STORY ... 37
AINT BERTHY CASTS HER LOVE SPELL ... 43
GITTIN DADDY'S PERMISSION ... 51
THE WEDDIN' CEREMONY ... 57
HILLBILLY WEDDING PARTY OF THE DECADE ... 62
FIRST NIGHT JITTERS AND THE CLIMAX ... 69
POSSUM ROULETTE AND COONHOUND MADNESS ... 73
HOW MANY TEATS ON A POSSUM? ... 80
THE HILLBILLY SUNSHINE CAFÉ AND FEED STORE ... 86
ZELBERT GITS CORNERED INTO MARRYIN' ... 105
PREACHER KESTER HITCHES ZELBERT AND OCIE MAE ... 109
OCIE MAE AND ZELBERT GIT CHIVAREED ... 112
ZELBERT WANTS TO BE A PREACHER ... 117
THE GHOSTS OF PANTHER HOLLER ... 123
ZELBERT AND OCIE MAE GIT INTO THE DIRT ... 128
THE WAMPUS CAT STARTED IT ALL ... 135

OCIE MAE TAKES UP FLINTSNAPPIN'	143
OCIE MAE AND ZELBERT HONEYMOON AT OPRYLAND	150
OCIE MAE GITS SIDEWAYS WITH THE PREACHER	163
THE GREAT BULLS GAP MULE RACE	169
FRANCES'S DINER IN HAZARD, KENTUCKY	182
JEZEBEL AT THE CHURCH POTUCK DINNER	184
CRAZY HILLBILLY PREACHER STORIES	191
PLUMGRANNIES	207
ZELBERT NICODEMUS MUSES APPALACHIA	211
THE HIDDEN CABIN ON ROCKY TOP MOUNTAIN	220
GRANDMA'S LESSON ON CUSSING	233
PREACHER JAMES JETHRO HUGHETT AND THE GOSPEL TENT	236
THE JAY BIRDS BOYS DEBATE CORNBREAD	242
THE CORNBREAD AND BEANS SHOWDOWN	247
THEY HUNG AN ELEPHANT!	255
INTERESTING AND CRAZY APPALACHIAN NAMES	261
SOUTHERN YAUPON TEA: THE FIRST JOLT DRINK	263
A NOISY, SPEED DATING FREE-FOR-ALL	266
MAMAW'S HILLBILLY CAVIAR	271
BEING SOUTHERN, SOUTHERNESS, AND APPALACHIA	277
HILLBILLY ELEGY, "Y'ALL, ARE THEY KILLING US SOFTLY?"	281

MUSING APPALACHIA
VOLUME 4

LOVE HUNTIN' AND OTHER CRAZY HILLBILLY STORIES

HARVEY HUGHETT

CRAZY RELATIVES AND WHERE MY STORIES COME FROM

I wrote this collection of humorous short stories with the intent of bringing to life eccentric and endearing characters that reflect Appalachia's unique culture, folklore, and traditions as I knew them. I don't have to make up much in the way of stories.

The stories are generally about authentic people with a little exaggeration. I was born into a dirt-poor family and raised in the mountains of rural East Tennessee. We had a big garden, a two-holer outhouse, and no electricity or running water. Our family raised and sold skunks to city folks as pets.

People think I'm kidding about me and Daddy being good "skunkers." We caught a hundred or so before I started dating and gave it up. I write a lot about skunks. I know my stink! I lived the things I write about. Poor folks do what they have to do. Nevertheless, we found humor in the hard times.

Some people have trouble believing stories about my family, but they're 80% the way they happened. I cut myself some slack on the other 20% because I'm 80 years old, and my memory is starting to go a little crazy. I wouldn't have anything to write about if I didn't have crazy kinfolks. My Momma says it's related to Hillbilly genetics, but that's a topic I don't want to get into. I've traced the family tree enough to know when to back off.

If you look closely, the general area of Appalachia probably has the highest ratio per capita of nuts, screwballs, religious zealots, and eccentrics in the country. If you don't believe me, just take a road trip and visit the dead-end dirt roads of Appalachia and rub shoulders with the locals. It wouldn't take long before you could write your own book! Of course, if you drive a fancy car and wear brand-name clothes, getting to know people will be much more difficult. Mountain people are suspicious of flatlanders.

My great-uncle, Bryant Gulley, is from my Mamaw's side of the family... the "more adventurous side." He was known throughout the area as an herbal doctor and sometimes referred to himself as "Dr. Gulley." His specialty recipe was a concoction made up of ginseng and other wild root extracts, heavily infused with moonshine. Was it good stuff? Let me put it this way. He had 14+1 kids, the last one fathered when he was 82. I rest my case. Momma always referred to him as "that old goat."

Then, there's Bryant's brother, Nathan. He was a moonshiner from the get-go in life, but he wasn't too bright because he too frequently got caught making likker and spent over fifteen long and hard years as a mandatory resident at Brushy Mountain State Penitentiary in Petros, Tennessee. I visited there last summer, and from what I saw, anyone would have to be flat crazy to risk going to that place. Ironically, it's now a museum, and, get this, it's also a moonshine distillery! If he were still around, I'm unsure whether Nathan would apply for a job there or be enraged at having been locked up.

I write about other kinfolks, too, but a few of them (or their kids/grandkids) get pretty upset about some of the things I write, so I am compelled to disguise their identities with fictitious names. Ocie Mae and Zelbert are two examples.

The old guys on the Jay Bird Store front porch are also based on real people that I knew. great-uncle Andrew Hughett was one of them, and, as a kid, I'd sit on the edge of the store's porch and listen to the old men's wild tales…and I'm sure that some of them were true. I took a lot of ribbing because I was a kid, but I learned a lot of really interesting stuff you don't find in books…and some stuff my momma would have whupped Uncle Andrew's butt for if she'd known.

My grandpa, my great-grandpa, and my great-great-grandpa were old-time mountain preachers who could shake the church rafters and make gospel tent walls flap like in a lightning storm when they were wound up. Several other close relatives were also preachers, and none of them were seminary-educated. Seminary-trained ministers who preached in the hills were viewed with suspicion. Appalachians wanted preachers who were inspired by God, not just reading something they'd learned from books or college teachers. The belief was that the less intelligent the preacher was, the better, because he wouldn't let his own worldly thoughts mess up God's message. My Papaw was a popular preacher, and it helped that he could hardly read.

I also write about other relatives and friends who led interesting lives. Most were God-fearing people who occasionally experienced "glitches" in life. I write about the more interesting and quirky anomalies.

THE JAY BIRD BOYS TALK TRASH

All across Appalachia, when the weather is good, older men gather on the porches of country stores and talk, or, when the weather is bad, they congregate around a pot-bellied stove inside. That's the way it was at the Jay Bird Country Store near Morristown, Tennessee when I was growing up.

The store's owner was OK with it as long as the guys obeyed a few basic rules: No cussin, no spittin' on the floor, and they had to buy something. Of course, the guys had to eat and buy chewing tobacco, so the third requirement was easy. The first two requirements could be problems.

All the Jay Bird Boys were in their 80s and in pretty good physical health, although the condition of their minds was always in question. They'd known each other since their youth and would often talk about the old times, what was happening in their neighborhood, who would win the next election, and so on. As you might suspect, the conversations sometimes got interesting when certain topics came up, such as who had the best coon dog, the smartest mule, or the best joke. Discussions were especially interesting when someone brought the others up to date on juicy neighborhood relationships or what a suspected errant preacher might be up to. In one form or another, women and/or mules happened to sneak into the conversations about every other hour, sometimes in the same sentence. They didn't talk much about cars or television because none of them had ever owned a car or a TV. To keep their hands busy, they whittled on cedar sticks with their knives and never stopped arguing about which brand was the best (Editor's note: It's *Hen and Rooster* Brand).

If you have ever wondered what old geezers sat around talking about, the paragraphs below will give you an idea. On a typical day, the following would frequently crop up.

For example, one feller would say, "You know, we wuz young and crazy, but we had fun, didn't we?" That would be the signal for someone else to respond with, "Yeah, do you remember that time that Nathan Gulley got hog-nosed and tied a stick of dynamite to a buzzard and turned hit loose in town?" That always got laughs. Each time the story was told, the more interesting it got.

Then another would say, "I remember when we wuz swimmin' down in Bent Creek near whar hit runs into the Chucky River, and some girls stole all our clothes. Did any of y'all ever figger out who did that? Hit's a good thang we didn't have no shoes, or they'd uv stole them, too. I 'spect they's all old and got grandkids by now. I clearly recomember that hit wuz a long walk home and us widout no clothes and havin' to hide in the bushes and all."

Then, someone would notice the weather and comment that the sky used to be much bluer in the old days or "Hit rained harder back in them days." Then, they'd all peer at the sky with their wrinkled faces and think about the years that had passed, the joys and pains they'd shared, and all the crazy things going on in today's crazy world. And their conversation would drift on to another topic.

They may have been slow to move, but their eyes sparkled for the most part, and their minds could still dredge up some humorous tidbits. They were friends. They had bonded years ago, and even though they occasionally fought loud enough that the store owner had to kick them out, they loved each other and always smiled and shook hands when they left after a long day's session of jawin.

Occasionally, I had a chance to sit on the porch with them or around the stove inside and listen. I was just a kid, so I wasn't allowed to say much, which was fine by me because it was intimidating to be surrounded by guys with such broad wisdom. I learned a lot about the ways of the world from them...along with some nice stories. I'll include a few to give you a better idea of the diversity of conversations they had.

Delroy once mentioned that he'd found out that Berthy Hughett had made an anniversary quilt for Ocie Mae and Zelbert Nicodemus. The design was the traditional "Liberated Wedding Ring" quilt block design. It was made of material from old clothes, sheets, and flour sack material that Ocie had been collecting since they'd gotten married. Jake asked, "Delroy, why in tarnation would you bring up such a boring thing as quilts here among guys like us when we could be discussing somethin' interestin'?" Pinkie also put in his two bits by expounding what a dumb idea it was because "Heck! They couldn't afford no weddin' ring, and because they' uz married, they shore in heck wasn't liberated!" Delroy was ready for that response and wryly mentioned that the quilt was "extry special" because, in honor of their marriage, some of the quilt blocks were made from Ocie's bloomers and Zelbert's underwear." You can guess where the conversation went from there. On the porch, intimate conversations weren't forbidden but were shared in hushed tones.

To move away from a growing topic that might get them thrown out of the store, Jake asked, "Has anyone uv y'all seen that speckled, brindle cat what's only got one eye? I want you boys to know that I DID NOT dump hit off at one of you'all's houses! But I will say that whoever dropped that poor thing off on the night of November 13th must have been inspared. They had to uv knowed that one of yore wives would take pity and start feedin' hit. The fur on hits rear half will eventually grow back if you nurse hit. I ain't never seen that cat, but I'm told that it's not really mange. You can tell if you look real close. Unfortunately, hits tail may not grow back but you never know. Whoever would drop off a fine cat like that ought to be shot! I heard it was a purebred."

Pinkie wanted to know what he meant by "purebred." Jake replied that the cat's daddy reportedly was a genuine Persian and that someone had dumped it on his back porch just a few days before at about 8 p.m. That conversation went nowhere, but it was a sure bet the cat would soon find its way back to Jake's house.

Then, Delroy asked if anyone knew if Ida Mae had finally quit drinking. Jake said he'd heard she'd taken to drinkin' something new that Bryant Gulley had mixed up from his crazy herbs and whatnot. Everyone knew that "whatnot" implicated Nathan Gulley, a close relative known to make medicine-grade "preservatives" made from corn. Andrew Hughett commented that it must be some major kind of effective medicine because he'd seen her guzzling the stuff straight from a fruit jar, and then she'd burp louder than a Frenchman. No one had heard a Frenchman burp before, and Pinkie offered that maybe a Frenchwoman like Miz Kitty would know the answer. Then, before anyone could respond, he added, "Do you think that Miz Kitty really skinny dips in that pond of her'n uv a night? Has any of you'all been up thar?"

Jake was quick to warn that it was rumored that her husband Squint had once killed a man and might not take lightly to such a question about his attractive wife, so the conversation drifted to the mountain etiquette of passing fruit jars around to friends. Andrew said the practice of sharing saved on "warshin'" so many dishes."

Then someone asked if they thought the new woman they'd hired at the Bulls Gap Feed Store and Deli was hired because of her looks or because her daddy bought a lot of feed. No one knew the answer to that puzzle, but Aint Berthy (as everyone called her) had once suggested that the woman probably was Jake's Second Cousin, "thrice removed", that is, divorced three times. Jake said he'd rather not talk about his family's private life but offered that Berthy had offered to check with her crystals and find out for sure if they were related or not. In any case, none of the boys dared get close to Berthy for fear she'd throw a hex on 'em like she did on the delivery guy at the feed store. No one was fond of stuttering.

The conversation then drifted to Leroy (May the Devil bless him), who was still remodeling his trailer after fourteen years. His intent was to enclose the bottom with a skirt so the chickens could stay warm. Jake said, "You probably remember, he's the one whose girlfriend had eight kids out of wedlock by twelve different men and whose genealogy is going to be a huge mess to untangle. I heared that he just remodeled the outside... the trailer, not the girlfriend...although she is in serious need of some eye shadow and a brain. Offhand, everything else appears to be functioning OK."

Then he added, "By the way, do any of y'all have a use for a three-legged pit bulldog? Hit wandered into my yard shortly after that ole stray cat appeared. Free delivery if you furnish the cage. I have a rope and pepper spray. Him and the cat make an entertaining pair. Hit's fun watching the cat try to chase hits tail. That reminds me of an "acquaintance's girlfriend"; only the cat has more kids, but no one faults her for not trying, given the neighborhood she lives in.

Jake then said, "Did I tell you all that Ida Mae can burp the Star-Spangled Banner? Patriot, her! Ha ha! I'm extremely proud of that woman! She amazes me. I know, I know...you are probably still holding to your claim that, with a family-size pot of pinto beans and a jar of Mountain Dew, your wives might be able to outperform her. That would be unfair, however, since Ida Mae knows how to read music. I wonder if she can do Country/Western? That's an entertaining thought, but I still say it could be dangerous."

Then, the conversation again shifted back to house cats. Pinkie claimed to be an expert on cats and explained that "If cats are not really happy and are just tolerating the moment, they'll ignore you and might scratch you if you mess with them. However, if they sticks their tail straight up in the air, hit means they is delighted to be headin' to the food bowl. You won't see a cat's happy tail on any other occasion."

He continued, "Suppose the tail snaps and whups crazy-like back and forth. In that case, hit means that they is really mad and waitin' for the right moment to get even with someone for bothering them. If you has one of them disadvantaged tailless cats, yore out of luck telling their mood, but you'll be right 90% of the time if assumes they'd like to harm you if given the opportunity. Cats is easier to understand than humans because most people don't have much in the way of a tail to wag. However, I saw a few exceptions to this the last time I was in Nashville."

Then, he gave a warning. "As a comparatively tailless human, I ain't recommendin' trying to communicate with yore cat with yore tail. You could end up in the looney bin if yore neighbors see you talking with yore butt. And it would just irritate the cat. You might not think cats is watchin' you carefully, but if you look close, even when they appears to be sleepin', one eye is always slightly cracked open and taking in their surroundings. And remember, if you ever git romantic, the cat's always watchin'."

And another warnin': "I probably don't has to tell you that cats is curious, playful, and equipped with razor-sharp teeth and claws that can rip. I has a friend whose name I ain't goin' to divulge, but one day, old Nathan Gulley had worked hard all day and come home all wore out from workin' in the woods. He took a shower and fell dead asleep nekkid as a jaybird sprawled out on his bed. His curious cat was not sleepin' but saw something very interesting to pounce on that reminded him of a mouse. After an innocent lack of judgment and a quick leap, that house cat instantly became an outside cat, but one with a smile on his maw. If you know what the word 'maw' means, that unfortunate event will take on added meaning."

When I found out why Nathan was limping, I reminded him that he was fortunate that his eyelids weren't wiggling. Nathan wasn't in no mood for joking. Yes, they ain't no doubt about it. Cats is cute!"

Jake moved to a new topic, "Boys, I have to tell you. I'm gittin' old, but I can still cut the mustard. I've been thanking about buying a hammer, a screwdriver, and a pair of pliers and taking up gunsmithin'. Do you think they's enuff work around here in the hills to keep me busy? I have an idear for a new gun caliber. I'd call hit the 23 Caliber Jaker Special. When my daddy died, he left me a full case of dynamite that I could use for loadin' the shells with powder. By my calculations, hit would be a humdinger load for groundhogs. They's a guy over to Mosheim who says he'll give me his trade secrets and learn me all about gunsmithin' for $16.75. I think I'm on to somethin', but first, I need to borry some money for the lessons. Any takers? I'd work on yore guns fur free. I don't take checks."

Nobody picked up on the gunsmithin' idea, but they suggested checking with Lynbo Webb to see what he thought. Lynbo arguably was the most intelligent man in the county. He once had a hernia and, after consulting a Sears Roebuck Catalog, fashioned a support truss out of a rubber car innertube. Lynbo had a good head on his shoulders and always had good advice.

Then, the conversation drifted back to Ida Mae's last husband. Ida Mae married him to civilize him and tried hard to give the old rascal a much-needed education in "personal improvement." She'd been working on him during six long years of marrriage. Unfortunately, he is now probably even more of a swindler, double-dealing, dishonest man than he ever was before. She got him to attend church once or twict, but his conversion didn't last long. When the collection plate got passed around, Darla told Delroy's wife that she saw him pull two dollars out of it."

This started the conversation on religion, a topic that frequently got them tossed out of the store. Andrew asked if anyone was attending the big tent revival they were holding over at Johnson City. The rumor was that the preacher was tired of other ministers claiming to heal the sick, so he was going to one-up them all and raise the dead.

Jake, the sanest of the group, said, "If I wuz that preacher, I'd be keerful. Iffen he don't come through with his claim, hiz name ain't goin' to be on the roll when hit's called up yonder."

The day was getting late when Pinkie asked, "Did you'all hear 'bout that 96-pound catfish I caught in the Chucky River last week? It's true, boys, I ain't lying this time."

Old Country Store Where Tales Were Told (Photo by Author)

Jake, putting a new chaw of Lame Mule Tobacco in his mouth, said, "Friends, I'm gittin tard. I think I'll go home, sit down, and spit for a spell.

So, when you see a bunch of old guys sitting on a porch somewhere and jawin', you now have an idea of what they talk about. That said, one last question needs some consideration: "Do you think Appalachia has more screwballs, crazy people, and everyday nuts than anywhere else in the entire universe, or does it just seem like that? Read on, and you'll find out.

THE SNUGGLE INN
HALF-STAR HOTEL

The Saturday after Christmas was always a big day for folks from the hills around Bulls Gap, Tennessee. It was the time of year when stores offered half-off prices, and a festive spirit still lingered in the air. The women would fix up better than usual, and the menfolk attempted to make up for giving lame Christmas gifts to their loved ones or make a new attempt to attract someone who might be considered marriageable material. It was an exciting time of the year, and people wanted to start it off right.

Ocie Mae Sutterfield had been saving money to buy a long-coveted bottle of perfume. She'd never have considered such a purchase until she married Zelbert and moved in with him and his beloved herd of hogs. He claimed the porkers smelled like money, but she never let up, claiming they smelled like shayt. She hoped the perfume would help.

Byant Gulley delighted in the new year because most people wanted to start off with a good attitude. Since he was in the business of selling herbal tinctures and medicines that altered one's perspective on the world (or the opposite sex), sales always surged at that time of year. Herbal elixirs that promised to improve vigor and good interpersonal relationships were especially popular. He vehemently claimed that his "prescriptions" even helped cure rheumatism and could put lead in the dullest of pencils... "but only if used properly." Of course, people being people, not many remembered the fine print instructions on anything and just chugged his stuff down, thinking that if three drops under the tongue were good, gulping down a tablespoon would give them an extra advantage. He also claimed that his "holiday special mix" could result in wise and stable relationships, cleanse one's body of negative energy, and enhance one's love life.

If you wanted something that would promote fidelity and protect you from heartbreak and betrayal in romantic relationships, he would refer you to Aint (Aunt) Berthy and her crystals. Bryant and Berthy were devout Christians, but they had differing views on crystals and competing ailment cures.

Due to a non-disclosure agreement, I can't give you details on the processing of Bryant's favorite prescription. But I can tell you that critical components of Potion # 9 included juices squeezed from lavender, rosemary, ginger, creeping Charlie, mullein, spotted wintergreen, and a liberal dose of his mystery ingredient, along with "a little extry stuff from the woods above Panther Holler." Coincidentally, Nathan Gully had one of his copper stills located up Panther Holler. Even though he didn't use copper much anymore, he continued to craft the batches from locally produced Jimmy Red dent corn, and they were always of premium quality.

Bryant only mixed this after-Christmas recipe once a year because it required a lot of roaming the steep hills and digging herbs, some of which were very scarce and had to be collected at different times of the season. I also wish I could tell you what the "mystery ingredient" was, but he didn't trust me with the information. But I will tell you that he went to his grave with a grin on his face, having lived to a ripe old age and having fathered fourteen "plus one" children. The "plus one" child was the contribution of a no-longer-friendly neighbor woman who liked his elixirs.

Nathan Gully also loved the week-after-Christmas atmosphere in town because many of the men were depressed by seeing their year-long savings drained, and they bought more hooch than usual to drown out their sorrows. If he had a good corn year, and the revenooers had a lousy catching year, that was always a good combination. Nathan was proud of his product and openly boasted, "I don't make no mean likker."

The Bulls Gap general store owner disliked that part of the season because people spent much of their money in the larger towns buying fancy stuff he didn't stock. Money was always tight, and people would squeeze a penny so tight that Abraham Lincoln would pee his pants.

Ever the entrepreneur, Booker T had accidentally won some money in a game of questionable chance and saw an opportunity to make "big money" after his momma died. He inherited an old five-bedroom house on Bulls Gap's main street and went to great lengths to turn it into a hotel. It wasn't much to look at, but it was strategically located, and, at that time, it was the only budget lodging in town, with an emphasis on "really low" budget. He figured that business would boom, given the tight money situation and people having little choice but to stay at his place. Hoping to attract only quality customers, he named it the "Snuggle Inn Half-Star Hotel." The old building was extraordinarily flammable, and he couldn't afford fire extinguishers. He didn't want to take any chances, so he put cigarette ashtrays in every room with "No Smoking" carefully painted on the bottoms of each ashtray. Hoping to attract good, honest lodgers, he put a sign on the front door, "No Smokin', No Likker, and No Whorin'." Booker T was a quality man.

When he opened for the post-holiday season, the Half-Star Hotel wasn't quite finished. He planned to use the profits from the first season to complete the small details that didn't have to be done but would add a nice touch to the rooms, such as installing doors on the bathrooms. However, to his credit, he had hung curtains in every room, although some opened to just a blank wall in the "privacy rooms." If the clients wanted air conditioning, he'd rent them a room with a window that opened to the outside. Two bathrooms were oddly shaped, and the toilet paper rolls were located out of convenient reach across the room, but he was working on a plan to rectify that. He had a stroke of luck when he purchased a bulk pack of ten cardboard pictures to hang on the walls. He hung two of them in each room. Two in the bedroom and two in the bathroom. All the prints were identical, of two cows leering out of a faux wood frame. He felt that the bovine images in a classy hotel in Bulls Gap, with the lovable name of Snuggle Inn, were appropriately matched.

This holiday season turned out to be a good one. Booker T offered free transportation to Morristown for after-Christmas shoppers who would either stay at the Half-Star Hotel or make a deposit for a future reservation. He had to recoup part of his investment to buy and install used carpet in the rooms. He was sparing no conveniences!

It was with great reluctance that women who knew Booker T would frequent any sort of business he had a hand in. However, because very few hill folk owned cars, the transportation offered was attractive. There was also a glimmer of hope that the hotel accommodations would be acceptable to out-of-towners. Most local couples were taking a jug of Clorox with them, just in case.

Promptly at 8 a.m. on the first Saturday of the month after Christmas, Booker and two friends loaded their cars with eager people headed for Morristown. He would make two stops: The Parks Belk Store, which is on the corner of Main and Henry Streets, and the Stockyards, which are just outside of town. Most of the women went to the former, where they slowly dispersed to other stores around town, and the men eagerly headed to the stockyards.

A few of the men disembarked at Parks Belk so they could walk up the street to the pool halls. They were busy places, the Sportsman and Speck's Place being two. The owner of the Sportsman was reputed to be a gambler and bookie. I won't mention his name for fear of a visit in the night. A high school friend's father owned the more respectable Speck's. His friends called him Speck, but that wasn't his real name. There was also another pool hall frequented by the Black community, but I can't remember its name. Sometimes, a couple of my darker sheep kinfolks would slip into the Black-owned pool hall via the back door in the alley. They did this for two reasons. One, there was less chance of being recognized by someone who knew his preacher, and two, they had sympathy for the Blacks. At that time, there were separate drinking fountains and back door entrances that were labeled "Coloreds Only" for certain businesses and government buildings.

When the mountain folk came into town, some people sneered and called them rednecks and hillbillies. Being treated like a minority gave them a feeling of some kinship with their black brothers, and, in a subtle kind of friendly protest, they would often drink from the "Negros Only" fountains and use the back doors.

There were Parks Belk department stores in Morristown, Johnson City, Bristol, and Clarksville. They sold a variety of merchandise, including clothing, home goods, cosmetics, shoes, and jewelry. I remember buying my first pair of shoes there. It was fun. I put my feet in a machine that x-rayed my feet, and I could see my bones. The salesman used this to custom-fit shoes to my feet. Of course, the government shuts down practical things, and you never see these machines anymore.

The Parks Belk in Morristown was also a popular social hub for the area, sometimes hosting dances, concerts, and civic meetings. They even sold camping and other gear for Boy Scouts.

The Stockyards offered something for everyone, not just the men. Some women avoided the yards because of the class of men that often congregated there, my great-uncle Nathan Gulley being one. He sold moonshine from the trunk of his car to regular customers. If he didn't know you, he didn't acknowledge your existence. He also ignored the women and preachers who mocked or sneered at him.

Of course, farmers would bring livestock to the yards to sell and buy, but the broader attractions were the other activities. Local musicians and wannabe Nashville greats would perform and play bluegrass, gospel, and country tunes on various instruments. Eventually, these impromptu activities developed into "The Stockyard Opry" and gained a broader regional following. When people started performing rock and roll music and shaking their butts around, they lost some of the stricter mountain folks. My grandpa, Rev. J. E. Hughett, would not go there, although his brother, Andrew, was a regular at the whittlin' and talkin' sessions with the old men. Even though he didn't drink or chew, he fit in. He was a regular until he died at age 98.

Eventually, all this developed into *The Stockyard Heritage Festival*, featuring live music, arts and crafts, historical exhibits, children's activities, and more. Of course, when I was growing up, everything there was smaller and more comfortable. As a youth, I spent a lot of Saturdays at the stockyards. I was most interested in listening to the old guys tell tall tales about the "good ole days." They'd sit around whittlin' and spitting tobacco and spinning tales, some of which I can't get out of my head no matter how hard I try. I was also amazed to see the wide variety of fish that locals brought to sell. I remember a massive catfish from the Nolichucky River that was so large that I could put my head in its mouth. I wish I had a photo of that, but we didn't own a camera.

I also enjoyed the flea market, where you could trade or buy a wide variety of items, including garden produce, canned goods, knives, guns, traps, antiques, clothes, food, herbs, and practically anything else imaginable. I got two of my best coon hounds at the stockyards. The Bluetick was a guaranteed "stepbrother" to the state tree-dog champion. I traded a pocket watch for him. Both the watch and that hound ran too slow to be very good at their function. However, the Redbone I traded for made up the difference. I loved that hound.

As you gather by now, the stockyards and downtown events were serious social events as much as practical shopping opportunities. When people would run into their hill folk neighbors, they'd always make a note to think of a compliment of some kind. To avoid embarrassing some of my relatives, I'll be careful and attempt to avoid some names here.

That said, Uncle Bryant garnered his share of compliments from the kind women in the crowd who dared approach his spread of herbal wares. A few nicer comments were: "Mister Gulley, I have to hand it to you. You is way smarter than you looks." His response to this kind of compliment was to say, "Thanky, Miz XX. I has to tell you, yore so good at making yore face up with all those eye shadders and sech, you should be a perfessional. And I notice that you've lost so many dad-blamed pounds of weight, I didn't recognize you. I liked yore old look better. You always wuz a looker. And, by the way, I have a special on an herbal cure for yore shortcomin's. I'll give you two-for-one 'cause it looks like you gonna need hit." Few people could come out on top when talking with Bryant Gulley. However, Miz XX did pretty well when she accused Bryant of being a "smart-arse" and "uxorious." That caught him off guard, and he returned his attention to selling herbal elixirs. He also made a mental note to check the preacher's dictionary and see what uxorious meant. Given the source, he suspected it might not be complementary, but maybe she was making a pass at him?

Soon, the day in town was over, and Booker T and his boys picked up the shoppers and returned them safely to Bulls Gap. Those who had booked a room in the new Snuggle Inn Half-Star Hotel were in for an experience, but not quite what they anticipated. I'll give you an example.

Nathan Gully, the local moonshiner, who some people considered a ne'er-do-well, had been married for a dozen years and just happened to be out of prison on this particular holiday. His wife (whose name I'll suppress, her poor soul) was glad to have her man back in town, bringing in much-needed money for the family again. His last stint at the Brushy Mountain "Gray Bar Hotel" had been hard on the family. The marriage wasn't broken, but it had some cracks that needed repairing. On the surface, she thought that a few days in the Snuggle Inn Half-Star Hotel might just be the ticket.

At first, Nahan argued against the idea, saying that the still on the mountain needed to have the fire stoked up and business cooking again. But, like many men, he gave in when confronted with reason and threats of being forced to sleep in the smokehouse. The thought also occurred to him that there might be a silver lining or two in the general idea. He'd sold all his liquid inventory that day and had some spare cash in his pocket for a bit of frivolity. Nathan was generally a serious man on a mission to craft the best product in East Tennessee. Still, sometimes he'd let his guard down, as the revenooers well knew.

He'd met Popcorn Sutton and considered him a show-off grandstander. Nathan wasn't jealous of the old moonshiner, but he did resent losing some of his business to nearby Cocke County. Life would have been better for Nathan had Popcorn been apprehended more often.

In any case, he had sweet thoughts of a nice soft bed with a genuine mattress instead of the hard thing he shared with his spouse on the mountain. In anticipation, his wife, on the other hand, talked in some detail about things like heartfelt conversations, quality time, emotional intimacy, trust-building, rekindling the spark of romance that had died while he was away, finding common ground and shared goals, being willing to accept each other's flaws and strengths, and starting a new phase in their relationship. Overwhelmed, Nathan didn't understand a thing she was saying, but he picked up on the part about laughing and playing together on the new bed Booker T bragged about and its possible therapeutic effect.

I won't go into detail about their evening and night's climactic events, but I will say that after a tiring day in town and enduring some of the heartfelt stuff his wife was crowing about, it wasn't long before they drifted into dreamland and were snoring.

At about midnight, noises started coming from the room above theirs. It was evident that a couple was having a domestic dispute over who had used up the last of the tobacco. However, it wasn't long before things quieted down, and Nathan and his wife were again "snuggling inn," just as Booker T had calculated.

At about 3 a.m., they were again jolted awake by loud and unusual noises. They sounded like bellows and were followed by terrible smells that came through the cracks in the wall. A bunch of Hells Angels bikers had checked into the room next to theirs. Thinking they might be under attack, Nathan charged into the hallway in his tighty-whiteys, but it was empty. After about an hour, all got quiet, and they figured the bikers had left. Unfortunately, their room now smelled like Nathan's great-aunt's house. Once things had calmed down, they again drifted back to sleep.

After what felt like a never-ending night, daylight came into the room from under the door. It was time to pack up and watch the sunrise over glorious Bulls Gap. Overall, it had been a wonderful stay, and the cost of the Snuggle Inn Half-Star Hotel was almost worth it.

A CHRISTMAS VISION
THE PREACHER COULDN'T UNSEE

Celebrating Christmas in the mountains and hollers around Bulls Gap, Tennessee, wasn't much different from what was happening in other parts of Appalachia. There was always a blend of old and new traditions, reflecting rich Appalachian culture. For even the most curmudgeonly of people, the season tended to bring out their best. Below are some things I remember…and how newlywed Ocie Mae's Christmas gift backfired. Monies were scarce in the hills, but people everywhere did as best they could with what was available.

Most traditions revolved around the birth of the Christ child, although Santa Claus and other flatland traditions were making inroads. Bible readings and stockings with candy and nuts were pretty well universal.

There were always special church services. Preacher J. E. Hughett at the Mountain Valley Church in Mohawk took pride in assembling a small choir of serenaders who would travel around and sing hymns and carols for shut-ins and the less fortunate members of the community. Also, there were the traditional Christmas sermons and pleas for people to help their neighbors. Preachers

Jeff and Kester did the same, but their sermons included a lot more fire and brimstone, tempered with pleas to remember what the season really represented.

Gift exchanges tended to be very simple because resources were scarce. Most gifts were handmade and reflected resourcefulness and creativity. Practical gifts were the norm, such as quilts, gloves, tools, pocketknives, underwear, knitted garments, and, where possible, shoes. There'd be a new gun or sewing machine in a really good year.

There usually were special meals of whatever could be had. Some families were fortunate to have hams from their last hog killin'. Others got lucky and were able to harvest a wild turkey or other game from the forest, but a Christmas dinner of a fat hen was more common. Cakes and pies were a seasonal favorite, but they required sugar, which was usually saved for holiday celebrations. Buttermilk Sky-High and vinegar pies shared the table with the usual apple and pumpkin pies in our home. Also, stack cakes were popular. These were made of pancakes stacked high with apple or peach butter spread between the thin layers. That tradition had existed for hundreds of years, and different families had varying recipes.

An interesting tradition handed down was the belief that at the stroke of midnight on Christmas Eve, animals could talk. I tried to listen in on our cat, Kitty Tom, but he was never in a talkative mood.

Firecrackers, celebratory gunshots into the air, clanging cowbells, and other loud noises could be heard up and down the hollers as people celebrated.

Rufus Cobb had a personal tradition of setting off a couple of sticks of dynamite at 4 a.m. on January 1 to greet the new year, and the hills would echo like thunder.

Of course, when the explosions occurred, it was no longer a private celebration. Often, even those with hangovers would wake up and curse Rufus.

The doors of homes were often adorned with bouquets of wildflowers, pinecones, berries, mistletoe, and fronds from pine or cedar trees. Candles were lit and placed by the windows to illuminate the early darkness of winter and to welcome Mary and Joseph as they searched for a place to give birth to their baby and take shelter. Evergreen Christmas trees were readily cut from the forests and decorated with popcorn, cut paper strings, and cookie ornaments. Tiny rag dolls, stitched by hand, and small toys carved from wood were popular. In our area, Red Cedar trees were preferred because they were common, and some believed they had a better fragrance.

An event that drew a lot of attention was the New Year's Day Turkey Shoot, where a genuine turkey was awarded to the lucky winner. "Lucky" was the operative word because they didn't shoot at conventional bullseyes with rifles but rather at a piece of paper hung on a tree 40 yards away. It had a big X drawn on it…and shotguns were used. The person whose tiny pellet came closest to the center of the X was the winner.

A few of the more interesting gifts I recall include the following:

Miz Kitty Lededder gave her husband, Squint, a box of shotgun shells. Squint gave his wife a new brush for her (and his) hair.

Jake gave his wife a new heated water dish for her chickens, but they didn't have electricity, so it didn't work well. Nevertheless, she was appreciative and gave him a framed, cross-stitch poem she'd written. Unfortunately, he couldn't read, but he treasured the thought.

Delroy from the Jaybird store gave Pinkie a toothbrush with the admonition that he should use it to "kill the disease" in his mouth. Andrew gave Delroy a bar of Ivory soap, and he carved a small dog "effigy" out of it. It didn't look much like a dog, with only three legs and one ear.

Bryant Gulley created a special elixir for the holidays, which sold out quickly after the word got out about its positive effects, with "frisky" being the primary descriptor. He regretted not having enough supplies to make a new batch. It was a mixture of extract from yaupon leaves he'd harvested from the hills, ginseng root extract, teaberry leaf juice, some cloves, and a secret ingredient he wouldn't divulge...all steeped in Uncle Nathan's best moonshine. By the way, yaupon is the only plant native to the USA with naturally occurring caffeine and is only found in parts of the South.

The most memorable gifts I recall were those given by the newlyweds, Zelbert and Ocie Mae Nicodemus, to each other. Ocie Mae claimed to have some Cherokee blood in her lineage, so he carved a little deer out of a piece of walnut wood to give it to her. Ocie Mae had seen him working on it and was touched, pondering long and hard what she could give her beloved husband. Money was almost nonexistent, and she worried about what to do for a week. Then, she had a stroke of luck. Crazy Daisy dropped by her cabin and gave her a roll of Saran Wrap that she'd gotten from an aunt in Knoxville. Ocie decided to wrap herself totally up in the clingy, transparent plastic stuff, place some ribbons and bows at a few strategic locations, and greet Zelbert at the door dressed as a gift...an absolutely and *totally naked* gift. She planned to spring the gift on him on Christmas Eve when Zelbert returned from taking a ham over to his parents. No one ever came by their modest cabin on the hillside, and the gift was sure to be appreciated!

So, on the afternoon of December 24th, she stood at the door, waiting for her beloved husband, Zelbert. At precisely 4:15 p.m. (as everyone in the holler remembered), she heard Zelbert approaching the porch. She flung open the door and yelled, "Merry Christmas!"

Only it wasn't Zelbert, it was Preacher Kester.

THE JAY BIRD BOYS
GIT DRUNKER THAN SKUNKS

The Jay Bird boys, all pushing 80 years old, were getting bored of sitting on the porch of the Jay Bird Country Store and spinning yarns, but the one with the least amount of encroaching dementia came up with an idea that captured other guys' interest. Pinkie said, "Do you boys recomember that ole reprobate moonshiner who died about a year ago? What wuz hiz name…Cletus? Or wuz hit Clyde?"

Jake chimed in and said he was Clyde Carter, and he was running from the law over in nearby Carter County. While he was well known as a moonshiner, not many people knew that he died of "white-livered widder's disease." Pinkie asked, "What in tarnation is white-livered widder's disease? I hain't never heered uv sech." Jake lowered his voice and whispered, "I kin see you boys hain't been learned about certain thangs. White-liver people suffer from an abnormally strong sex drive." Still confused, Pinkie continued, "Well, whut's that got to do with Clyde?"

"Well, if Andrew Hughett wuz here, I couldn't tell you 'cause hiz daddy's a preacher. I hain't gonna give you no details anyway 'cept to say that Clyde died of a heart attack in bed at a real bad time." Pinkie said, "Wait, they ain't no good time to die of a heart attack." Jake replied, "Well, take my words fur hit, they is."

Then Jake went on to explain that there wasn't a lot of information floating around about white-livered widder disease because it was taboo for mountain folk to talk about bedroom stuff. Then he said that Clyde's woman was a lively, buxom, and good-looking lady who'd had three other husbands die on her. People claim that her tremendous passion killed them off…and that earned her the reputation of a white-livered widder.

By now, the boys were caught up in the story and wanted to know more. He said that university researchers who had nothing better to do with their time over in Nashville had discovered that "high-natured" women had white spots on their livers, and it was believed if they married three times, their liver would turn white. And it was a known fact that in parts of Appalachia, white liver was related to someone who had a "bedroom disorder."

Jake went on to explain that none of the local women would marry Clyde, so he went to Knoxville and brought back "the best woman that money can buy." Being a moonshiner, Clyde had plenty of money, and a white-livered woman seemed to be a fit match for him.

Jake's wife had talked to Clyde's sister, and she told her about all this stuff. Also, Bryant Gulley's wife had told her that Clyde had traded some of his second-run, doubled moonshine for a special ginseng elixir so he could keep up with his new "day-to-day, after-work chores."

Pinkie wanted to know more, and Jake continued with the topic at hand. Jake asked, "Do you boys remember that Clyde used to put fruit jars of moonshine in a hole in a holler tree up on Chicken Run Road, and you could drop three dollars in a box and take a jar?" The boys all remembered and shook their heads. People liked the idea that they could buy alcohol anonymously, and the honor system worked pretty well in a community where privacy was valued.

"Well, I got to wondering if there might be a little white whisky still stored that his widder forgot about. After Clyde died, she run off to Knoxville again with an old red-headed boyfriend she once had, and nobody's heard hide ner hair uv her since."

This got the guys to thinking as a group, and that usually ended badly. The last time they started thinking like that, they ended up taking a fishing trip to Lake Guntersville in Alabama. They came back all crippled up and broken. Then, the time before that, they went to the Smoky Mountains and got lost on a fishing trip on the way back in Cade's Cove, on Abrams Creek. That trip required a year of recovery time and several doctor's visits. But they got over their aches and bruises, and even though they couldn't walk very well, they still longed for the good old days when they could get around and have fun. They hardly ever went fishing anymore, but the thought of the possibility of moonshine still being in the old tree gnawed at their feeble minds.

It was about this time when Booker T dropped by the store and joined the conversation. Booker was far from being a tee-totaler and was always looking for a quick way to make an easy buck. If the boys would show him where the tree was, he'd take them there in his old "Woodie" station wagon and give them half the take, if anything was left in the tree. By this time, Delroy had hobbled over to the store and joined the team. Having been there numerous times, he knew exactly where the old tree was, so they crowded into the station wagon and took off.

Right away, the old car got a flat tire not a mile from the store. Booker wasn't happy about doing manual labor of any kind, but the old guys chimed in and gave him way more advice than he wanted. Soon, they pulled up next to a grove of old oak trees, and the boys unloaded. The tree wasn't more than twenty steps from the road, and just as Delroy remembered, there was a hole in the side of the tree. Since Booker was the most able, they voted him to reach into the hole and see if there was anything in it.

When he stuck his hand inside, he let out a blood-curdling scream and leaped back. The scream unnerved the guys, and two of them fell down in an attempt to run away. When Booker jerked his hand out of the hole, a really mad boar raccoon was firmly attached. When the coon saw all the guys, it let go, fell to the ground, and scurried off into the woods.

Booker was whining like he was going to die, but the old boys' laughter caused him to buck up and quit complaining. Booker refused to put his hand in the hole again, so they sat and pondered the situation.

Pinkie came up with a plan. He gathered up a handful of dry oak leaves, stuffed them in the hole, lit a match, and tossed it in. Soon, smoke poured out, and a mama coon and two babies scurried out and took off for the woods. After this, Pinkie pulled a log up to the tree so he could get a better look in the hole. Then he yelled, "Jackpot! They's four half-gallon jars uv 'shine in hyar!"

Booker took the boys back to the Jay Bird store, where they hid their share of the jars in paper pokes, and Booker got on his way.

Then, the boys pondered what they should do next. Delroy and Jake were all for dividing the hootch into pint bottles and selling it, but then they realized that if they were caught selling illegal likker, they could be arrested as bootleggers. Pinkie suggested that they open a jar and sample it to make sure that it was still good enough to drink. He did so and proclaimed that it had aged just about right during the past year, and, because of that, it was now better stuff than when Clyde first sold it. The other guys had to take a sip to see if Pinkie was current in his assessment.

Delroy then took a sip and, after a thoughtful pause to allow his throat and breath to recover, said only one word, "smooth!" He claimed that it had the taste of Rye Malt in it like Popcorn Sutton over in Cocke County used to make. Hearing this, the other guys had to take a swig to see if he was correct in what he claimed. Jake disagreed and said that he was pretty sure the mash had been made of Jimmy Red corn, which was the best stuff to make 'shine from. Of course, like any other discussion they had, they seldom agreed. Pinkie took another taste and claimed that it had the smooth taste of Yellow Dent corn raised in the flatlands. Then, each of the boys had to take another sip to see if he was right. Long story short, the sips turned into unhealthy gulps, and eventually, they were wobbling around like three-legged skunks and about to fall off the porch. They were two-thirds drunk and quickly heading for three-thirds. Clyde's recipe was so smooth that it snuck up on them before they realized what was happening.

This is where their conversation veered off track and loosened up their tongues, and soon, they were talking crazy stuff that would get them in trouble if Preacher Kester had heard what they were saying. The longer they talked, the lighter the fruit jar got, and they commenced to taking turns telling stories.

Jake said, "Did you boys know that Union General Samuel P. Carter fought at the Battle of Bulls Gap, Tennessee, and fought Confederate General John C. Breckinridge in battle?" None of the boys knew enough about the history of "The Big War" to know if that was true, so the turn passed to Delroy.

He asked if they knew anything about the Gulley Murders. They didn't, and he went on to describe how Samuel Osborne Gulley's son and his nephew were ambushed over near the French Broad River and killed by the Bill Sizemore Gang two weeks after the war was over *(Writer's note: I plan to write about this true story at some point as Samuel Osborne Gulley is my direct relative)*.

Not interested in war stories, Pinkie wanted to know more about white-livered women but gave it up when Old Lady Gooch walked by them and went into the store. The boys usually tried to keep track of what people bought, but forgot about it this time, preferring to talk about more exciting things. On most days, Miz Gooch was a good topic for conversation, but all were pretty positive that her liver wasn't white or even slightly pink. All agreed that her liver had to have been coal tar black. If she'd known what the guys were talking about, she'd likely have given them a tongue-lashing and kicked them off of the porch. She'd done that once before, but even with the drinks in them, they were still sober enough to keep their mouths shut.

Pinkie took another draw from the fruit jar and commented, "Did y'all know Mason Carter? He's the one that people got tired of wasting two syllables on his name and jist started calling him 'Jar.' They were going to name his younger sister 'Kerr', but the Preacher said that meant 'mean dog,' so they named her Sweetie instead. However, as she grew older, most people agreed that they should have stuck with the name Kerr, given her personality.

For an inexplicable reason, that reminded Delroy of Imogene Jarnigan, who could charm a rattlesnake out of its skin. They figured that she should have been named Sweetie. Everybody liked Imogene. She knew the history of everyone in the holler and was the area's only genealogist. Her daddy, John, gained some local fame when he turned a tractor engine into a barbecue smoker. He was also the first person in the area to buy a real car, a 1928 A-Model Ford sedan. It was used, and the engine made strange noises. Some people suggested that he probably should put the barbecue engine in the car.

Delroy declared that he and his wife started having good luck right after her missing cat showed up after six weeks of being gone, purring away under their porch. They believed in signs. Delroy had dropped the mangy thing off in Newport next to the Fighting Cocks High School and hoped never to see it again, but its return was a sign he couldn't ignore. Newport was twenty-one miles away. They were superstitious and also felt that having mice in the house was bad luck. Jake offered that maybe the cat would get lucky this time.

Pinkie said he was getting hungry and wished he had some of his Mamaw's cornbread. She made it the proper way, without sugar. Sweet cornbread is called cake…and there were no ifs, ands, or buts about that, and he'd fight any man who disagreed. And a woman too, if it came to that.

Jake mentioned that his sister, Sherry Sue, who worked at the Little Dutch Café in Morristown, wouldn't allow hip-shakin' rock and roll music on the jukebox and always kept it stocked with Patsy Cline and Conway Twitty…" good, honest music." She also would sing "Coal Miner's Daughter" on a makeshift stage on Saturday nights," but last weekend was a disaster when she started crying in the middle of the song. Someone snuck another record into the machine, and Sherry Sue had a hissy fit when people started dancing to "Ring of Fire" like it was their last night on Earth.

After the Talley girl from Cocke County passed by the porch, Pinkie commented that she made his heart flutter faster than a hummingbird on caffeine. Jake countered with, "Hush yore mouth! She's 'sposed to marry one of them Sutterfield boys as soon as he gits out of the Army. Besides, if yore heart wuz to git to a fluttering, hit would flutter you right straight to Hell. Remember what the Preacher told you?"

Now that the conversation looked like it was heading towards the topic of love, someone asked if Zelbert Nicodemus had recovered from when he accidentally kissed an alligator snapping turtle while showing off to the neighborhood kids. No one had an update only to say that "Hit served him right for being an ignoramus. Besides, hiz nose wuz too long anyways."

When the first jar was half empty, the boys started listing the oddest foods they could think of. Here are a few food items mentioned as they tried to outdo each other.

- Coon Liver' n' Onions
- Southern Fried Muskrat
- Poke Weed and Ramp Sallet
- Catfish and Peach Gumbo Soup
- Squirrel Shanks (they got 'em too).
- Pickled Paw Paws
- Smoked Crawdads
- Grits' n' Possum Gravy
- Hand Slung Chitlins
- Coot Cobbler

But that topic of conversation came to a halt when Pinkie offered up "Boiled Mule" and swore that his daddy once brought home a whole mule loin strip. Then he mentioned that Zeb Ledbedder had a mule he wanted to get rid of, and it would be an excellent opportunity to feed the whole community. When the guys protested, he reminded them that Miz Kitty, Squint Ledbedder's French wife, said they always ate horse meat in Europe. He claimed that horses and mules had to be the same when it came to meat, and they were missing out on an opportunity.

That prompted the conversation back to the topic of women with white livers, and the boys dispersed when it dawned on Pinkie that his wife was in her third marriage. He said, "Boys, I gotta go. My wife has some 'chores' for me at home." As he stumbled off, he mumbled, "God willin', I'll see y'all tomorrow."

APPALACHIAN BOYS WHIZZING GAME

Not all family reunions were fun. There was one where I received one of the worst whuppins I ever got. Of course, the food was good, and playing with my cousins was a highlight, but sometimes bad things happen to sorta well-meaning kids.

First, you have to know that backhills mountain boys are used to roaming the woods and fields, and whenever nature calls, they just unzip and let fly behind the nearest bush. I mean, if you're three miles from the cabin, what are you going to do?

A group of us boys was stuffed with potluck family reunion food. Bobby, Buddy, Ronnie, Johnny, Jimmy, and I were there. Buddy was the oldest. We were in the middle of a contest to see who was the bravest and could jump the farthest from Uncle Commodore's barn loft when Jimmy said, "Hey, I drunk too much lemonade, and I gotta go. Let's have a "sprinkling" contest and see who can make the highest wet mark on the side of the barn. That sounded like a great idea, and in preparation for the competition, we all ran back to the food tables and tanked up with more lemonade. We didn't want an audience, so we snuck around to the back of the barn to determine who the champion would be. Jimmy was the Huck Finn of the group, and he came up with the idea when he overheard Uncle Bryant tell Nathan Gulley that trying to fight the sheriff would be "like having a whizzing contest with a skunk."

The game was simply to see who could wee-wee the highest up the side of the barn. Jimmy was pretty short and suggested a competition to see who could last the longest or shoot the most accurately, but he lost out because most of the boys were taller than he was. The majority ruled.

Nobody wanted to go first, so we decided to go from youngest to oldest. I won't go into the competition details or creative techniques because these guys are still alive as I write this, and we always tried to swear secrecy about stuff like that, mostly.

The first guy backed up about two feet from the wall and let go. It started off weak and crept up slowly, but fell short and ended up on his shoes. It was going to be a grueling competition. The next boy aimed higher, and the arc began strong but maxed out a few inches short of the wall. Embarrassed, he claimed that bad lemonade had jinxed him.

Ronnie was over-ready, and he was still thinking about his next step when his fly got stuck, and he wet his pants before he could even get into the game. He started to cry, and we consoled him by saying, "That would have been good, Ronnie, but you'll have time for a rematch at the next reunion. From the looks of yore pants, you probably would have won."

Next was me, and I stood closer to the barn wall and moved into the lead. If I'd started the day knowing it would end in a competition like this, I'd have saved up all morning for the contest. I stepped back, proud of my three-foot, two-inch splotch. It beat Johnny's best effort by eight inches.

Then, the oldest guy, Buddy, boasted that he was aiming for the roof, stepped back to the three-foot mark, and his arc made an impressive three feet and five inches up the barn wall.

That was when we heard Aunt Mandy's daughter's voice. She had been peeping from the edge of the barn and said, "What are y'all doing?"

In unison, we all said, "We ain't doin' nothin'. Now you go back and play dolls with the girls. This is a boy game."

I won't tell you Mandy's daughter's real name, but without hesitation, she marched up to the "firing line," hiked up her dress, bent forward, and grabbed her ankles, with her rear end aimed high toward the barn wall. She then yelled Oorah and let go a stream that arced upward and sparkled in the sunlight. The result was easily a foot above the highest mark on the wall! She was the undisputed hands-down champion!

Then, she ran off, laughing and yelling, "Whatever boys can do, girls can do hit better!"

> *(Note: In the interest of full disclosure, I must tell you that her daddy was a Marine in the 1950s, and "Oorah" had become a family tradition).*

It was at that point that the parade got rained on. I was attempting to vindicate my reputation and was just starting another run at the wall when my daddy came on the scene. He'd heard Aunt Mandy's daughter brag. At first, I thought he'd not punish me with all my friends watching, but I was dead wrong. He pulled off his leather belt and tanned my hide until I got blisters. Sometimes, even the sunniest days end with a rainstorm.

Hang in there and watch your back. Someone's usually looking, and a few of them can make you repent. I've been repented a bunch of times. Oorah!

A STRANGE HILLBILLY LOVE STORY
(Part 1)

This love story may seem unusual to city folks from the flatlands. Such doings as I describe in the stories that follow were natural stuff to people in the hills of Appalachia. We grew up differently there. That said, on our side of the mountain, we didn't always follow traditional mountain protocols for marrying and such, but we found ways to get the job done. As a first step, we'd need to meet someone. This usually happened at church events, neighborhood dinners, hog killin's, or school. Geographical circumstances made it unlikely to meet someone from somewhere else. Then came the courting phase. To city folk, this was known as "dating."

Courtships usually lasted only a short time, three weeks or so being common. Anything longer and an "arranged marriage with a shotgun involved" was increasingly likely. Most Appalachian families didn't have much money, but honor was of paramount importance. Fists or guns helped ensure that the right thing was done. Chaperones were the norm to help protect the lady's chastity. This almost always worked except for when the suitor slipped some money to the chaperone.

Some guys would give their girlfriend a "love spoon" carved from wood and engraved with knots and hearts to signify they were serious. Rings were an uncommon luxury in the early days. If the woman reciprocated the man's feelings, she'd make a nice quilt for him. Some couples would slip off and get married by a justice of the peace, but most tried to be married by a preacher. The type of wedding depended on the support they received from their parents and their circumstances. It was very bad taste to move in together without getting married. If a couple had that in mind, they would be better off running off to Cincinnati or Detroit, where living in sin was not frowned upon so much.

In the remote hills in the early days, marriages were commonly held in the bride's or the preacher's home and were short and sweet. Special wedding dresses were uncommon except where the families could afford such an extravagance. Kissing rarely happened, and only when no one was looking, and a peck could be snuck in.

I'm getting along in years, and the young kids of today don't seem to be getting married like they used to back in my day. Nevertheless, many old-time marriage customs persist in Appalachia, and getting hitched with a genuine marriage license tends to be one of them. I have to be cautious about how I talk about this stuff because my wife of fifty-seven years will kick me out of the house if I start going into too much detail about courting, bedroom antics, and such. I don't want to risk ruining a good thing at my age. I hate cookin' and sleepin' alone, although I admit that I am almost getting used to spending nights on the couch. Depending on the offense, I sometimes have little choice but to face the consequences, which can range from the couch to worse. Still, I will tell you that getting kicked outta bed and spending the night on the front porch swing in the dead of winter is more than just a friendly "training exercise."

Now that I have that preface stuff out of my system, back to the story.

Earl "The Squirrel" Carter and Sherry, his wife, have been happily married and frolicking with each other for more than fifty years like a couple of horny teenagers. Ninety-nine percent of the divorced people reading this may ask, "How on God's green earth is that even possible?" In case you're curious, in the following paragraphs and the following few stories, I'll tell you how Earl and Sherry courted and came to tie the knot so tight. That said, my wife will insist that I put a veil over the details of the sections outlining witchcraft and aphrodisiacs. I'll try to be careful, but I do have a clumsy memory.

Earl was raised in the backhills outside of Bulls Gap, Tennessee, on a steep hillside up a dark holler where only a footpath led to his folks' cabin. Some claim that his family is kin to June Carter, Johnny Cash's wife. Although June was raised just sixteen miles away in the Clinch Mountain area, it is unknown whether they are related by blood. Either way, Earl couldn't carry a tune in a paper poke, so that's probably just a rumor.

Earl's kinfolks hail from the Laurel Fork community in Carter County, which borders North Carolina. The family is proud that their ancestors played a role in helping to defeat the British at King's Mountain during the Revolutionary War. The Carters always loved a good fight, a tradition they continued into the Civil War and up to the current day. Earl and most of the men in his family continued the military tradition in World War I, World War II, Vietnam, and elsewhere, where they were assured of excitement and a chance to escape the hills. Earl's tough as a pine knot, and a few scars are witness that he can carry his own. An interesting side note is that, like many other Highlanders, the Carters chose not to take sides in the Civil War, so as to be free to fight whichever army happened to be at hand. This may sound crazy to you, but in their way of thinking, it was the only way to get involved and, at the same time, stay neutral.

I digress a lot when I write, but if I don't follow up on thoughts immediately as they pop into my head, I tend to get "my-brain" headaches. That said, some of you may recomember that my Uncle Nathan Gulley spent more than fifteen long, hard years locked up at Brushy Mountain State Prison in the remote town of Petros. In 1976, Nathan was a forced resident there when Johnny Cash performed for the inmates with his band, *The Tennessee Three*. Cash was never incarcerated there, but he felt sorry for those who got whacked harder than he had been. The objective of his visit was to give hope and faith to those who were incarcerated. Most were there for violent crimes, but Uncle Nathan never did anything more violent than stoke a fire in the woods and make moonshine…but, to his wife's dismay, he frequently got caught. I wouldn't go so far as to say that he was a slow learner, but I will say that he loved the thrill of his risky profession. He loved the excitement of chasing around the woods with guns and evading the revenooers. This gave him ample incentive to exercise his legs when there wasn't a war he could get involved in. I liked Uncle Nathan and write a lot about him. Of all my kinfolk, he's likely the only one for whom a really exciting movie could be made. I know a lot about Nathan, but he would only relate a few stories to me directly. I got others from my Mamaw, who was less worried about statutes of limitations and such. Where was I before my mind wandered over to Uncle Nathan?

The Carters were proud and hardworking descendants of the Scotch-Irish, with some Cherokee blood occasionally mixed in. Most people in the area could trace part of their lineage to Indians because, in the early days, more than a few Native Americans calculated that living among the crazy white people would be an easier road to travel. This may have been true in the Wild West, but not so much in the hills, where every day also required a tremendous amount of work to put food on the table and clothes on their backsides. In any case, Mother Nature almost always gets her way, and intermarriages like that were not uncommon.

My headache has been avoided, so back to the love story with some tips on courtin' in Appalachia.

Like in any society, courtships, marriages, affairs, secret rendezvous, quirks, and other intimacies were talked about, discussed, scrutinized, and analyzed in great detail by both males and females. In Appalachia, some topics were never discussed in mixed company and were reserved for same-gender discussions.

Hillbilly Love Story That Ends Well

The men talked about every permutation of the more physical stuff at every opportunity whenever they happened to be together. The "stuff" usually included many colorful adjectives, exciting verbs, and strange nouns that appealed to bizarre male desires and imagination. Often, these discussions evolved into unfounded boasts and a competition to see who could tell the biggest lie. Everyone suspected the boasts were exaggerations, but the entertainment factor was higher that way. Usually, the person who boasted loudest was the one who cowered the most when approached by his wife at home. It was the real quiet guys one had to watch out for.

Conversely, women often delved into high gear and provided greater detail in their discussions about interrelationships. These often were at their peak at quilting parties. Of course, if the quilts were being crafted in the church's basement, the juicy parts were whispered in hushed tones. Unlike men, and being women, actual lies were few and far between, and discussions were never overtly raunchy. However, they did sometimes delve into the steamy and exciting interactions they'd observed in "somebody else's family." Dreamy discussions about "true love and affection" were punctuated by occasional forays (accompanied by blushes) into the more adventurous and passionate romances they knew of…again, in "other people's families." I'm sorry that I digress again, but the topic of this story keeps making my "man mind" wander onto thin ice.

AINT BERTHY CASTS HER LOVE SPELL
(Part 2)

Although Earl was strong as a mule and smart as a wild hog, his "presentation" to the opposite sex lacked a few essential details regarding attracting a mate. To remedy this, he consulted with the boys on the porch of the Jay Bird Store in Morristown. This was a mistake, of course, but it was a start. They guffawed and made fun of the mountain boy's naiveté, but they did share some pivotal advice. They suggested if he were really desperate to attract a woman that he consult with my great-uncle, Bryant Gulley, or my great-aunt, Berthy Hughett.

As you might suspect, not everyone agreed. Delroy strongly advised Earl to avoid going to Berthy for advice because "that thar ole witch'll put a dang hex on you that you cain't scrape off with a Barlow knife and hit has lots of real bad side effects." He went on to describe how it took him six months to shake a spell she'd once placed on him, and all he did was yell at his "lawfully wedded woman." He didn't get much sympathy from Jake, who adamantly claimed that Berthy had fixed his marriage when he thought it was beyond repair. He went on to describe how she'd burned a ceremonial candle and, from then on, he and his wife had been like two flirty love birds. He offered that he had eleven kids to prove it.

Although their strategies varied considerably, Bryant and Berthy each often succeeded in helping people "couple." *(Note: I have to be very careful here with my choice of words in case my lovely wife reads this. If you knew her, you'd understand.)*

Uncle Bryant was a locally known mountain herb doctor and was often practical in his advice. When Earl approached him, Bryant immediately recommended several "prescriptions" he could concoct from ginseng mixed with a half dozen other highly effective (but secret) herbs he gathered from the woods and ridgetops near his cabin.

Being a cautious Christian man, Bryant told Earl that he'd only give the elixirs to him on the morning of his wedding, due to their extreme potency. Everything he sold came with a money-back guarantee, and he was proud to boast that he'd never had to reimburse anyone. Of course, the guarantee was void if it was God's will that the elixirs did not work. Nobody trumps God. Disappointed by the wait but highly enthused, Earl then sought out Berthy.

My Aunt (Aint) Berthy was more challenging to approach than Uncle Bryant. When Earl came close to her small clapboard house, he was faced with a loaded shotgun and a warning, "One more step, you heathen, and I'll drop yore ass right thar! What's you awantin'?"

Earl's first impulse was to run, but his hormonal incentive moved him to blurt out, "Please listen! I'm 17 years old and I still caint git married. I'm in a bad way, and people are a makin' fun of me, and I needs yore help. Ole Man Gulley said you could fix me up to git a woman. My momma says she's goin' to kick me outta the house iffen I don't git on wid it."

Berthy could be a hard woman, but she did have a soft spot for the underprivileged, and with one look at Earl's face, she knew he needed help. She said, "If you has a gun wid'ja, I'll shoot you.

If not, come on into my treatin' room." Her treating room was a bare table in the middle of her small living room. On it was something covered with a colorful, hand-knitted and crocheted cloth.

They sat down at the table, and Berthy interviewed Earl. He carefully explained how he had been looking hard for a wife for the past four years but had hit dead ends at every attempt and that he'd even gone so far as to brush his teeth and promise girls that he'd someday get a job making big money.

In the meantime, he had a successful business going collecting muskrat and coon hides and selling them at the farm store in Bulls Gap. He boasted that he had amassed more than a hundred and eighty-seven dollars from his sales in the previous twelve months and still had time to plow, plant, harvest a garden, and raise a few hogs.

Berthy, ever observant, noticed the scars on Earl's sun-browned skin and the holes in his overalls. These, coupled with the pained look on his face, moved her to take him on as a client. So, she said. "Okay, if you want's my help, you'll have to come back in seven days. Before returnin', you gotta go dip yoreself seven times in Lick Creek and warsh off with a bar of lye soap that's only been used seven times." She also said she'd need something belonging to the girl he wanted to marry.

This presented a problem for Earl. He didn't have a specific girl in mind, as they'd all pretty well rebuffed him. That didn't bother Berthy, and she just said, "Don't you pay no nevermind, we's can work around dat. You has potential. Now, listen here real careful-like. When you come back hyar nex' time, frum my gate you has to take seven steps to my porch. If you takes eight steps, go back home 'cause I won't be able to hep ya. Iffen you takes six steps, go back to the gate, and start over."

Ever excited and anxious, Earl did as she said and found himself again sitting at her front room table, where she removed the cloth from the objects underneath. A pink candle encircled by some fresh rose petals and seven quartz crystals were revealed.

Berthy carefully explained that, when it came to casting love spells, it wasn't with the intent to control someone's free will but to put them *in the mood* to make them lovingly think of you.

She proceeded to carve the word "Earl" on the side of the pink candle. Then she wrapped a piece of paper that was saturated with rose oil around the candle a quarter inch below the wick. In the room's darkness, she lit the candle and had Earl chant: "Thinking of me, thinking of me and only of me, fill my future wife's heart with love for me." He repeated this seven times. Then, Berthy passed one of the crystals over the flame seven times and blew the flame out.

She then gave the crystal to Earl and instructed him to keep it with him everywhere he went. Further, she instructed him to travel to a distant location for a few days, identify a girl, obtain a hair sample from her, and then return to her. His uncle happened to be going to Gatlinburg the following weekend, and he arranged to hitch a ride with him.

Gatlinburg is a tourist town where many people go to relax, recreate, and generally nose around the stores and look at other people. It's a magical place, and a lot of sparking and honeymoons happen there. Berthy's instructions were to travel, watch people, look at all the single girls he encountered, and visualize them falling in love with him as he clutched the crystal.

Earl hadn't been in Gatlinburg more than an hour when he noticed a really cute, slender girl about his age looking at a puppy that an old man was petting.

He felt a strong urge to approach her, so he grasped the crystal in his hand, approached the girl, and said, "I have a puppy at my house. In fact, I have twelve puppies. Missie, my Bluetick hound just littered a bunch." He grasped the crystal tighter and said, "You can have one if you want."

Taken aback, the girl tried to ignore Earl, but when she took a quick glance into his eyes, something inside her stirred, and she couldn't help but stare. At first, it scared her, but, almost as if she had no control, she found herself blushing and saying, "I'd like that, but I don't know you from Adam's housecat. Who are you and where are your puppies?" Earl explained that he lived in the hills near Bulls Gap and was visiting a cousin in Gatlinburg for a few days.

Earl learned that the girl's name was Sherry and that she was a mountain girl who was raised and lived in Cades Cove, not far away. Being about the same age and feeling a mutual attraction, they walked around town, looked into gift shops, and shared an ice cream and hot dog at Howard's Restaurant. The most intimate moment of the two-hour-long rendezvous was when Earl reached up and removed a loose hair from Sherry's sweater. He clutched it tight, wrapped it in a napkin, and secretly put it in his pocket.

Three days later, he was back at Berthy's place with the hair. They went to the table and uncovered the candle and crystals. The candle with Earl's name on it was still in place. She took a sharp knife and etched Sherry's name beside Earl's, rubbed the crystal with rose oil, and had Earl visualize the desired outcome. She then had Earl hold the hair and crystal against his heart and say these words:

"By the power of love and light, I ask that Sherry fall in love with me. I consecrate a space in my heart for this love's arrival. So be it." At this point, Earl was surprised to feel the tingling energy of the quartz flow into his heart and link up with his personal energy. The spell seemed to be working!

Berthy instructed him to carry the crystal everywhere he went, to make contact with the girl of his interest again, and, with the caution that the final outcome would only happen if it was God's will, she would fall in love with him. He was to visualize the two of them together, happy and in love, but nothing more than that. There would be ample time for future spells to accommodate the sexy stuff if needed. In Berthy's experience, that kind of spell wasn't needed until the couple approached middle age.

Before turning Earl loose, Berthy gave him some courting advice. She told him, "Earl, I don't have much use for menfolk, but you seem to show promise. Now, lemme give you some womanly advice. Don't you listen to none of those yahoos at the Jay Bird Store. They's all losers, 'ceptin Andrew. He's my brother, and family respects family.

Firstest, when you courts a woman, you needs to unnerstand if she has potential. You don't want to land up with no Jezabel. If this girl you met seems happy to see you, that's a good sign. Look at her eyes, and you should be able to tell. Of course, if she's not there when you return, I'll need to cast a new spell on'er. Look into her eyes double-close as iffen yore tryin' to talk to her with yore thoughts. If she blushes and turns her head, she likes you. If yore eyes lock together on each other on a regular basis, two things might be goin' on. Either you has a big zit on yore face or a booger on your nose, and she don't know how to tell you or, more likely, hit's a sign that she likes you a lot and is trying to figure out if you'd be a good husband. If you find yoreself blushing when she looks at you, it don't mean nothin' cause honest men does that around good-looking wimmen. People caint control blushing.

She continued, "If they like you and they don't know you good enough, they'll be all nervous. That's 'cause they's tryin' to make a good impression on you and they's under pressure to not mess up. It's a good sign when they's nervous. Here's how you can tell. Sometimes they plays with their hair or blinks a lot. Some rubs their face and sneak peeks atcha when they think you ain't lookin'. If you both git to the point that you start talkin' easy-like and she smiles at you a bunch, that's a sure sign that the spell we put on her is a workin' good and a high chance that things is goin' to work out in yore favor. Dependin' on how you acts as a husband later on will determine if hit's working in her favor or not. If you git outta line, I'll promise I'll put a hex on you that you won't like."

"And take notice if yore eyes wander to her lips. And if her eyes wander to yore eyes. When you both git to the point whar you and she don't look away when you do this, it's a done deal, and hit's high time to start arranging for a preacher."

"Also, you gotta keep in yore mind that men only want one thing from a woman, and it ain't what your sinnin' mind thinks. Men wants their women to treat them special, sorta like a hero. Women wants to be appreciated and respected for who they is and what they can do. That's the secret to holding a woman's love and devotion for life. If you do that, all the sexy stuff will happen automatically, but if hit don't, you come back hyar later, and we'll burn a bright red candle and cast a different kind of spell to fix that. But we have to be careful. If you fall for Bryant Gulley's elixir AND my candle spell at the same time, you could be in a heap of trouble and land up with fourteen plus-one kids like Bryant and mebbe some mad husbands up and down the hollers wantin' to shoot you. I run a professional service here, and I don't mean to git on the wrong side of the Bible."

Earl had arranged to meet Sherry at noon the following Saturday at Howard's Restaurant. He hitched a ride with a neighbor and met up with Sherry. Right off, he clearly visualized them together. As he shook her hand, he felt the crystal's energy flowing through his body into hers. By the end of the day, they'd pretty well agreed to marry. It happened just like Berthy had predicted.

Later, Earl was at the Jay Bird Store, and the porch gang demanded a detailed report. Pinkie cut to the chase and asked, "Did you all git to he-ing and she-ing? (hugging and kissing). Andrew wanted to know if they were going to "jump the broom" (get married), and Jake followed up with "Didja swap slobber?" (kiss).

Feeling embarrassed, Earl quickly excused himself and returned to his momma's home in the hills. The report overwhelmed his mother with joy, and she said she'd set up the backyard for the wedding the following Sunday and start cooking.

However, despite the excitement, there were a few details to consider first. Earl would have to face Sherry's father and hope he would approve of giving his daughter's hand in marriage. If not, they'd have to decide to call it off or run off together. Bryant Gulley told Earl not to get his hopes up and that there was a 50/50 chance of her daddy saying yes or shooting him. Offhand, he figured that Sherry's daddy would be glad to marry her off because she was already sixteen years old and unmarried, which was unusual in the hills.

Berthy's Incantation

Then, if he passed the daddy test, Sherry would have to decide if her Sunday-go-to-meeting dress would be good enough to get hitched in. Then Earl would be faced with finding a place to spend a honeymoon and, most difficult of all, a place for them to set up house and live. Although he had yet to clear it with Sherry, he planned to borrow a pup tent from Ocie Mae Nicodemus to cover the honeymoon part, but finding a place to live that would fit their budget would be a problem unless he could buy a larger tent to hold them together until he could get a job and find a house.

Contemplating all the complexities of getting married, Earl began to wonder if Sherry was sending him a positive signal with her eyes, one that said yes to marriage, or if a gnat had just flown into them. Berthy calmed him down by saying, "Don't you worry even a teeny bit, Earl. I already has you covered with another spell, and this'un hyar will be a doozy!"

GITTIN DADDY'S PERMISSION
(Part 3)

Earl and Sherry had known each other for three whole weeks, and time was a'wastin'. Even more pressing was the unfortunate fact that both were getting old, and neighbors were starting to call Sherry an old maid. By Appalachian standards in those days, 16-year-olds were pushing the envelope on whether one was marriageable or not.

With the agreement to get married out of the way, Earl gave Sherry a Bluetick puppy instead of a ring. Backwoods engagements in those days were infrequent or none at all. Rings were mostly for flatlander city folks with money to blow. Sherry appreciated the hound but had plans to extract a ring from Earl after they were married. She was young but already knew that women had their ways.

The next step was to get permission from Sherry's father, John Johnson, to marry Sherry. In total, he had seven sons and three daughters. Earl figured her daddy wouldn't miss one of them. Besides, boys kept sniffing around the Johnson homestead, wanting to court Sherry, and he was tired of having to run them off. The price of shotgun shells expended while changing their interest was taxing his budget. He liked Sherry and didn't want her to marry just any hooligan who came around. Also, he was secretly hoping she'd marry someone who owned a large farm with fancy horses he could ride, so he was holding out on allowing her to get married. He figured the chances were good for the horses because Sherry was one of the prettiest girls in all of Cades Cove. Mischievous and full of vinegar, for sure, but cuter than a three-week-old brindle kitten.

If you've ever experienced the Appalachian Mountains on a clear day, it's always impressive. The mountains cast long, dark shadows. Because of that, some claimed that the Devil used to live in Cades Cove. In prehistory days, Indians used to hunt there, but there's no evidence that they ever set up camp in the area. Cades Cove is nestled in a beautiful valley, shrouded in the mists of the Great Smoky Mountains in East Tennessee, and is teeming with wildlife, majestic trees, and a peace that many would die for. And, if strangers were to come around at night, they might do just that.

Thunderstorms in the Smokies were really fantastic, with all the booming and light shows that came with them. A downside of all this was that there was a neighbor whose house got struck by lightning, and the young couple inside died in their bed. A metal bedframe was deemed the cause, and, of course, it was God's will to take 'em at that time. You might mess with some things, but don't ever doubt the will of the Almighty. Ever cautious, Mr. Johnson made his bedframe out of wood. The bed was comfortable, but it creaked horribly at the slightest movement; however, they got used to it.

Earl wanted the marriage to take place on the porch of the Jay Bird Store with J. E. Hughett officiating, but my papaw wouldn't agree to such "because it wouldn't be right." Weddings were seldom performed in churches or on the front porches of stores in those days, so it was finally decided that it should happen at the bride's home in the Smokies…but only if Earl could get permission from Sherry's protective daddy. That was a big concern. The couple didn't want to elope, and they genuinely wanted their father's blessing.

Earl was very nervous about talking to Sherry's father, a strict and intimidating man. Sherry had told him about all the guys her daddy had run off with a shotgun earlier. So, he prepared.

Earl practiced a compelling speech for Sherry's father and got it down in memory. "Mr. Johnson, Sir, I'm Earl Carter and I come hyar to beg of you somethin' vary important. Sherry and I is in love, and we wants to git married. I wants to spend my whole life with her. Can I have permission to marry yore daughter? I promise to love and cherish and take good care of her and be a good son-in-law to you."

The Jay Bird Store group thought what he proposed to say was good. Still, they had some slightly different suggestions, all of which included inappropriate innuendos involving baby-making processes.

So, prepared with his memorized spiel, Earl traveled to Cades Cove and knocked on the Johnson household door, and the father answered. Before Earl could say anything, he was slapped with some questions:

"What do you want? Whose boy are you? Didn't you see my *No Trespassin'* signs? You might arta git outta here while the gittin's good. This hyar shotgun is loaded with double-aught buckshot and hit's itching to git on with bidness."

This caught Earl off-guard as he was prepared for a response more along the lines of "Well, young man, I'm happy to hear that you love Sherry so much. She's the apple of my eye and deserves the very best there is in a husband. You certainly have my blessing to marry my sweet Sherry." But, in actuality, Earl didn't catch even a hint of that attitude in her father's voice.

Panicked and searching for something to say, Earl responded to the questions thrown at him with:

"Hi, Sir. I'm from over near Bulls Gap. I'm Preacher Hughett's nephew, and I wuz just out walking around and saw that old truck in yore yard and wondered iffen hit wuz for sale? Sherry told me all about hit. Hit's sittin' on blocks and looks like hit needs some wrenchin'."

Sherry's paw said, "Really? You think that old rust bucket could be made to run? I give up on hit 'bout ten years ago." Then he said, "Now, what's this I hear about you huggin' on my daughter? Didja git my permission? I'd kill a man what hurt my daughter."

"Uh, no, Sir. I mean, Yes, Sir. I wuz just a holdin' her hand, and one thang led to another, and afore long she touched me on the cheek, and I just put my arm around her innocent like. Honest, Mr. Johnson, that's all we did. Not a thang more. Please believe me, Sir. We's in love, and I wants to marry Sherry and make her a husband you'll be proud of."

Johnson paused and looked at Sherry, who was peeping from behind the door, and asked, "Is that right, Sherry? Tell me the truth or I'll tan yore hide worse than that time I caught drinking my cough medicine."

"Yes, Daddy, he's right; me and Earl's in love and needs to git married, and we wants yore permission."

Her daddy pondered the words and replied, "Wait! You NEEDS to git married or you WANTS to?

"No, Daddy, we don't HAS to git married like that. We has to because we's in love and haint nuthin' gonna change that. And we don't want no baby kids until we has a good house to put 'em in."

Sherry's father stared at Earl and his daughter for a long time. He didn't know what to think or say. He stared, scratched his head, and said, "Well, I can't tell whyar to go wid this. How much property does yore daddy own, and how many horses does he have? Does he have one of them spotted Appyloosys?"

Earl replied that his dad had died but owned 30 acres of prime mountain land, two mules, three hogs, and a dozen chickens. He added that he and Sherry planned to move in with his momma and take over the farm. He didn't mention that the land was too steep to farm in most places and covered with so many rocks that the mules needed help finding enough grass to eat.

Sherry's dad continued to think and finally said, "I don't know if I should give my permission or kick both our yawls' asses all the way up to Gatlinburg."

Together, Earl and Sherry said, "Please, daddy, give us permission to git married."

Sherry's father sighed and said, "I don't know. I wuz a looking forward to riding good horses instead of a couple of flea-bit mules." A tear started down Sherry's face.

Finally, Mr. Johnson said, "OK, I've made up my mind. The problem is, iffen I says no; y'all probably slip off and go to Cincinnati or some other place where Satan has took up permanent residence, so, yes, I'll give you my blessin'…on two conditions."

"What's that, Mr. Johnson?"

"That you name yore firstborn after me and that you drag that dad-blamed piece of junk pickup truck outta my yard! It's a snake magnet, and the missus wants rid of it. I kinda like snakes myself, but she don't cotton to them, none."

Relieved, Earl said, "You bet, Sir. Yes, Sir. Not a problem, Sir." (What none of them knew at the time was that their firstborn would be a girl)

Then he said, "Now, let's git on with it. I'm demanding that the weddin' take place here on the property and that we do it up right with a party that'll shake up the mountains all the way to Nashville. If the preachers complain, so be it. They'll git over hit. Last time I jus threw a twenty-dollar bill in the offerin' plate, and the preacher 'bout shook my hand off."

Sherry hugged her daddy, and he put his arms around her. Mountain people don't hug other men, so he shook Earl's hand and said, "Remember all yore promises, boy. I got a long-reachin' shotgun, and I hain't afraid uv usin' hit."

All in all, the day went well. Now came the work part...pulling off a wedding and party on a tight budget without anybody getting killed. Usually, in the hills, the preacher would spend only about five or so minutes with the ceremony and another five giving some advice. The couple would then pack up and move in with one of their parents until they got on their feet. Honeymoons were rare, but Earl and Sherry were planning something that didn't involve a pup tent, although that was the backup plan.

THE WEDDIN' CEREMONY
(PART 4)

Rev. J. E. Hughett performed the wedding at the Johnson homestead at Cades Cove. The ceremony was short and sweet, but the after-marriage celebration lasted thirty-four hours, unlike most Appalachian weddings. Mountain people got pretty tired of working their butts hard and looked for excuses to celebrate. What they celebrated was not as important as breaking away from the monotony of hard work on the farm and "cutting loose" a bit.

The wedding party mainly consisted of the best man, Zelbert Nicodemus, and the maid of honor, Wanda Mae Sutterfield. Zelbert was dressed head to foot in camo hunting gear. Wanda Mae wore a camo dress with matching canvas ballet flats. Earl's brother, Gatley, and Sherry's brother, Ricky, were the witnesses. The couple was nervous, and it didn't help that, during the ceremony, the maid of honor excused herself to run off to the outhouse, either to pee or to throw up from a job she had that morning, probably the latter. Did I mention the maid of honor was a taxidermist? She had taxidermied a brindle cat the week before and was real proud of it. After the ceremony, she went into the house, where she slept for several hours until the kids kicked her out of the bed so they could jump on it.

The ceremony started off when a makeshift choir sang the hymn, *Whither Thou Goest*. The song is based on the biblical story of Naomi and Ruth, encouraging the loyalty and devotion of a spouse to follow their partner wherever they go. Then, the preacher performed the ceremony.

He quoted Bible scriptures that speak of God's design for marriage. He cited Genesis 2 18-24, Corinthians 13:4-8, and Psalm 12:7-1 to encourage, instruct, and bless the couple. This took about eight minutes.

Next came the part where the preacher asked Earl and Sherry to exchange vows, promises made before God and the witnesses. They included the phrase "I do" or "I will." Sherry was eager and promptly said, "I do," with excitement and enthusiasm in her voice. Zelbert, on the other hand, by this time, was a nervous wreck and starting to get a bad case of premarital jitters. Not knowing up from down at this point, when asked, "Does you, Earl Carter, frum this here day forward, take Sherry Ann Johnson to be yore wife, for richer or poorer, in sickness and health, to love and cherish, till death do you apart?"

To this, Earl paused a few seconds; his voice creaked, and he muttered timidly, "I reckon so." This response was adequate at the time and would not be mentioned again until three weeks later when Sherry pinned him down and asked, "What on God's green earth did'ja mean by just mumbling, "I reckon?" This was just the first of many tiffs that Earl would end up losing during his long marriage.

The actual marriage stuff took relatively little time. Immediately after the I-dos were over, Preacher Hughett prepared to high-tail it for home and grabbed a plate of fried chicken to take with him. He said he wasn't much of a party man and "sensed that sin was a'brewin'" with the various bootleggers and backsliders he saw in attendance.

Not all attendees were backsliders. Stokes Carter. A WWII South Pacific Marine was a hardshell Baptist of the strictest order. He got into a heated argument with Jack Johnson, who was leaning towards the Methodists. They nearly got to fisticuffs when Stokes accused the Methodists of "dry cleaning" instead of baptizing.'

It's interesting to note that before the preacher left, he invited people to make donations to the Lord's work. He said the Lord mostly paid him in blessings, but it took hard cash to buy hymnals and paint the church. Afterward, as he counted the money, he noted a twenty-dollar bill in the collection hat. When he saw that, he pulled Zelbert Nicodemus aside and told him, "Find the kind soul who put this in the hat and let me know who it is. We need a person like that in my congregation!" Zelbert did as he was told and reported back later, "He's a friend of Gary Carter, and nobody knows much about him except that he sings like a Methodist, shouts like a Presbyterian, and his breath smells like a Baptist." Preacher Hughett replied, "I don't worry about our differences. I love that man!"

At this point, Robert Carter stepped into the fray and said, "Now, lemme tell all you all the truth, God loves everbody, even the Hardshell Baptists whose shells is so hard you cain't crack 'em, and the Presbyterians who is so mean you can smell the brimstone on 'em. Now, personally, I ain't never met no likker what I didn't love. And when I'm in the woods huntin' and fishin', I see God's handiwork everwhar I go. Now, you all quit your bickering, go fishing, and tell your differences to God. I catch fish in the same part of the river you baptize in, and the fish all taste the same." That calmed everybody down.

Not long after the ceremony, the embarrassed couple was coerced into "swappin' slobber" to add a bit of romance to the event.

Unlike most brides of today, Sherry didn't have a fluffy, white wedding dress, but her daddy had traded an old rifle for a fancy wool dress at a store in Knoxville and made her wear it instead of the camo. It was made of wool and serge, a far cry from the feed sack clothing of Earl's family. She was pretty already, but the dress made her look stunning. He'd borrowed a suit for Earl to wear.

Everyone was impressed...except Wanda Mae Sutterfield, Ocie Mae's single sister, who was green with envy and jealousy. Wanda Mae was almost fifteen and still unmarried, and the clock was ticking loudly. Earl felt uncomfortable in the flatlander suit with a white shirt and bolo tie he'd borrowed from Booker T for the occasion. Booker had lots of fancy clothes. The month before, Booker had won a poker game and walked away with big money. Since then, he's had lots of friends.

In those days, newly married couples usually just moved in and lived temporarily with one of their parents until they could find a place, often the bride's parents. Earl thanked Mr. and Mrs. Johnson, but plans had already been made to move in with his momma on the farm near Bulls Gap. Mr. Johnson was agreeable with this arrangement and went further and kindly offered to take his kids and wife and spend three days visiting his aunt in Sevierville to free up their house for Earl and Sherry so they could get some private "gittin'-to-know-each-other" time. It was just a hop, skip, and jump down the road to Sevierville. Unlike Earl's family, Sherry's folks owned a running car.

But there was another wedding practice. In front of everyone, Sherry's daddy ceremonially lightly smacked her on the left cheek with his shoe (Yes, he wore shoes). It was widely believed this would bring good luck to the marriage. Sherry's momma then gave her a poke full of sunflower seeds to assure she'd have a passel of grandkids. Earl, accustomed to saying the wrong thing at the wrong times, blurted out. "I guarant-dang-tee ya, we'll give hit our absolute best shot!"

Earl felt like he was the luckiest man in the world because Sherry had said yes to his marriage proposal. Or did she propose to him? He was so shook up he didn't remember. Either way, life was good.

HILLBILLY WEDDING PARTY OF THE DECADE
(Part 5)

The courtship and marriage customs of old Appalachia reflect the unique and charming character and rich cultural heritage of the Southern Highlands. However, one must remember that some activities are frowned upon, immoral, or illegal. Of course, depending on where and how one was raised, the boundaries between one or the other can become blurred.

For example, displays of affection in public were often discouraged. Wedding parties were popular because this was a reasonably safe location in which to look for a marriageable mate. Still, one had to be cautious because fathers and tattletales were usually nearby. Couples were chaperoned whenever possible, and people from outside the community were scrutinized and watched closely. Young couples were generally watched to help ensure that the women's chastity was protected. Other than getting married or having a chaperone around, there wasn't much time to be together alone with someone of the opposite sex.

That said, unlike what you may see in the movies, Appalachian marriage celebrations weren't just pulling taffy and shucking corn. These were also good excuses and opportunities for young folks to play post office and other creative games. When the adults weren't looking, a girl would go into a separate room, call out a boy's name, and tell him she had a letter in mind. If he guessed it, he could go in and kiss her. Of course, she determined if he guessed the correct letter or not. Otherwise, after three unsuccessful tries, the opportunity went to the next boy in line. Or they'd play spin-the-bottle. This was a non-discriminatory game where the boy spins a bottle and kisses the girl to whom it points when it stops. If the bottle stopped on a boy, it was re-spun. Other variations of these games got made up as the night went on…if the chaperones let their guard down.

In any case, at wedding parties, there were ample opportunities for young people to slip out the door to sneak off to the two-holer outhouse to tinkle or take a whiz. If the line was short, say a boy and a girl who found themselves alone, opportunities sometimes presented themselves wherein freedom opened up and doors were closed…or they'd wander off into the woods for a spell "to wait their turn" and to get a breath of fresh air. Sometimes, the air got so hot and heavy during the waits that entire new weddings were initiated.

Since the Johnsons' house couldn't hold all the people who came, they spilled into the yard, and cars and pickups packed the field next door. There weren't enough chairs, so hay bales were scattered around the lawn. The night air was pretty cool, so there was a bonfire in a makeshift fire pit dug into the yard, and weenies were being roasted. Despite being cool, the Johnsons had arranged some hay bales into a rectangle, draped a tarp over them, filled it with water, and had a swimming pool for those who liked to swim. This was a real hit until someone dumped a water snake in it. Ruben got the blame because he collected rattlesnakes for fun and profit. He also provided eastern diamondback rattlesnake "mystery meat" for the event. He labeled them "Mountain Round Steaks."

Most of the drinking happened in the parking lot to avoid offending the bride's family, although half-pint bottles were seen being passed around when the Johnsons or Carters weren't looking.

A highlight of the evening was a group of country western singers accompanied by a small band. Carol Hughett got them going by singing, *"Will the Circle Be Unbroken?"* Carol sang this song in bars and roadhouses throughout the South and even owned a sequined suit for his performances. Everyone was invited to sing along. This popular Christian song was about the hope of reuniting with loved ones in heaven after death. It was a favorite of the Carter family, Johnny Cash, Nitty Gritty Dirt Band, Randy Travis, and others.

As the evening wore on, the music got louder, and the dancing got faster. The only dancing allowed at the Johnson place was cloggin' and flatfootin, two Appalachian dances that didn't allow touching the opposite sex.

In the South, there's always plenty of food whenever there's a celebration. It's a bottom-line requirement. Zelbert and Ocie Mae provided three country hams, eight pints of blackberry jam, and a large platter of chitlins. This was mainly a potluck event, and several tables overflowed with food for the nearly eighty family members and friends attending.

A sampling of foods available included deep-fried chicken, macaroni and cheese, collard greens, cornbread, buttermilk, peach cobbler, chicken and dumplings, meatloaf, mashed taters, corned beef and cabbage, coleslaw, grits, smothered turkey parts, pot roast, dressing, hoppin' John, deviled eggs, baked beans, fried catfish, tomato/watermelon salad, creamed corn, banana pudding, peach cobbler, fried okra, catfish, green trout, fried green tomatoes, sweet tater pie, buttermilk sky-high pie, apple pie, pecan pie, ambrosia, carrot cake, sweet tea, RC Cola, hibiscus tea, lemonade, and a wagon load of other food and drinks. There was no shortage of food, and people came and went at the food tables all during the day and evening.

Now, let me make it clear here that neither Earl nor his bride, Sherry, nor their parents drank alcoholic beverages. They were teetotalers from way back. On the other hand, whenever you gather this many people into one location with that much food and chaos, someone will sneak in some liquor.

Although Nathan and Bryant Gulley, and Berthy Hughett were invited, all three said they'd rather not get involved in "all that foolishness" and didn't attend. They agreed, "It's jist a weddin', after all!"

Some noticed that, sitting in the shadows near the bucket of lemonade, someone had placed another bucket they called "Coon Dog Punch," and kids were discouraged from dipping into it. Into that, people were invited to toss any variety of drinks, as long as it wasn't water.

Another table included rare meat offerings and was accompanied by a sign indicating that the table hosted a "Mystery Meat Contest." Each meat was numbered with a tag, and people were invited to guess what animal the meat came from after tasting it. The platters were numbered 1 through 10. What meats were offered? I'll tell you, but the attendees didn't find out until the evening was about over and the plates were mostly empty.

Ruben Carter said some people got sick to their stomachs, but that it was all in their minds. Of course, Ruben was in charge of the table. Platter # 1 was heaped up with *No-luck doe* venison that Forrest Johnson had "harvested" with his pickup on the way to the wedding. Platter #2 contained *'57 Pontiac wild turkey* "straight from the grill," Platter #3 was full of *filet of raccoon*, Platter #4 had *creamed possum*, Platter #5 was overflowing with *fried drum fish*, Platter #6 contained very carefully prepared *Chunk-of-Skunk* polecat hors d'oeuvres, Platter #6 was full of *"didn't quite make it" fried squirrel*, Platter # 7 contained highway *pavement quail*,

Platter # 7 was full of *steamed crow*, Platter # 8 boasted *fricasseed frog* legs, and Platter # 9 contained *rattlesnake round steaks*. Finally, Platter # 10 contained *beer-basted prime steak meat* from an Angus cow that somehow had wandered onto Jake's property. When the identity of the meats was unveiled, it was interesting to see the various reactions and even more interesting that the Angus steak meat only ranked number 4 in popularity. There was food for every taste! By the way, Robert Johnson was the winner of the taste test. The grand prize was a box of ammo and a skinning knife.

An interesting aside is that the venison was tender as all get out. It turns out that as Forrest was driving up the "Tail of the Dragon" highway in the Smokies, a deer bolted out, and he had to react quickly in order to hit it. The bull bar on his pickup was mangled and the headlights were broken, but the meat was immediately tenderized and perfect for feeding a lot of people at the wedding reception. He hung the carcass from a tree in the side yard, skinned, dressed, and cut the meat into bits for the Mystery Meat Competition. Grandma Johnson was impressed that Forrest was so thoughtful and complimented him on his choice of meat but hadn't expected him to bring so much to the reception. Forrest just smiled and asked her if she'd like more meat to take home; he had plenty to spare.

There were lots of flowers at the wedding. The bride held a bundle of red roses, and the groom clutched a bunch of white ones. These were supplied by Grandma Johnson, who was ever frugal. There'd been a funeral the day before, and the flowers were just tossed out on the ground. She lived by the motto: "Waste not, want not!"

No celebration is worth anything without fireworks. Cousin Gary came from Hickory, North Carolina, via the Cherokee Indian Reservation and picked up a basket of fireworks for the kids to play with. Some of the men were jealous and organized their own fireworks. Andrew lined up a row of pumpkins on hay bales, filled them with water, and let people take turns shooting them with a 12-gauge shotgun he'd borrowed from the Johnsons' house. It was impressive to see the pumpkins explode after each gun boom. At Gary's urging, the little kids lit bottle rockets and shot them at each other in a pseudo-war. He got the idea from the water balloon fight. However, the grand finale was when Sherry's brother, John, set off a stick of dynamite high in a tree where it could make maximum noise. Once their ears stopped ringing, a few proclaimed the moment as "glorious."

David was a barrel of fun and carved out some party time to plan a follow-up "ATF Party" (Alcohol, Tobacco, and Firearms). Roy contributed to the fun by removing the door from the outhouse and monitoring a knife-throwing competition with the kids. Pretty soon, there was a line of adults wanting to compete. Ever the creative person, Ricky set up a game for the boys to see who could pee the highest up the side of the barn wall. The competition was tight until Earl's sister, Lynda, happened along, hiked her dress up, touched her chin to her toes, and let fly… backward! She won the contest by eight inches, but Aunt Mandy dragged her away by the ear before she could bask in the winner's limelight. Life is not always fair, even to the very talented.

Willie Sue got fed up with her kid's antics and yelled so loud that the windows rattled: "I GAWT ONLY TWO WORDS FER YEW DAD BLAMED KIDS: BEE HAV!!!" I have to admit that the young kids were full of vinegar. Once grounded to the house, little Eura got her hands on a dead squirrel that was in the icebox and was chasing the other kids with it. When yelled at again, she finally calmed down and played with Johnson's three-legged, one-eyed dog, Lucky.

It's fortunate that there was only a single fight during the festivity that I know of. Forrest Johnson got into an argument with Robbie Carter for using his tobacco without permission. In the midst of the discussion, Forrest bit Robbie on the arm, then Robbie knocked Forrest's false teeth out. Last we heard, Robbie went to the Johnsons' next-door neighbor to borrow some Merthiolate and Band-Aids. The neighbors were very hospitable people. They had a front yard ornament made out of bowling balls that was supposed to represent a solar system for their tomato plants. Their house was comprised of two single-wide trailers hooked together side by side with a hole cut in the walls so you could step from one to the other. The neighbor was really handy with a chainsaw and duct taped around the doors to keep the drafts out. Appalachians are creative people. You learn a lot of valuable tricks at family get-togethers.

I probably shouldn't mention this, but Forrest was a delightful person in his own way, although some less tolerant people might be tempted to describe him as "filthy of mind and dirty of body." In life, he was an unfortunate victim of alcohol abuse and spent more time than a man should locked up in the "gray bar hotel." Eventually, he recognized the downside of moonshine and spent the rest of his life helping street people in Knoxville. Also, on the plus side, he was an ingenious trader of anything of value; watches, guns, coon dogs, or whatever. People claimed he could swap a three-legged goat for a racehorse and get twenty dollars to boot. Remember, God loves the sinner too, just not the sin. Forrest was a lot to love.

FIRST NIGHT JITTERS AND THE CLIMAX
(Part 6)

After the partying crowd had gone home, and at about 4 a.m., Earl and Sherry put out the candles and prepared for the honeymoon bed. Both were extremely nervous, but Earl still had hold of the crystal Berthy Hughett had given him, and Sherry had a ton of advice from her girlfriends. Her parents had never dared to provide any sex-ed advice other than, "Watch them hogs, and you'll larn all you needs to know about them birds and bees; only don't pay no mind to the squeals. Mother Nature will larn you the rest."

Sherry entered the bedroom to dress in her nightgown as Earl waited for her. As they were undressing, they could not shake the feeling that they were being watched by something from the woods. They figured it was just their imagination because they were anxious and embarrassed.

Earl sat by Sherry's side on her parents' wooden bed. He kissed her gently on the lips and looked into her eyes. They sparkled like stars. He whispered into her ear and suggested that they make themselves more comfortable.

Just after they had timidly removed most of their clothes, they heard strange sounds coming from the woods outside the window. It was horrible, as if several dying cats were being attacked by dogs. Earl went to the window to check things out, and the sound got louder and louder. He looked in the closet for Mr. Johnson's shotgun, but it was not there. Then, they heard all manner of caterwauling, banging, cowbells, hollering, and a few blood-curdling screams. Earl grabbed the fireplace poker and ran to the door in his underwear. The door flew open, and amidst yells and more screams, a blanket was thrown over his head; he was gagged, his hands and legs were tied up, and he was drug kicking and yelling into the woods behind the house where he was left to think about how grand being married was.

It finally dawned on them that the young folks in the neighborhood were giving them an old-fashioned shivaree or 'serenade.' These take on various forms. City folks write cute sayings on car windshields and tie tin cans to bumpers. Mountain folks are considerably more creative.

I write of the shivaree custom in considerable detail in Volume Two of Musing Appalachia (Available on Amazon), but I will only say here that Earl and Sherry got off easy. In any case, he was dumped in the woods about a hundred yards from the house for an hour or so until he could work himself loose. Sherry was horribly worried but too terrified to go outside and look for Earl. Then the door slung open again. Sherry's girlfriends tossed a sack of self-rising flour in her face, causing temporary blindness and covering her head in white. Another slipped a handful of sugar into the top of her panties "to sweeten things up." The intruders then promptly left.

There was no shower in the house, but there was a towel and a bucket of water at the base of the bed used to wash road dust off, but it wasn't enough, and there was no way she was going outside. So, she hid under a blanket in a corner and contemplated her next steps, the major one being what would happen to her if she broke number six of God's ten commandments.

For sure, shivarees are good fun! However, they can get a little out of hand. Shivarees were great entertainment for the mountain kids and always anticipated with glee, but Earl wasn't a good sport and saw absolutely no humor in the frivolity.

Eventually, the revelers got tired and went home. Earl worked himself loose, washed himself off with a fresh pail of water he drew from the well, and attempted to resume his married life where he'd left off. Unfortunately, Sherry had hardly slept for the past four days, what with all the marriage preparations and excitement, and had fallen into a deep sleep. She was dead to the world and, for all practical purposes, out of commission for conjugal pleasures.

Earl fell asleep clutching the enchanted crystal Berthy had given him and had sweet dreams of a sweeter awakening. The nightmare was over, and his life's dream was just beginning.

But things got better. Although there wasn't a shower and they didn't have running water in the house, Mr. Johnson had placed a porcelain-covered steel bathtub in the backyard behind the rose bushes. Mrs. Johnson would carry buckets of hot water (heated on the kitchen wood stove) to the bathtub, and she and her husband would have a nice soak.

When everyone was gone from the homestead and they were finally alone, Earl got out of bed, stoked up a fire in the stove, and heated water for the outdoor tub. Then, the newlyweds basked together in the warm, soothing water. All was good until they heard a car coming up the driveway. They took off running for the house, only they forgot to take their clothes. Later that evening, Earl made a mental note to get a larger tub, put it on cinder blocks, and build a small fire under it to heat the water when he could afford a house. AND, it would have a privacy wall around it.

The rest of the day was paradisical. The last thing they remembered was just how loud the creaking wooden bed was. Their firstborn child was a girl, and they named her Johnna.

And they lived happily ever after...sorta.

POSSUM ROULETTE
AND COONHOUND MADNESS

The first time that Uncle Nathan was released from Brushy Mountain State Penitentiary in Petros, Tennessee, he was paroled on the condition that he no longer make moonshine. This presented a problem because that was all he knew how to do to put food on the table for his family. Fortunately, while locked up, he learned some new tricks from the other inmates, and one of the most promising was gambling. He'd never had much luck at gambling, but a creative twist came to his mind and inspired him to try, promising to make him rich —maybe even enough money to buy a car.

The idea for his new venture was born while coon hunting with his bluetick hound, Sooner (He'd "sooner" eat than anything). They'd surprised a possum in the woods, and it took off running for the base of a cliff where there were two burrows. The possum ran into one of the holes, but Nathan wasn't sure which one. In reality, there was only one hole, but Nathan had been drinking and, for the time being, was seeing double. It was in this condition that the idea for possum roulette was born.

The plan was simple. He made seventeen wire cages and set them up in a circle in an open area in the woods behind his cabin near Bulls Gap. Each enclosure was assigned a number from 1 to 17. This was a high-stakes game for mountain folk, and in order to play, each participant had to pay $1 per round in hard cash. Nathan's cousin Jimmy was the scorekeeper and cashier. His job was mostly to keep the game on track, collect the money, and pay out to the winners. It would be a game that combined luck, strategy, and a hint of mischief.

The procedure involved the guys standing around the outside of the circle of cages, hoping the possum placed in the center would enter the numbered cage they had bet on. For example, with 17 cages and only 10 guys betting, there often would be times when no one would win, and the money would stay with the "house" (that is, Nathan). This was how Nathan would make money. If the possum entered the number that a guy had bet on, that person would get $17. However, to increase the odds of winning, a person had the option of making a "holler bet" on three consecutive numbers, and he'd win if the possum entered into cages with either of the numbers. However, a holler bet costs $4 per round. By Nathan's calculations, he would be the biggest winner when the dust settled.

The night before the games, Nathan and Sooner rounded up a bunch of wild possums. There were two big males, a feisty female, and two small blue possums. Of course, it was anticipated that when a possum was released in the center of the circle, it would run into one of the cages to hide and, hopefully, identify a winner...or not. Nathan didn't want many winners.

Each possum was given a name. The big males were named Pawsome and Booger. The female was given the name of Peepers because of her eyes. The little blue possums went by the names of Sprout and Squeaky. Squeaky was not a good name for a possum because possums don't make any kind of noise, and that includes squeaks. They just grin. Of course, Sprout was a dumb name, too, but they served the purpose.

He invited some of his moonshine-drinking buddies and trusted friends to participate in the first game of possum roulette. A few of the more colorful guys were:

Nathan's brother, Bryant. He showed up wearing a cowboy hat and a toothpick dangling from the corner of his mouth.

Then there was Berthy's old man, Tom Dyer, a trickster. He snuck along a high-pitched dog whistle in his pocket, hoping it would appeal to the possum and lure it into a cage. Only animals, including possums, could hear the whistle call.

Also, there was Earl Carter from the Carter County clan. He always had lots of plans, but they often backfired. Like most of the Carters, he was a wiry fellow with a knack for getting into trouble. Earl was known for his quick thinking and even quicker feet when attempting to evade trouble. Despite his best efforts, he never seemed to win, but that didn't stop him from trying. However, on the plus side, he had the best-looking wife, although she'd have kicked his butt had she known he was playing possum roulette.

Uncle John was the oldest of the group and had a natural talent for training animals. He figured he could outthink the possums. He raised skunks for profit, figuring that possums would be attracted to the way they smelled.

Booker T was also in attendance. He was the laziest of the bunch but was also usually the luckiest. If you don't already know it, dumb luck always trumps talent in this world. With his infectious grin and easygoing attitude, Booker thought he could charm the possums into the cage he chose. It never worked with the women he tried to corner, but he figured that possums were way more intelligent than the women he'd met, and his charm might just be the ticket for possums. He asked Earl what his secret was for attracting a good-looking woman, but Earl only said, "You ain't lookin' at 'em with yore eyes right. Let yore eyes do the talkin'."

Tiny Cobb was nicknamed "Tiny" due to his 340 pounds of boasted but unproven muscle. Despite his imposing exterior, he had a soft spot for animals and considered possums to be his friends.

With this colorful cast of characters, the Possum Roulette was bound to be a success. Of course, in this group, there was a good chance that someone might accidentally cheat, so several preventative measures were taken. To this end, Nathan's cousin, Jimmy, wasn't allowed to bet. He had to remain neutral, oversee the game, and pay the winners. Also, between rounds, the cages would be randomly rearranged. Jimmy would regularly check the cages to ensure no external influences, such as food or scents, were sneaked into a particular cage. None of the spectators or participants was allowed to enter the circle or physically interfere or try to guide the possum. Only Jimmy was allowed to release a possum, and he made sure to place it in the very center of the circle and ensure the possum was calm before he turned it loose. If anyone was caught cheating, he was banned from playing the current round or future games.

Under the canopy of the towering trees, the circle of seventeen cages sat in the middle of a clearing, and, finally, it was time for the games to begin. In the first round, ten men gathered around, each with a pocket full of cash, ready to bet on the cage they figured the possum would scurry into. Possums are unpredictable, so it was anyone's guess who would win, but Nathan was banking on being the biggest winner because he'd thought hard about the odds while making his last run of likker.

Jimmy announced, "OK, boys, place yore bets!" The men lined up and threw down their money, each one confident they'd go home that night with a pocket bulging with money.

The first possum to be turned loose was Pawsome, the largest of the group and, from outward appearances, an absolute stud.

As soon as the last bet was placed, Jimmy gently set Pawsome in the center of the circle. The possum looked around, bewildered by the sudden freedom. The anticipation was palpable, with each man holding his breath, eyes glued to the critter.

Within seconds of being released, all the men cheered and yelled for Pawsome to run and hide in the cage they'd chosen. Despite his large size, Pawsome turned out not to be awesome. Hearing all the racket, he just lay down on the ground and fell asleep. Nothing would wake him up. He lay there with his tongue hanging out and drooling until Jimmy carefully picked him up and gently placed him in the woods, where he could return to his family. An hour later, he was still "playing possum."

Next, Jimmy turned loose Peepers, the female possum. True to her name, Peepers promptly peed, then took a tentative step towards cage 13, then she quickly changed direction and headed for cage 11. When the crowd erupted in cheers and groans, Peepers reversed direction and ran to the other side of the circle and hid in cage number 7. With a grin, Tiny Cobb ambled forward and collected seventeen dollars.

Then, Jimmy released Sprout, one of the little blue possums. Sprout must have been too dumb to be afraid because he calmly ambled over to cage 6, took a sniff, then moved to cage 9 before making a sudden detour and scampering into cage 3. Unbeknownst to Jimmy, Earl Carter had hidden a piece of cheese under cage 3. With a knowing look in his eyes, Earl stepped forward and collected seventeen dollars.

At this point, Nathan started panicking because he wasn't making any money. The men burst out into laughter and applause, congratulating Earl, who danced a little flatfoot while waving the money.

The next possum to be released was the other male, Booger. Booger got that name because he smelled like all possums…like a bad booger. When released, Tom Dyer turned his back to the guys to fake a cough, slipped the dog whistle into his mouth, and blew in anticipation of luring Booger to cage 2, where he'd placed his bet. Interestingly, Booger was heading towards that side of the circle, but when he heard the whistle (that only dogs and animals can hear), he came to a screeching halt, wrinkled his nose, and looked confused. Then he high-tailed it to the opposite side of the circle and beelined it towards cage 16. No one had bet on 16, so Nathan was already dancing a jig. But his celebration was premature.

Possum Roulette

Blowing the dog whistle proved to be a bad move because when Tom blew the whistle, Old Sooner and four coonhound friends came running, jumped across the cages, and took off, chasing Booger into the trees. They upset the cage with the remaining possums in it, and they all ran into the woods. It was chaos, with possums, hounds, and men running around and yelling.

It was at that time that the game warden showed up. One of the men's wives had heard where her husband was going, and she objected by alerting the Warden. He said, "You boys know that using wildlife in your games is illegal. You cain't do that. You're all under arrest! Ever one of you!"

The men stood silent, their laughter evaporating in the face of authority. Nathan, ever the spokesperson, stepped forward. "Hit's jist a bit of fun, occifer. They ain't no harm being done."

The ranger shook his head. "Fun or not, it's still against the law. Possums deserve to be in the wild, not part of your games. Now, line up."

To this, Nathan replied, "Warden, what possums is you talkin' about? I don't see no possums nowhere around hyar." Luckily, all the possums had escaped, but the baying dogs could be heard in the woods.

So, the night ended well for everyone except for Nathan. He just took a flask from a pocket in his overalls and thought about resurrecting a spare moonshine still he had hidden in the brush up on Piney Mountain.

HOW MANY TEATS ON A POSSUM?

Do you know how many teats a momma possum has? You won't believe me when I tell you. I've studied possums and I know more about them than 99.9% of the people in the world. Read on, and you will too.

Here's the answer: Thirteen (13) TWELVE TEATS ARE ARRANGED IN A CIRCLE ON THE MOMMA POSSUM'S BELLY, AND THE THIRTEENTH IS FOUND RIGHT SMACK DAB IN THE CENTER OF THE CIRCLE! Now, you gotta admit, that's amazing! When people cuddle possums, I guess they fail to look inside their pouch where the little suckers are hidden. The pouch is sorta like Mother Nature's organic bra.

Kangaroos also have pouches in which to carry their young. They generally only give birth to one baby at a time. I don't know why, but they call them "joeys." In a way, kangaroos are a bit more complicated than possums in a dairy sort of way. While they have only one baby at a time, they have four teats and get this... each teat can produce milk with varying nutrient compositions! For example, the lowest teat in the pouch provides milk that is perfect for a tiny newborn joey and has an exceptionally high protein content for initial growth. In contrast, other teats located higher up in the pouch produce milk rich in fats and carbohydrates. As the joey grows to the level of the higher teat, that one is specially formulated for more energy. Try topping that! Don't believe me? Google it!

My Uncle Bryant told me that his cow had a teat that gave chocolate milk, but he lied. My cousin and I tried for 30 minutes to get some once, but never had success.

Unlike kangaroos, possums and humans are somewhat disadvantaged when it comes to nutritious titties. I suspect that says something about us, but it is what it is.

When born, baby possums are the size of a bumblebee. That said, if you could get them away from momma possum, up to 20 would fit into a regular tablespoon. I've not tried this because possums have sharp teeth and, like all mothers, dislike having their babies stacked into a spoon. Nevertheless, I urge you to try it and let me know how it goes.

Although you'd think that thirteen would be plenty of babies, even for most Appalachians, they (the possums) can bear up to twenty young'uns at a time. With only 12+1 teats, competition among the babies is fierce. People who study this stuff more than I do claim that only the first 12 or 13 to latch on to a teat will survive and grow up. I'm guessing that more than 13 baby possums might make it if one loses a grip and another quickly sucks itself into place, taking turns.

The only question I have is, how did scientists figure all this stuff out, given that possums rear their babies hidden inside a pouch? Do they put little GoPro cameras in there? As a kid growing up and studying possums, I didn't have a camera, but I did have a pet possum. Clyde wasn't a female and didn't sport a pouch.

But all this does bring up the question: If a humanoid has squalling triplets or quadruplets but only two milk outlets, how do they manage? My momma only had one kid at a time, so I had a free-for-all.

Because this is a family publication, I'm not going to go into detail on the following totally true fact, but I would be remiss if I didn't tell you that possums are extraordinarily gifted in another way. The females have two vaginal tracts and two uteri, and males, in turn, have a forked pecker. Please don't take my word for it; Google that too. I don't make stuff up. In Appalachia, some people believe that the male possums impregnate the females through the nose, but that's not true…as far as I know.

It's true that possums ("opossums" if you're a Yankee) play dead. Actually, in my experience, if you scare them enough, they faint. Those are really seizures that cause them to flop over on the ground, where they can lay for hours just staring blankly, drooling, and sticking out their tongue. You'd swear they're dead. They have no control over doing this, but stress seems to bring it on. I'm told that pointy-head university professors claim that this same play-dead tactic occasionally works when a bear attacks a person. If true, I guess humans learned that trick from possums, but I don't know if you're supposed to let your tongue hang out and drool when attacked by a bear. In any case, the lesson here is, if you find a possum that appears dead, don't bury it unless it's a totally flattened pavement possum you encounter on the highway. Or you can feed it to your cat if it's been there for a while. It's like jerky. If I were you, I'd suggest not eating it yourself. Possum in any form is an acquired taste.

As I mentioned earlier, I once had a possum as a pet. I named him Clyde after Clyde Snowdon, a former Sheriff at Morristown, Tennessee. I forgot why I chose that name, but it seemed like the right thing to do at the time. Like the sheriff, Clyde wasn't overly friendly, and although he was threatening, he never bit me. *Note: If a cop pulls you over and he's grinning like a possum, it's going to be a bad day for you.*

You ask, do possums stink? Clyde never smelled bad for the whole two years he owned me. However, in the wild, when I scared a possum enough, they sometimes smelled putrid. That's another part of their protection strategy and may help explain why they've survived as a species for 65 million years, from the time of the Cretaceous-Paleogene era. For example, to add to their show of playing dead, they sometimes secrete noxious, smelly stuff from their anus and empty their bowels. I swear to you on a stack of holy land travel brochures that after this happens, a possum is not something you want to take home to show Momma. However, if you're ever attacked by a vicious bear or your ex-wife, I suggest that you try this novel possum technique. Common sense says that it would work 99% of the time.

In their defense, except for when they're trying to scare predators away from them, possums are constantly grooming themselves, kinda like narcissistic cats do. They regularly and thoroughly groom themselves. Part of this is due to the fact that they hardly have sweat glands, so this helps them stay cool and pretty well odorless (except when really irritated). This reminds me of an angry woman I used to know, but I'm sticking to the topic of possums in this essay.

Possums eat about anything. I fed Clyde mostly leftovers from our dinner table, and he loved them all. He'd eat lettuce right along with country ham. He'd even eat kale, although I never touch that stuff. He once ate a jalapeño pepper and didn't even belch. He was great at eating bugs or mice in our house. We never let him outside because the dogs are never nice to possums.

Out in nature, when they get lucky, possums eat a lot of dead and rotten animals. This helps build up their resistance to diseases. Also, they don't get rabies. Pointy-headed university professors say this is because their body temperature is pretty low. Poisonous snakes, except for coral snakes, can't kill possums because they're immune to the venom. Coral snakes have the same venom as cobras, and that's really bad juju. When possums come across snakes, they're just another meal...and that includes rattlesnakes. In this way, possums are your friend and should be loved.

People think possums are dimwitted, and, in my study, I pretty well have to agree, although, if you think about it, they've existed for millions of years. That's something that no human has been able to accomplish. Very few animals and no humans have been able to survive that long, although Elvis is giving it a shot. If being dimwitted and having lots of kids promotes longevity, I have some kinfolks who may never die. Now that I think about it, there's an old feller who lives up Gulley Holler who appears to be just one step above a Neanderthal. I gotta remember to ask him about possums.

That reminds me of an old joke: "Why did the chicken cross the road? To prove to the possum that it could be done." Yeah, that's pretty lame, but there are worse jokes about blondes.

Possum tails are snake-like and come in handy as an extra arm or leg. They can carry things with their tails, hang onto tree branches, and do whatever else strikes their fancy. I once asked my Aunt Berthy why it was that possums didn't have hair on their tails like squirrels and raccoons, and she said that in the earliest days, possums were vain creatures with beautiful, bushy tails. Being proud and boastful, they showed them off at every opportunity. The fox was considered to be wise, so the possum asked for advice on how to make its tail even more stunning. The fox was fed up with the possum's vanity and told it to soak its tail in a concoction that would make it shine brightly and be more beautiful than ever. Unfortunately, the mixture caused the opossum's hair to fall out, leaving its tail bare. From that time on, possums have had hairless tails. Aunt Berthy warned me not to get vain or boastful, or that something bad might happen to my own tail. Berthy was smart.

Possums are your secret friend in various ways. They are immune to Lyme disease and eat about 5,000 ticks each season.

Please don't hurt them. They may be saving your life, and you don't even know it!

When it comes to remembering where they have found food, they have better memories than dogs, cats, and even rats. And they have a great sense of smell. How do we know this? Your hard-earned tax dollars helped fund scientific studies that uncovered this vital information.

I saved the best for last. Do people eat possums? Absolutely! My family is from the Bulls Gap area of East Tennessee, and possum was common table fare with some of my kinfolks. Of course, when we discovered hamburgers, our diet changed a bit. Possum was considered a readily available source of protein during hard times when other food was scarce. However, it's less commonly eaten in modern times except in certain areas (like West Virginia). Historically, possum meat has been a part of traditional diets in various cultures, particularly in the southern USA. It's often prepared in stews or baked, and the taste is sorta gamey, similar to swamp rabbit or dark meat poultry. I have a recipe for possum stew, but we usually ate it roasted like a small piglet with apples, raisins, and other taste-averters stuffed inside them.

So, nestled in the rugged beauty of the Appalachian Mountains lies a treasure trove of moonshiners, granny women, ramp-eating people, stunning scenery…and lots of possums.

> *Sorry, no photo here. Possums bite when you start messing with them. Can you imagine holding their pouch open and trying to take a photo while they are snapping at you with their sharp teeth? If you don't believe this story, use Google or AI to verify. Mother Nature is amazing.*

THE HILLBILLY SUNSHINE CAFÉ AND FEED STORE

"You'uns git thet dad-blamed moonshine outta my kitchen. They ain't gonna be no drinkin' in this eatin' place. Sinners can go nex' door to the Half-Star Hotel and buy hit iffen they wants hit! Now, git outta my way; I got some serious cookin' to do."

In the 1950s, Bulls Gap, Tennessee, had very few eating establishments, except for a small counter in the corner of the Bulls Gap Feed Store, where they served baloney sandwiches, RC Colas, Moon Pies, Tom's Peanuts, and similar essential food items. The town was ripe to have a genuine restaurant. To this end… and in an attempt to get filthy rich…several local families banded together to fill the Gap.

The last major feeding operation in the Gap occurred shortly after the town was established by an important Civil War battle, when soldiers needed to eat. The Confederates had built important earthwork fortifications to defend a critical east-west transportation route where the East Tennessee and Virginia Railroad crossed Bay's Mountain. This was along the route from Chattanooga through Knoxville and across the Appalachian Mountains to Lynchburg, Virginia. Union Brigadier General Alvan C. Gillem had a big battle with Confederate General John C. Breckinridge and got his butt whipped. He claimed it was because he had run out of ammunition and food. After the Big War was over and the soldiers left, there wasn't much in the way of a classy food place until the Hillbilly Sunshine Café and Snack Bar came to life.

From the start, the 'Shine Café, as it came to be known, had the honorable intent of bringing genuine Appalachian mountain food to the locals and hapless touristers who might have gotten lost and ended up hungry in Bulls Gap.

The original idea for the restaurant originated with Booker T, a local man who was working pretty hard on "turning over a new leaf." He was trying to quit his sinnin' ways and make some honest money for a change. He inherited a house on Bulls Gap's main street from his momma and remodeled it into the occasionally busy Snuggle Inn Half-Star Hotel. He billed it as the town's major (actually, only) "sleepin' place" in the area and started out by not allowing any "drinkin', gamblin' or whorin'." Generally, he was pretty successful at sticking to his guidelines. In actual practice, the hotel's guidelines were just "suggestions," and he struggled to build a good reputation while still bringing in enough money to fund his major bad habit…voracious eating. He lived to eat. This was exacerbated by the sad fact that he was more than a bit lazy when it came to any kind of labor, which extended to cooking. This was a significant handicap for a person who had never attracted a regular spouse and was living in a small town with no restaurants. He was getting tired of eating Spam sandwiches, Moon Pies, and cola drinks and yearned for some variety.

No one would believe it, but Booker T was a thin man at one time, but his predilection for food had brought him to a new level of 363 very enjoyable pounds. His actual weight depended on what he ate that day, but he didn't keep track.

His late momma had been renting out the property on which the feed store sat, but the lease contract was for fifty years, so even though she'd died, he couldn't kick the feed store out. He'd always wanted to put a restaurant there in its place, a dream of his that never went away.

About once a month, Bryant Gulley would venture out of Gulley Holler, over near Whitesburg, and come to town to sell his herbal cure-all elixirs and organic potions. He claimed they would cure pretty well anything known to mankind (and women) except death. Of course, he accepted no responsibility for people who happened to pass into the other world, leaving that option open to God. He was not one to argue with God.

His regular customers used his "recipes" for healing, enhancing well-being, and what he called "magical enhancements." He claimed that extracts he'd squeezed out of wild herbs and plants found in the hills could make one's body "extraordinary." That meant that using his concoctions could alleviate pain and diseases and, most notably, enhance one's love life ... sometimes by a considerable amount. Bryant's energy elixirs were his most popular anchor products, and they never failed to keep his fourteen kids fed, but shoes were not always possible. He had a plan for that, and the café idea was a crucial part of it.

Despite the shoes, even in the rural mountain community, Bryant's business was thriving enough for him to purchase forty acres of steep mountain scabland and construct a cabin almost adequate for accommodating the overflow of children, his chickens, and a couple of mules housed underneath the downhill side. Life was good for Bryant, but he occasionally longed for a new challenge.

At one point, he got into a conversation with Booker T, and Booker shared that he wanted a restaurant but wasn't interested in setting one up himself. He was not attracted to the idea of cooking and serving food to others. His interest was primarily in eating… in large quantities. He dreamed of a friendly establishment where he could get free meals and still take advantage of the feed store's strategic location next to the motel where he lived.

Bryant was a thinking man known to be the most intelligent person in the surrounding hills. He could even read, and it was known that he actually owned several books. His favorites were the Bible and "*A Thousand and One Formulas: The Laboratory Handbook for the Experimenter*" by Sidney Gernsback.

From the Gernsback book, he learned many exciting things, including practical recipes for crafting new elixirs and making explosives. In the 1950s, the head of the Soviet Union, Nikita Khrushchev, created hysteria and fear in the United States by threatening nuclear war. Just as a precaution, Bryant attempted to use homemade dynamite to blast a bomb shelter into a rock cliff in front of his cabin. That didn't end well; he blew the porch off his house, and flying rocks caused a lot of holes in his tin roof. Since that didn't work out, he decided to try a different approach to protecting his family from imagined Russian invaders and bought a shotgun and two boxes of shells instead.

> *Note from the author: This was an actual event, and old-time locals still talk about Bryant's failed attempt to build a bomb shelter, as well as his fame for selling elixirs and fathering 14+1 children. However, some of my relatives have disputed the exact number of children since the publication of my book, Musing Appalachia: Volume 1 (available on Amazon). I was going off the number that Bryant himself told me. My mother always claimed that 14+1 was "on the low side." Perhaps only God knows the actual number? In any case, he clearly made a strong case for the efficiency of his elixirs when he fathered his last documented child at the age of 82. He told me that he planned to live until 110 years "unless hit's God's will to take me afore then."*
>
> *I also wrote about the "plus one" child. Here, I will only say that he didn't get shot by an irate husband,*

but he did end up being found guilty by the Hamblen County court and had to make payments for child support. That story was written in the newspapers, and his "special recipe" sales increased.

Another book in Bryant's library was *"The History of the Decline and Fall of the Roman Empire"* by Edward Gibbon. From this, he gained a deeper understanding of human nature and psychology. I apologize for digressing from the café story, but when Bryant's name comes up, I have many old memories, and I want to write them down before I get Alzheimer's, "unless hit's God's will to take me afore then."

The outcome of Booker T's conversation with Bryant Gulley was that Bryant would go back to his cabin and see what he could do to organize a plan for a restaurant and recruit staff. For Booker T's part, he would give the feed store leaseholder the good news that "the best restaurant to ever come to Bulls Gap" would soon share space in his establishment. That way, people could buy meals for both them and their animals just by stepping into the other side of the store. And, they only had a short walk next door to the Half-Star Hotel for the other creature comforts that human bodies desire.

And the planning began!

Bryant returned to his cabin, devised a plan for a café, and organized a meeting with his trusted neighbors. He limited attendance to only those with an entrepreneurial spirit and who wanted to get filthy rich by extracting money from hungry people who craved genuine country cooking…not the sissy foods served in the restaurants in the flatlands.

The Bulls Gap Feed Store was located in the heart of the community and had a good reputation. If they didn't sell it, you probably didn't need it. Also, in addition to rubbing elbows with people at church, it was also a good place to meet people. The café didn't dare compete with the church and stayed closed on Sundays.

Bryant's "café elite team" consisted of the following people with varying skills and culinary-related talents. Of course, there was Bryant, who knew every medicinal herb and edible wild food growing in the hills. He also knew which mushrooms were edible, which were poisonous, and which ones would "perk you up and make you feel like you could do a week's work in about ten minutes." However, ginseng root extracts were his specialty. His wife, Annie Evans Gulley, had a collection of cast-iron skillets and could make cornbread and beans more desirable than the best caviar. And, of course, with so many kids, getting someone to help run the homestead was not a problem, although outfitting them all with shoes was a goal that was often beyond his reach.

His primary goal for the restaurant was to create a cozy setting in the foothills of the Great Smoky Mountains, where the air smells of pine and honeysuckle, and folks could gather together, trade stories, and find comfort while eating their favorite mountain food.

Concerning a dress code for employees, he surmised that having the restaurant workers go barefoot and wear bib overalls and flour sack dresses would lend an air of authenticity to the operation and cut down on their costs because they could just simply wear their everyday clothes.

Then, there were Zelbert and Ocie Mae Nicodemus, a newly married couple anxious to find their place in life, build a homestead, and populate it with kids and more pigs. Wanda Mae, Ocie's feisty sister, also joined the staff. She had two pet rattlesnakes and dreams of becoming a chef. Already, she was pretty good at making biscuits and red-eye gravy and had made a pie once. Her Aunt Flossie volunteered to be the chief cook in the small kitchen. Flossie was sassy but could fry chicken with a blindfold over her eyes and both arms tied behind her back.

Nathan Gulley, the moonshiner, was too busy with his booming business to be sidetracked by such "triflin' foolishness." Still, his wife, Luly, was excited to get out of the house and learn a trade that could tide her over during those times when Nathan was hauled off to jail for illegally making "nature's old-timey blow out and starter."

Aunt Berthy Hughett, Crazy Daisy, and Miz Kitty Ledbedder would be brought in to teach the team the best recipes handed down in their families. Squint Ledbedder had brought Miz Kitty back from France after World War II as a "War Trophy Wife," and she was targeted to add some knowledge of French cooking to the menu offerings.

For music, they'd feature Carol Hughett on the guitar, often wearing his sequined suit and western hat when he was in town between gigs around the Nashville area. He generally hung out in "music city" itself, hoping to break into the big time. In the meantime, while waiting, he played in bars and dives wherever he could. Occasionally, he'd get asked back for a follow-up performance. (Note: *Carol Hughett was great-uncle Commodore's son who made an intermittent living playing and singing in honky-tonks. Commodore was known for several things, but the most noteworthy was being struck and killed by lightning. I wrote about Commodore's demise in Musing Appalachia).*

The problem of where to locate the new restaurant had been solved by Booker T's offer to dedicate part of the space in the feed store. He had the feed store owner over a barrel since he technically owned the property. Along with the feed store and the Half-Star Hotel, he had a little "restaurant startup" money left over from his momma's inheritance. There were enough resources to move sacks of feed from one side of the store to a shed out back and hang a curtain between the two enterprises. Except for when Carol played his music, all was pretty quiet. The two adjacent businesses got along relatively well, except for the animal feed smells permeating the restaurant and the food aromas disrupting business on the feed side as people hurried to make purchases in order to get something to eat.

The team's first dilemma was deciding on and coming to a consensus on a menu of recipes that were true to their roots and steeped in Appalachian tradition.

Zelbert offered to keep the restaurant supplied with pork from his hogs and wild game he'd harvest from the woods. However, he offered this service with the caveat that if Ole Sooner, his coon dog, were to die, he'd be up Bent Creek without a paddle. Barring that, he saw no problem meeting demands for main dishes such as squirrel, raccoon, catfish, and "marsh rabbit" (muskrat). An occasional deer or wild turkey would round out part of the menu when the game warden was out of town. Zelbert also offered to buy some calves and raise beeves as soon as he could patch the holes in his pasture fence.

In the meantime, he figured that if Earl Carter's danged old heifer came into his yard again, prime beef would be on the menu. He almost shot it the last time it came onto his place, but Sherry, Earl's good-lookin' wife, threatened to beat the living Hell out of him if he did. Ocie Mae, Zelbert's wife, threatened to beat even more stuff out of Zelbert if he even got close to Sherry.

Wanda Mae Sutterfield would supply dandelions, watercress, and assorted seasonal vegetables and fruits. She knew all the good collecting spots and everyone with a garden or fruit tree. Her continuity plan was that the locals would be eager to earn extra money by planting a few additional rows of corn, beans, potatoes, tomatoes, and other vegetables. Wild blackberries and huckleberries were free for the picking, and the mountain kids could be hired to collect them. The teenagers were capable of canning food for the winter months.

Nathan Gulley insisted they sell moonshine from under the counter, but he was soundly voted down. They didn't want the preachers in the area picketing the restaurant, as they had done the liquor stores in the wet counties. Newport, Cosby, Del Rio, and the other towns had been hit hard.

They didn't do much in the way of remodeling, but cleared out a space, hung a few curtains and pictures, and made colorful strings of lights from empty shotgun shells. They would use Mason jars for glasses. The signs on the walls consisted of one that said, "THE GUVMENT AIN'T TAKIN OUR GUNS!" and "JOHN 3:16, READ IT BEFORE YOU GO TO HELL!" However, the most prominent sign read, "MAKE BULLS GAP GRET AGAIN! EAT HYAR!"

They also hung some treasures on the walls: rusty tools, a couple of animal hides, a likker jug, a few stolen hubcaps, some counterfeit Elvis memorabilia, and less valuable antiques.

Behind the restaurant/feed store, they made room for a wood stove, a Bar-B-Q grill, and six cords of split hickory wood. Carol had found a fiddle player to back up his guitar, and the kitchen staff would ensure the air was full of nostalgia and good smells.

After much work and arguing, and with the remodel finally out of the way, The Hillbilly Sunshine Café and Snack Bar opened its doors to the public.

"Y'all ready for this, boys?" Bryant grinned, adjusting his overalls as they stood in front of the rustic Feed Store. Then, the restaurant came to life with a sprinkle of Aint Berthy's "energized" moon water and a dash of moonshine on the doorstep. The aroma of fried chicken and French fries filled the air, and in no time at all, a crowd of hungry and curious people started rushing in the door and filling the chairs. Good food had come to Bulls Gap! Booker T's chair was filled to capacity and a bit more.

One doubtful person wrinkled her face as she looked over the menu. She asked, "What's good to eat here?" Bryant answered, "Everthin' we sells is good food, but we figger that the "enchanted apple pie" will be the best seller. Hit's a secret fambly recipe that I oversee myself." A doubtful look crossed her face as she looked the rugged old mountain man over and perused the menu. "Ever bite you takes will give you a flavor you'll not ferget soon, and you'll be back for more. Howsomeever, you must eat one uv our entrées to get the full effects of the pie, and together, you'll git more than yore money's worth. Hit's guaranteed, or we'll give you a free Moon Pie."

With skepticism, the snooty lady ate a modest meal and followed it up with a slice of enchanted apple pie, even though it cost 50 cents more than the regular pies. From the outside, it looked like any other apple pie, but from the moment it hit your goozle, you couldn't put it down until you licked the plate. She was hooked and became a repeat customer.

It didn't take long for the enchanted apple pie's reputation to take hold in the community. Soon, even restaurant owners from Gatlinburg were snooping around in an attempt to discover what made the pie so special. Word spread like wildfire about the magical dishes from the simple feed store/restaurant in what some jokingly referred to as Resume Speed, Tennessee.

But some things could have turned out better. Wanda Mae had been slinging hash browns since she was eight years old, and she accidentally set the kitchen on fire while experimenting with some fried pickled peaches. They weren't bad, so they put them on the menu as "deep-fried crispy peaches." They became another hit on the menu, perhaps because she'd marinated them in Nathan's moonshine overnight before cooking. When caught by Ocie Mae, she claimed that it tenderized the peaches. Ocie countered with, "Hit also tenderized yore dad-blamed brain! Now, quit it afore the preacher gits on our case!"

Wanda Mae tried to work the tables as a waitress, but it didn't work out. She once asked a guy from Tri-cities if he was happy with the food, and he looked at her wistfully and asked if he could lick the plate. Misunderstanding him, she started a firestorm when she replied, "Mister, "you can lick whatever you want, jest don't risk gittin' a lickin' frum my pa. He'll kick yore licker into the middle of next month and tie yore tongue into a Boy Scout squar knot!"

What no one but Bryant Gulley knew was that the enchanted apple pie, the crispy peaches, and most of the wild game meat served had been marinated in Nathan's best run moonshine, liberally infused with ginseng, and sprinkled with a special seasoning prepared by Aint Berthy in her own kitchen…on her table with her candles and crystals. Bryant allowed Berthy to set up a display table in the restaurant's corner, where she placed a small stock of elixirs and potions for sale, accompanied by a note stating that "special orders" were her specialty. In addition to the aroma of the fried foods, the air smelled of various dried herbs and cedarwood.

All this was happening while a few less strict people were squirreled away next door in the Snuggle Inn Half-Star Hotel, sipping Nathan's mood enhancer and laughing about life's mysteries. The latest topic of conversation over there was the puzzle over why the stray cat just outside the hotel's door had winked at them when they checked in. They finally decided it was just an anomaly of it being a full moon that night, and then they sent someone next door to the 'Shine Café to fetch their wives and pie refills. Bulls Gap had become a place where laughter, love potions, and specialty ginseng intertwined. Nathan's wife joked that all it took was "a lot of hope and a little root."

Because Berthy didn't like crowds, she only came around to replenish her lotions and potions on the sales table and to drop off her latest offerings. People loved her despite her eccentricities, one of which was that six times out of ten, she'd show up wearing mismatched socks and red long-handles under a colorful dress made of bright ribbons collected from various cemetery flowers. Had she tried to mix in with the hippies in the flatlands, she'd have likely become a significant role model.

They almost had a disaster once when Nathan Gulley wandered into the restaurant carrying three full quart jars of moonshine. Before Zelbert started to kick him out to the street for bringing alcohol into a "dry restaurant," Nathan yelled, "Boys,

I've got somethin' hyar in these jars what'll make yore hearts flutter faster than a teenaged hummingbird on caffeine."

Ocie Mae responded, "They hain't nuthin' special about that evil stuff. Hit'll addle yore brain and make you think that all women you run across looks like Dolly Parton. And that don't never end well."

Nathan replied, "Watch your language, Ocie; this hyar is a special batch what's been infused with a double dose of Bryant's secret root extracts. I notice that you hain't got married yit. The stuff in this fruit jar will fix that."

Sherry Carter overheard the conversation and asked, "Is that stuff shore enuf a love potion? My old man has been a little off-ish lately, and I need to make shore he don't stray off with one uv them flatlander girls who comes sniffin' around and what don't wear many clothes to kivver up their pasty lookin' skin and skinny arses."

Nathan didn't hesitate to answer, "Iffen you kin git Earl to drank this special batch the night before a full moon, he'll soon be a chasin' you like a love-sick, double-spotted hound dog after a squirrel."

So, Sherry had her man drink the potion disguised in a glass of Dr. Enuf Cola. The very next day, Earl rode his mule to a meadow beyond the ridge above the house, gathered up a bouquet of dandelion and rhododendron flowers, and declared a renewed love for her. Hoping not to be outdistanced by her man, Sherry gulped down a double dose of "Nathan's Love Brew" for herself and waited for the potion's magic. She didn't have to wait long, and the results were amazing. The next time she ran into Nathan, she complimented him on his recipe. Nathan responded, "Hit's the nature of the craft. You'd better buy some uv this batch afore I run out. Since the café started up, business has been a'boomin'."

Even though there were a few fits and starts, the Hillbilly Sunshine Café's reputation quickly grew. It became a go-to place for mountain folks, and laughter, love, and wild recipes created delightful social and eating experiences. The café's success was a testament to Appalachian community kinship and the magic of good food.

It wasn't long before the café's team felt compelled to call a "Jesus Meetin'" with Booker T because he was eating up too much of their profits. In exchange for rent, they cut him way back to just four meals a day and five snacks.

They set up a few tables outdoors, and on warm summer nights, people could eat while the stars twinkled and the fireflies danced in the air. As the word spread, the little café was regularly busting with hungry souls seeking comfort and a taste of the Appalachian back hills.

In addition to providing full meals to the public, they boasted the best selections of pies and non-alcoholic drinks in the South. By definition, Hawkins County was a "dry county," and generally, East Tennesseans were teetotalers. Despite not serving alcohol, they were starting to build a healthy clientele of discriminating customers who'd drive over from Cocke County. This didn't sit well with Popcorn Sutton, Newport's most popular moonshiner, but it was what it was.

Sales were steady throughout the day for drinks like Co-Cola and Pepsi, along with other soft drink offerings, including the ever-popular Dr. Pepper, RC Cola, Double Cola, Tru-Cola, Cherikee Red, Mountain Dew, Dr. Enuf, and beverages from the Williams Bottling Company over at Morristown.

They also served sun-tempered sweet tea and coffee. Booker T had found an abandoned refrigerator in town, laid it on its back, and filled it with ice and bottles of drinks. First, they'd tried using an old wheelbarrow, but it kept tipping over.

They complemented the drinks with several desserts that included the traditional Moon Pies and Honey Buns, supplemented by "Pertater" Cake, Sorghum Stack Cake, Skillet Cake, Red Velvet Cake, Aunt Berthy's Angel's Food Cake, Devil's Food Cake,

Confederate Coffee Cake, Buttermilk Sky High Pie, Egg Scones, Roasted Chinkapins, Chocolate Persimmon Cake, White Cake with Buttermilk Frosting, Black Bottom Pie, Hickernut Pie, deep-fried Ding Dongs, and Enchanted Apple Pie (which 50 cents more than the other pies).

Not surprisingly, the Enchanted Apple Pie was far and away the most popular menu item. These were custom-made and delivered daily to the restaurant by Bryant Gulley's wife. The recipe had been a family secret for generations. Rumor had it that it was liberally infused with "mystery root" extracts, wild teaberry essence, ginger juices, and an additional secret ingredient that Bryant claimed to be the only guy in Tennessee who knew where it grew. The pies were cooked with a special run of "product moisturizer" made by Uncle Nathan. Most people returned for seconds and left the restaurant in a really frisky, good mood. Some even got sleepy and rented a room in the Half-Star hotel. A few fell asleep in their chairs and had to be carried to the hotel.

Some people experienced strange side effects from the Enchanted Apple pie. For example, they were very impressed when Miss Edna Mae started speaking in rhymes, something she'd never done before. Bryant wanted to put her on stage and have her recite rhymes while dancing the flatfoot, but she claimed to be too shy.

The café's menu was a work in progress and changed frequently depending on the seasons: squirrel season, duck season, fishin' season, and lovin' season. Frankly, in that part of Appalachia, the only season that wasn't year-round was garden season.

As mentioned earlier, Zelbert Nicodemus was designated the full-time "Outdoor Food Gatherer." This was to keep costs down and improve profit margins. In other words, he supplied a lot of wild game foods from the woods and creeks rather than spending a wagonload of money on expensive beef, hors d'oeuvres, and fancy stuff from the stores in town that mountain people weren't used to eating. Backwoods authenticity was the operant word (actually, that's two words, but we can work with that: "backwoods-authenticity."

The restaurant gained a devoted following of regulars, and after three months, Booker T wanted them to increase their hours and hire additional cooks and servers. As a block, the staff balked at his proposal because the café work was starting to interfere with other things they wanted to do, and they didn't trust "strangers" to take their place and work among them. The menu was tremendously ambitious, with many Appalachian food favorites, and not just anyone knew how to prepare the food correctly. Special orders were discouraged, and to accommodate those who couldn't read and to speed up orders, they numbered their more popular combination plates:

Each entrée came with a choice of a salad (turnip greens, collard greens, mustard greens, watercress, or dandelion greens) and one's choice of dessert (peach cobbler, blackberry cobbler, paw paw cobbler (seasonal), persimmon cobbler, Yankee cornbread (contains sugar), and "redneck grinner" cookies, or you could substitute a small cup of soup of the day.

The menu read as follows:

> #1 Our signature house dish is the "Hillbilly Reuben," a tasty sandwich made of homemade bread, fried baloney, mayonnaise, pickle relish, and a side helping of deer jerky. Like every meal on the menu, it comes with your choice of a drink, a salad, and a dessert. This dish is extremely popular because it is priced competitively (the cheapest item on the menu), and everyone loves baloney! $1.25
>
> #2 "Love Me Tender" Fried Chicken with buttermilk biscuits, Spam French fries, and your choice of a salad and dessert. The drinks available are listed elsewhere on the menu. You'll have to inquire at the Half-Star Hotel

if you want something more than what we've got in the ice box." $3.00

3 Catch-of-the-Day "Butt Shank Steaks" (This could be deer, bear, wild hog, or "other"). It comes with fried green tomatoes, cornbread, and a dish of pinto beans stewed with hog jowl. $2.00

#4 "Lick Creek Swamp Stew" (a blend of catfish, crawdads, frog legs, and cattails). It comes with fried okra, a baked tater, and cornbread. $2.50. "Bent Creek Stew" can also be had, but it costs fifty cents more because the snappin' turtles there make the harvests more dangerous.

#5 "Skillet Cornbread and Milk" (choice of sweet milk or buttermilk) and the *pièce de resistance* is "Squirrel Dumplins" with a side of *"Foie Gras* of Raccoon" (Note: Squirrel Burger may be substituted, depending on whether Zelbert got out hunting yesterday or not). $3.00

#6 "Fried Spam Sandwich" served with an egg, a side of macaroni and cheeze with cornbread and real grits (like God intended, that is, they ain't no sugar). $1.50

#7 "Marsh Rabbit" smothered with Sawmill Gravy and two biscuits, with a side of Beenie Weinies and Confederate Crackers. $1.50

#8 "Fried Catfish and Peach Gumbo" with a side of rattlesnake pole beans and souse "whore derves" on fresh-made salt-rizing bread. $1.50

#9 Porker Special: "Hog Jowl and Black-Eyed Peas" with hang-slung chitlins, pickled pig's toes, and cornbread. $2.75

#10 Subject to availability, Genuine One-pound "Beef Steak" from a local cow (no bull!), grilled with hikery wood and served with mashed taters, white gravy, garden carrots, and a side bowl of "Lick Creek Stew." You will note that our steaks are so tender that *"you don't need no teef to eat our beef."* Also, as a service to our customers, if you lick the plate, you can rent a room at the Half-Star Hotel at a 25% discount." $6.00 per plate and worth the money!

#11 The "Hunka Hunka Burnin' Love Burger" Make a tribute to Elvis and buy this burger. The jukebox will play the song whenever anyone orders the "hunka catch-of-the-day" meat on a bun. It comes with a bowl of greasy greens and cornbread. $2.00

> *Note: Because The Hillbilly Sunshine Café was a "fine dining" restaurant, it chose not to serve wild ramps or possum in any of its published recipes. However, they had been considering adding possum balls to the menu because of persistent customer requests (mainly Aunt Luly). She was voted down by the management, who had once tried eating possum. Actually, they only ate half of a bite. As Berthy says, "Hit's an acquired taste, and we haint a 'quirin hit."*

Unfortunately, all good things have a way of coming to an end, and the 'Shine Café was no exception. It all started to unravel when a state health inspector dropped in to check to see if they had a permit and ensure that cleanliness and other laws were being complied with. After a quick glance at the menu, it only took the inspector a New York Second to recognize that there were game law violations. Chaos erupted when he took a look at the kitchen and discovered that the "organic" food they advertised was not only illegal but sometimes comprised of roadkill.

The café team tried unsuccessfully to derail the inspector and his several pages of infractions but failed.

When Aunt Berthy heard of the inspector's intention to shut the place down, she burned some candles and consulted her crystals in an attempt to ward off the health inspector. Unfortunately, she must have made a mistake because all this did was delay the inspector for a while.

Ocie Mae did her part by serving the health inspector a complimentary plate of "Forgiveness Grits" along with one of the genuine enchanted beef steaks that Earl Carter's wandering heifer had unknowingly contributed. His free meal was followed up with a large piece of Enchanted Apple Pie and some of Aunt Berthy's love potion mixed in his sweet tea.

The results were just short of amazing. After eating the magical meal, the inspector was too busy licking his fingers to write up any violations. Also, he fell in love with Wanda Mae and proposed to her on the spot, with pie still dripping out of his mouth. At this point, everyone felt that they'd won the battle, so the local eating sensation, which served up hillbilly nostalgia and comfort food, could stay in business.

Hillbilly Sunshine Café

Unfortunately, a disastrous attack by Mother Nature and a stroke of additional bad luck dealt the *coup de grâce* to the café.

A mother skunk and six babies lived underneath the restaurant's porous floor. Attracted by the smells from the restaurant above, Mama Polecat decided to drop in and sneak a bite to eat. Unfortunately, as she tried to slip into the kitchen, a door slammed on her, squeezing Hell's worst smell out of her, a noxious odor that made people sick to their stomachs as they rushed for the doors. It took several weeks for the odor to go away, and by the time the smell was tolerable and they were ready to reopen, the earlier inspector's female boss paid a visit. That led to the quick and final end to the Bulls Gap Hillbilly Sunshine Café and Snack Bar. No one gave the inspector a complimentary piece of Enchanted Apple Pie, and not one of the café's staff got filthy rich.

ZELBERT GITS CORNERED INTO MARRYIN'

When the stars started lining up against Zelbert, he didn't have much choice about getting married. Let me tell y'all about it.

One day, I was killing time with Uncle Andrew on the porch over at the Jay Bird store near Morristown. The boys were all worked up and talkin' about Zelbert Nicodemus gittin' roped into marryin' Ocie Mae Sutterfield. I didn't know Zelbert very well, but I did meet Ocie Mae's Aunt Flossy once up at my Uncle Bryant's place in the hills above Whitesburg. Flossie was a strange and unpredictable woman, and I don't write much about her, my biggest fear being bodily harm…mine! Admittedly, I'm crazy but I ain't dumb!

On the porch, the "boys" (all over 70 years old) were known to discuss all kinds of important stuff. They never paused a conversation any longer than it took to stuff a fresh chaw of Red Coon Brand tobacco in their jaw. They'd talk about politics, women, guns, watches, knives, who made the best likker, preachers, huntin', fishin', people they didn't like, why the government was behind weather changes, as well as things they knew something of, and even things they didn't have a clue about. They talked about everything under the sun. There was never a lull in the conversations.

On the day I dropped by, they were busy discussing the merits of various breeds of coon dogs, with nobody agreeing with anyone else. Five different men favored five different hounds: Blueticks, Plotts, Redticks, Walkers, and several mixed breeds, and they were loudly arguing the merits of each...that is, until Zelbert Nicodemus dropped by the store lookin' for their advice.

Zelbert was just a young pup of twenty years and didn't know anything about women when his neighbor, Popcorn Cobb, told him the Jay Bird Store guys claimed to know everything and could give him all the advice he wanted, and more. Zelbert himself was no dummy and, being a do-it-yourselfer, once developed a cast for Uncle Nathan's broken arm out of a car inner tube. He got the idea from a picture he'd seen in a Sears Roebuck catalog. But, of women and their habits, he only knew his momma. This worried him because he didn't much get along with her. If other women were like his mother, he calculated that might be big concern.

Zelbert was a big ole boy, barely shy of six feet tall and 300 pounds. His major flaw was that he had poor eyesight and used dime-store eyeglasses when needed to see small details. Unfortunately, they were never strong enough, so he devised a method of putting pieces of tape on the lenses and poking small holes in the tape to peep through. That seemed to clear things up. He never went to school and couldn't read, but he claimed he could write well, and the glasses helped.

He told the Jay Bird boys that Ole Man Sutterfield wanted him to marry one of his daughters. He had two of them, Ocie Mae and Wanda Mae. He told Zelbert that he could have his pick of the litter. They were born about ten months apart, and, at 15 and 16, either one was ripe for marryin'.

Zelbert was interested because he was getting tired of his momma's cooking and couldn't figure out how to move out of the house unless he first got him a woman who could make vittles, wash clothes, plant and tend the garden, raise kids, make his bed, clean the mud off his shoes when coming in from the pig pen, feed the hogs and other stuff his momma did. Zelbert was good at huntin', fishin', and bringin' in meat for the table. And he had a reputation for being good at working mules, a skill of considerable value in Appalachia. His momma claimed this was because he was more stubborn than any mule she'd ever seen.

Of course, the boys at the store had all kinds of good advice, and they questioned Zelbert about the various merits of the two girls. This was like throwing a worm at a bunch of chickens as they all jumped to answer at once.

Zelbert explained that Ocie Mae was "real purdy," lighthearted, well-formed (that is, chubby), wore pigtails, sported a print dress, and always had some kind of flower or ribbon in her hair.

Her sister, Wanda Mae, was really pretty also; slender, combed her hair in lovely braids, and wore a cotton dress with frills on it, but never a belt. Zelbert noticed stuff like that.

The boys looked Zelbert over and asked if he had any clean overhauls without holes in them to wear because he couldn't get married looking like he did. They pointed out that he could air out his "junk" without opening the fly.

Zelbert mentioned another reason he needed to get married: his momma no longer appreciated his fine company and said she was going to kick his "lazy, sorry butt" out of the house.

Well, the boys had a little fun with Zelbert, bless his heart. In retrospect, he should've looked for advice somewhere else.

Jake advised that every man is supposed to get hitched at least once in his life. In his own case, it was more than once.

Delroy said that he should choose the chubby one because she could keep him warm in the winter and give him shade in the summer.

Pinkie countered that Delroy might be right about that because if he were to marry the skinny one, people would think she was pregnant every time she swallowed a grape. That got a laugh. Pinkie always had some good'uns.

Then Andrew, being the sanest of the bunch, asked, "What can you bring to the marriage that's useful besides wandering around in the woods chasing possums all night?"

Zelbert thought hard about that and answered, "Well, I've saved up $56.43 from selling furs, and I have a good sow hog and a pet rattlesnake. And, of course, I have Ole Sooner, my hound dog, and he's the best in the hills.

Impressed, the boys looked at each other and asked what he would do to bring in money to buy a spot of land and a trailer house, pay doctor bills, and buy all the stuff that babies needed. Zelbert had a good answer for that, too, and said he had been thinking about applying for a job at the sock factory in town during the past year or so. That satisfied everyone.

Long story shortened, Zelbert returned to the holler and asked Ocie Mae if she'd marry him. Ocie Mae had a mysterious but knowing look on her face as she stared Zelbert square in the face and said, "I'll marry you on two conditions, that ye git ya a new pair of overalls and git shed of that dadblamed rattlesnake!"

PREACHER KESTER HITCHES ZELBERT AND OCIE MAE

Ocie then told Zelbert, "I triple-dog dare you to propose to me. I bet you won't say 'I will.'" He finally did, but he had a lot to learn about being married to a mountain woman. Unbeknownst to him, Ocie Mae, like most women anywhere, even in the cities, planned to tame her man down. Of course, it's a major flaw in all women that they think they can do this, but they never stop trying. If God hadn't made them this way, maybe no one would get married, and civilization would peter out?

Ocie's daddy made sure the courtship was short because he didn't want any babies with sore feet. That's how he explained kids that made a nine-month journey in six. At any rate, the couple was guarded close until Preacher Kester could marry 'em up. It wasn't a fancy weddin' and it wasn't in the church, but the bride and groom each picked their favorite foods for the wedding celebration. Ocie Mae's momma made a special cake with genuine chocolate they bought from the "rollin' store." That was a wagon that came around the holler twice a week selling basic foodstuff.

Ocie also got some new plastic flowers for a fancy bouquet and pinned one in her hair. For a change, Zelbert got a brand-spanking new pair of overhauls with suspenders that both worked. Zelbert's momma fixed up his favorite meal. Because they raised hogs, she whupped up an old family recipe of sow belly soup and a buttermilk cake shaped like a possum. Zelbert loved any kind of hog meat, and he loved to hunt possums. When he was a small kid, his mother had to hide the bacon from him.

Although only a few family members attended, the wedding was lovely, and the couple was happy to embark on a new journey in life, even if their plans never extended beyond the holler.

Zelbert's momma was especially happy because Zelbert was movin' out of the house and into a back room at Ocie Mae's folks' place. Zelbert's momma was a wispy woman of few words. The words weren't many, but they certainly were loud. She wasn't shy about telling folks that Zelbert was getting too aggravating to be around, and she was glad he was marrying one of his own kind. Somewhere along the line, she got the idea that Ocie Mae was as fussy as a lost polecat with a sore foot but figured that, after gittin' hitched, she'd "skin Zelbert right good and learn him some long overdue lessons."

Preacher Kester was tall, rangy, and grinned a lot like a preacher should, although he did appear to be a bit slow-witted. At least that's what Zelbert's momma said. She took delight in telling people that she once saw a mule outsmart the preacher and bite him on the arse, but if you know anything about mules, that wasn't unusual. Mules are one of God's most intelligent animals, although some think the devil created the breed. To his credit, Preacher Kester was used to the craziness of some of the people who lived in the back hills because his wife was raised there. The preacher wore shoes, spoke a little slowly, moved even slower, and had a funny whine in his voice. Together with his white beard, somebody said that made him look "regal." I wasn't sure what that meant, but I guessed it meant snooty. Either way, he was a few classes short of being formally licensed by the seminary to call people to repentance and marry people up.

There was some confusion when Preacher Kester asked, "Do you, Ocie Mae, take Zelbert to be your lawfully wedded husband, from this day forward for better or worse, for richer or poorer, in sickness and in health, to hold and cherish, till death do you part?"

Ocie Mae later told people that she thought the preacher said, "Do you, Ocie Mae, take this reprobate to be yore lawfully wedded man, to hold and to scold, for better but not worse, for richer but not poorer, to loathe and cherish, 'till he might die?"

Zelbert didn't help things when he answered, "Yeah, Preacher, I do, sort of, but I ain't gonna do no woman work around the house." Then he capped it off by sayin', "Let's git this weddin' over with, cause hit'll soon be dark, and I plan to be in the woods wif Ole Sooner huntin' coons for us to eat tomorrer."

Ocie Mae wasn't offended by any of the bantering and figured Zelbert was just funning around. She countered with, "I agree wid Zelbert, Preacher. Now we all got the skinny for this weddin' over with, let's dive into that cake and git honkin fat together! I'm hungry."

OCIE MAE AND ZELBERT GIT CHIVAREED

After eating a nuptial meal prepared by their parents, the giddy couple immediately started preparing to go into lockdown together and get to the business of building their family empire in the hills of rural Greene County. Their goal was to get jobs in the sock factory in Morristown and save up enough money to buy a small spot of land near Cosby in Cocke County and raise as many hogs and kids as they could. Zelbert's family had raised pigs for three generations, and when the price of pork was up, their place smelled just like money. However, when the price of pork plummeted on the market, everything smelled like the stuff on the floor of the pig pens. The smell of people who raise hogs is an acquired taste, but it never smells like money.

For Ocie, getting married was the culmination of an obsessive dream. Being stuck back in the hills as her family was, and being on the biggie side, she worried that she might not get married at all, so she went all out in her efforts to encourage the "big day."

Discouraged, a month before even meeting Zelbert, Ocie went to Bryant Gulley's place in Gulley Holler and got advice. Bryant, a popular mountain herb doctor, gave her a bottle of his "secret recipe." Despite his grizzled mountaineer looks, Bryant was an intelligent man. He assured Ocie that she would get married and told her to guard the bottle of elixir from her pappy and save it for her future wedding night.

After giving Ocie a bottle of his best concoction, Bryant's wife had Ocie perform a mountain ritual to foretell if her eventual marriage would be happy or sad or if she'd even marry at all. Divination and spells were common among mountain folk to help calm fears about becoming a lone bachelor or an old maid and missing the economic security that marriage suggested.

Bryant's wife instructed Ocie to peel an apple in a single strand and toss the skin over her left shoulder. The idea was for the peeling to fall in the form of her future true love's initials. Ocie was excited because the peeling appeared to be a distorted S. From then on, she started looking out for guys with names that started with S. Of course, the name Zelbert didn't begin with an S but a Z was close enough. Bryant's wife was thorough, and also made a tea of Teaberry leaves, and read Ocie's future mate's character. Unfortunately, that was also inconclusive. Then she brought out a hand mirror and gazed over her shoulder in an attempt to see if an answer might be lurking behind her. All this was to help Ocie get some assurance that a compatible future mate awaited and to help curb her worries. Armed with the bottle of Bryant's "special recipe" as a future wedding gift and renewed knowledge that a man would come into her life, Ocie went home from Gulley Holler a happy person.

Now, back to the chivaree: In review, these were noisy celebrations of friends and family that took place on the wedding night of a loved one and were kept secret from the couple. I'm sure many happy couples hoped against hope that everyone had forgotten about honoring their marriage with a chivaree. In contrast, others may have had hurt feelings if they didn't get one.

To cut to the chase, after the wedding and the newlyweds had retired to their comfortable room for the night, the first thing that

Ocie Mae did was to light the kerosene chimney lamp and bring out Uncle Bryant's months-old wedding present. Then, as Bryant had suggested, they gulped it down. Zelbert said it had an unmistakable smell and taste of ginseng, teaberry, and corn likker. Ocie had never experienced ginseng but, after catching her breath, said that the taste was "interesting." All happy, they then turned down the chimney lamp and prepared for bed.

Because of Ocie's daddy's watchful eye, the couple hadn't had much chance to mingle and had been seriously limited in building a relationship through courting. They were giddy-level excited to get on with life's rumored marital bliss.

Unfortunately, things don't always go as planned. In this case, Ocie Mae's sister, Wanda Mae, organized a few friends to have some fun with the newlyweds. She and a group of friends gathered outside their window and waited until about thirty minutes had passed for things to calm down. This was calculated to give the couple enough time to shed a few clothes.

They intended to give them an old-timey "serenade" or "chivaree." Serenading with a chivaree, or, in French, *charivari*, is a custom dating from the Middle Ages and was still quite popular in Appalachia. This traditional mountain folk custom was staged during their first night as a bride and groom. These usually included some level of chanting or singing and merrymaking with loud noises to ensure no one was sleeping or getting much privacy. The noise would continue until the new couple greeted people at the door.

Some fear was involved because Ocie Mae's ill-tempered daddy, Ole Man Sutterfield, was on the premises and owned a shotgun, and nobody wanted to cross him.

Even today, city folks make weak attempts to carry on the tradition of chivarees by tying tin cans onto car bumpers, painting auto windows, sprinkling flour on the couple's apartment floor, short-sheeting the bed, taking labels off food cans, and sometimes worse.

Of course, Zelbert and Ocie didn't own a car, and their food was seldom in cans. I remember a time when revelers dismantled and reassembled a horse-drawn "honeymoon buggy" on top of a barn. But Ocie and Zelbert didn't own a buggy, and there wasn't going on an exotic honeymoon to Gatlinburg like rich folks did

Noah Gulley's Cabin Where the Chivaree Took Place
(Photo courtesy of Addie Gulley Hughett who was raised here)

Then, on cue, the overexcited group started hollering at the top of their lungs and banging on pots and pans, setting off firecrackers, beating on the windows and doors, and yellin' out the names of the newlyweds and yelling "Chivaree! Chivaree! Chivaree!" The intent was to scare the devil out of the newlyweds, which usually worked if they'd never heard about chivarees. If it weren't for Ole Man Sutterfield's long-reaching shotgun, the revelers would have beaten the door down, grabbed the bridegroom, roughed him up, or taken him outside and dumped him in the pig trough. Instead, they just made noise and hollered, "Chivaree! Chivaree!"

Zelbert, having never heard of chivarees, was wondering just what kind of crazy family he'd married into. After Ocie clued him in on what was happening, he resigned himself to making the marriage work with his newly acquired family and settled down.

Then, the celebration came to a booming and immediate halt. One of Zelbert's friends had gotten a stick of dynamite from his uncle, lit it, and tossed it into the front yard, and everybody started running. When it went off, the explosion echoed throughout the hills for miles. Rather than a celebration, a few people thought the Russians might be invading and got their guns out.

By this time, all the uninvited visitors were running down the dirt road with lanterns in hand, some still beating on their pots and pans and hollering out the names of the newlyweds and "chivaree." The commotion eventually faded into the distance, and all was again calm at the honeymoon house.

Zelbert had been welcomed into the family!

ZELBERT WANTS TO BE A PREACHER

I once wrote a totally true story of an experience I had while visiting an Appalachian church in Edwina, Tennessee, where Pastor Jimmy M preached and danced around while holding a handful of very dangerous and poisonous snakes. The following story is a melding of actual mountain customs and humor based on that and other similar churches I've visited. The characters Ocie Mae and Zelbert are made up of a mixture of cousins and neighbors. Coincidentally, my grandpa's name is Elbert, but he doesn't have a lot in common with zElbert in the following story. Papaw didn't preach with snakes. I hope this tale may bring back memories for those raised in the hills and educate others about what it used to be like (and still is in a few places). On your next vacation, you should roam the back roads of Appalachia. You can still see and experience much of what I write about, because it's not all gone yet.

Ocie Mae and Zelbert had gotten married, moved in with Ocie Mae's folks, and settled down in a back room that had been used to dry herbs. The aroma was pleasant, and the newlyweds welcomed the feather-stuffed bed. Most days, Zelbert would go by his old home, visit with his momma, slop his pet hog and her litter of future hams, feed his mule, and take care of his coon dogs. He still needed to get around to applying for a job in the sock factory in Morristown, but wasn't in a hurry. Ocie Mae's daddy, Ole Man Sutterfield, gave Zelbert a bad time about not finding work and referred to him as a "triflin' no-a-count." Tensions flared occasionally, and the couple was looking for another place to stay where the rent was affordable...preferably free. They hadn't given up their search when Zelbert got sidetracked by one of his hare-brained ideas. He wanted to become a preacher. Not just any preacher but a snake-handling man of God. As a preacher, he might even land a job where a free house was provided.

Even today, throughout Appalachia, there are still a few primitive churches that practice venomous snake handling and drinking poison (strychnine and lye being preferred). State and federal regulations prohibiting interstate commerce in selling protected snake species have made their worship more challenging. Fortunately, venomous serpents are common in the wild throughout Appalachia. For Zelbert, various poisonous snakes were "free for the picking" in the hills.

Churches that practice snake handling have special services in which people worship with snakes. They base the practice on the Bible (Mark, Chapter 16, Verses 17-18, and Luke 10: 19). The idea of handling snakes and drinking poison was intended to validate one's faith and demonstrate to others that they are "true believers" who are undeniably protected by God.

The excitement of the meetings he attended got Zelbert turned on to wanting to become one of those "specialized" preachers. In order to get the congregation into the spirit of things, there was usually a booming sound system wired to a band outfitted with electric guitars, a set of drums, and a piano. Sometimes, brass instruments were used, and occasionally, someone would keep rhythm with a pair of spoons. The music was motivational, followed by revved-up, passionate, and dramatic sermons that were sometimes filled with prophecies and faith healing. The excitement was infectious. Dancing, clapping, waving hands in the air, and shouting Amen! and Hallelujah! were common once the meetings got into gear. This greatly appealed to Zelbert but less to Ocie Mae. His in-laws especially disliked the idea, and their patience with Zelbert was starting to wear thin.

I can't emphasize enough how writhing and very real the snakes I saw were. That is no exaggeration. Depending on the snake's size, the preacher would have three to six at a time in his hands. As he preached, he'd hold them above his head, sway, dance in circles, and occasionally do "the stomp," which symbolizes stomping evil down or smashing the devil's head. Ocie Mae's heart would jump when the preacher did this, which always caught her off guard. Usually, there was a mix of rattlesnakes and copperheads but never water moccasins which emit a sickening odor. Even snake handlers have their limits.

On one occasion, Zelbert proved his faith to the congregation by taking up a handful of snakes and dancing around with them like the preacher did. When he did this, Ocie Mae "danced" right out the church's back door and went straight home, wondering what kind of crazy man she'd married.

After one of the meetings at the *Soul Fuel Faith Church,* in which he fully took in the moment's glory, Zelbert was so touched by the spirit that he decided to become a preacher himself. He knew where a den of rattlesnakes was, and there were always a few copperhead snakes in the brush pile behind his old house on the mountain. So, he built a wooden box with screen walls and a latching door and proceeded to populate it with a half-dozen nice-sized snakes, which he hid in a flour sack under his bed where Ocie Mae seldom looked. When Ocie Mae was away from the house for a few hours, he'd take the snakes out and practice preaching with them. This was all well and dandy, except that he overlooked a couple of important trade secrets that the preachers had yet to tell him. They often carefully milked the venom out of the snakes the night before they handled them. Also, they'd put them in a refrigerator overnight, so they'd be mainly in a hibernation state when taken from their box the next day. The rub was that Zelbert needed to learn how to milk venom out of the snakes, and the Sutterfield household didn't own a refrigerator.

At any rate, all was going pretty well until he heard a blood-curdling scream from Ocie Mae's momma. The snakes had somehow escaped their cage, and she had jumped up on top of the kitchen table. When Ole man Sutterfield saw what was happening, he grabbed his shotgun from over the stone fireplace, shot the snake, and blew a right smart big hole in the cabin floor. That would have ended it there, but more snakes were running around, and Ole Man Sutterfield was afraid of running out of shells. Woodrow Carter happened to be passing by, heard the commotion, and joined the hunt with his old H&R revolver, which he nicknamed "Gitter." Eventually, three rattlesnakes and two copperheads were killed (along with as many teacup-sized holes in the wooden floor).

Ocie Mae threatened the truth out of Zelbert, and he felt obligated to tell her folks that there were six snakes, and one was still loose somewhere in the house. By now, Miz Sutterfield was hysterical, still on the kitchen table, screaming, "A rattlesnake is loose in the house, and hit'll kill us all!" Zelbert was a little slow to come to his wits and said, "My pet rattlesnake! That's the Lord's snake! Stop shootin! Don't you hurt him! I'm gonna preach with 'em!"

Ocie Mae's daddy pushed Zelbert aside and said, "I'll git the rest of 'um before they kill somebody, then I'll take care of you! I'm saving out a special shell."

At this point, Ocie's sister, Wanda Mae, entered the kitchen and screamed, "I've been bit!" And to prove it, she pointed to what looked like blood on her leg. Ole Man Sutterfield grabbed his knife and wanted to cut the snake bite location where it was bleeding and suck the venom out, but Wanda Mae wouldn't let him. She tightly held her dress to her leg and looked frantically at everyone.

Ocie Mae then sprang into action with a big club and went poking around in the corners of the rooms looking for the last rattler. She told her sister to "buck up" and "don't you dare die on us or I'll kill you!" to which Wanda Mae whispered to Ocie Mae that she hadn't been bitten but had just scratched her leg with a fork to distract them from all their foolishness over a silly snake. Ocie Mae yelled back, "You'uz always the dumbest one in the fambly, Wanda Mae. You knows them dammed snakes can kill you!"

With all the stress and carrying on, Zelbert took all he could and, fearing that Ole Man Sutterfield might shoot him dead on the spot, high-tailed it out of the house and went to his momma's place, where he told her that Wanda Mae had been bitten by a rattlesnake and was going to die. He wasn't sure whose fault it was that allowed the snakes to escape their box. He then went out to tend his pet hog that had recently littered fourteen piglets, the only money crop he could depend on other than selling coonskins and ginseng roots.

For a while, Ocie tried to talk Zelbert into going back to her folk's house. His usual response was, "I'd rather be in Hell with my back broke!" Eventually, Ocie Mae's family pretty well calmed down, although they never found the last snake. They figured it must have gotten scared off by the commotion and slipped out the door. Zelbert stayed over to his momma's house for a week before eventually slurking back to the Sutterfield place and his new but tattered wife. Old Man Sutterfield informed Zelbert in no uncertain terms that he had better be cleared out of the house in a week or he'd personally strangle him to death with his bare hands and feed his carcass to his pet hog.

In short, Zelbert decided he wanted to be something other than a preacher after all because people were too danged finicky and not religious enough. He then started earnestly looking for a place for him and Ocie Mae to move to.

> *Note: While it is true that there still are a few snake-handling churches scattered across Appalachia, it would be irresponsible of me to prejudge their sincerity and deny that faith and God's will may be at play in their services.*
>
> *Interestingly, when someone dies of a bite or poison (it rarely happens), it is not necessarily interpreted by the congregation as a negative thing and is often passed off as "God wanted them and 'took them home' at a most appropriate time when they were openly placing their lives in God's hands." From that perspective, it may have been a good thing. It's not for me to say.*
>
> *Snake-handling churches are restricted in some states, and it's illegal to procure or own wild snakes in most areas. Not long ago, a Kentucky snake-handling minister was bitten by a rattlesnake and died. It's a serious thing. My advice? Practice your faith with rubber snakes.*

THE GHOSTS OF PANTHER HOLLER

In the last episode, Ocie Mae and Zelbert were kicked out of the Sutterfield house for harboring snakes that Zelbert intended to use to become a snake-handling preacher.

Unfortunately, some of Satan's favorite animals were injured in the melee that occurred when they accidentally got loose in the Nicodemus house, resulting in the newlyweds having to find a new place to live. Zelbert gave up the idea of becoming a preacher and set about looking for a new home for his wife. This was difficult because most of their meager income came from the occasional sale of pigs littered by Zelbert's pet hog, Sweet Pea. Also, he brought in a little money by selling raccoon hides and ginseng roots, but that income was spotty and seasonal.

However, luck was with them when they ran into Commodore Ledbedder. Squint, as he was called by most people, owned an abandoned shack just over the hill from his place that hadn't been lived in for years. Whoever had made the two-room cabin had done a good job, but time had taken a toll.

The former resident, a highly backwoods woman named Merti (short for Myrtle), had died there, and her body wasn't found for a month. Without going into the gory details, Merti had been complaining of ghosts and haints bothering her for several years, and folks figured they finally got to her. To make things worse, a wild panther had brutally killed her son a few years earlier, and she buried him behind the cabin. After Merti's body was found, her remains were buried beside her son's grave on the edge of the woods. People were convinced that evil spirits were somehow involved, and no one dared to touch anything on the property for fear it was haunted. Over the years, the house fell into disrepair.

Everyone warned Zelbert and Ocie Mae, "Don't you dare go near Panther Holler." However, not being superstitious, they proceeded with the deal. After all, Ocie Mae's daddy had a long-reaching shotgun, which became a growing concern the longer they lived with his wife's folks.

Squint touted the house as "fully furnished" because everything Merti owned had been hastily left behind. He claimed that the cabin just needed a "little bit" of cleaning up and fixing here and there. All the pots, pans, dishes, and everything else had been left as-is in the house. The mice had been living in the mattress, which needed a little cleaning. The door was missing from the two-holer outhouse, but it was serviceable, other than a crack in the seat on the women's side. The men's side was also acceptable, but it was stained and smelled a bit. This was no problem for Zelbert because he raised hogs, and the smell reminded him of money...but only when the price of pork was high. Ocie Mae wasn't raised that way and invested in some perfume and spread it around, giving the outhouse the quaint smell of a French bordello, but that was much better than the alternative.

So...Zelbert borrowed some tools from his momma's house, and Ocie Mae finagled a gallon of Clorox and a broom, and they set about fixin' the place up. The fruit of their labor paid off, and after the cracks in the walls were filled, and the glass in the sole window was fixed with some tape, and the ashes were cleaned from the fireplace, and the squirrels and their nest removed from the chimney, the place was transformed into a dream come true for the young couple. They were excited by their very first home and looked forward to no one listening from the next room.

Food was placed on the newly cleaned shelves, Grandma's quilts were carefully placed on the bed, and the animal pens out back were repaired to accommodate some of Zelbert's animals. The dogs found a place out of the weather underneath the cabin.

At first, Squint wanted Zelbert's pet hog as a down payment on rent, but Zelbert remembered that his grandpa used to say, "Don't you never sell yore mule in order to buy a plow," so he refused. Because the shack had a reputation for being haunted, Squint ended up charging the couple only a sugar-cured country ham and 30 pounds of pork every three months for rent. What a deal! Additionally, he was pleased to have someone clean the place up.

Zelbert's grandpa had lots of good sayings. A few he remembered were: "Life is a 'hol sight simpler when you plow around the stumps." "Two can live as cheap as one if one uv 'em don't eat." "I commenced to shakin' like a dog poopin' peach seeds." And, my favorite, "Don't pee on my shoes and tell me hits 'a rainin'"

Life promised to be good for the couple in their new home.

Well, some deals can have hidden flaws. A minor problem was fixing the outhouse door to keep critters from wandering in and interrupting business. Zelbert ignored the crack in the toilet seat on Ocie Mae's side until she complained for the twentieth time. When he returned from the repair job, he remarked that when he had his head in the hole to repair it, his beard got stuck in the crack, and it hurt like heck when he jerked his head out. Ocie Mae's response caused Zelbert to scratch his head when she responded, "I found out that crack shore was aggravatin' too. Hit hurt!"

However, cracks in the seats and mouse-proofing the cabin soon proved to be the least of their concerns. Neither Ocie

Mae nor Zelbert gave any thought to ghosts and such, but that ended about a month after they got settled in. Friends kept telling them about strange happenings in Panther Holler and even made jokes about it.

For example, someone asked Ocie Mae if she wanted to hear the story about the walking skeleton in Panther Holler, and her reply was, "No, I'd see right thru hit." Another was, "Didja hear the story 'bout the corduroy piller (pillow) on Merti's bed?" Ocie Mae quipped back, "I shore did. Hit made head lines."

Then, late at night, they began to hear faint but eerie sounds, including footprints and occasional screams, as if a woman was suffering in the woods. Each time, Zelbert would take his daddy's old Civil War gun and a lantern and creep outside to investigate, and the sounds would go away for several days. Intuitively, they felt that something wasn't quite right. Once, Ocie Mae thought she saw a faint red light near the ground in the trees near where Merti and her son were buried.

Then, stranger occurrences began to happen. After work in the evenings, Zelbert would carefully lean his tools against the front porch wall for the night. From time to time, the tools would be gone in the morning only to reappear a couple of days later, again carefully stacked against the porch wall. At first, they figured they had misplaced the tools, but it soon became clear that strange things were going on.

Once, on an exceptionally dark night, Ocie Mae got up to visit the privy. This time, she was positive she heard footprints following her as she walked back to the cabin from the outhouse. She ran into the house, locked the door, woke Zelbert up, and told him. Both of them were increasingly getting scared and starting to believe in haints and boogers.

The next day, Ocie Mae visited her parents and spent the night. Zelbert said he wanted to go too, but claimed he was running a fever and had better stay at the cabin. He was determined to end the ghost scares. So, he strategically hid himself and his rifle in a comfortable place in the woods not far from the outhouse and waited. He planned to spend every night there until he solved the mystery.

At about 2 a.m. on the first night, he heard the creak of the outhouse door as it opened. He shined his light and saw the blur of a dark image as it fled away. The following day, he found the tracks of a mountain lion. Apparently, it was drawn to the perfume scent that Ocie had sprayed in the privy.

This prompted Zelbert to visit with Squint Ledbedder. Squint was an accomplished trapper and said that panthers and mountain lions can scream "jist like a dad-blamed woman in heat." Here, I'm referring to the mountain lion, not Ocie Mae, though the idea does merit some thought. Squint agreed to trap the large cat and assured Zelbert that it would cure their problem.

What Squint didn't say was that, now that the cabin had been restored to livable conditions, the "mountain lion" was just a scare tactic he'd initiated to have Zelbert and Ocie Mae move out so he could free up a place for one of his old army buddies to move into. He'd mimicked the sounds and faked the footprints.

At any rate, he gave up the idea of scaring Ocie and Zelbert off the place when he found out that his old army buddy expected to live there for free. Hams were better than nothing.

ZELBERT AND OCIE MAE GIT INTO THE DIRT

One day, as Zelbert approached his modest shack at the head of Panther Holler, he noticed his wife of one year dancing and jumping around in the garden, stark naked and yelling. Initially, he was delighted that she was just welcoming him home. As he got closer, the tone of her voice and unusual curse words convinced him otherwise. She had sat down in the dirt to prepare a bed for a particular strain of Romaine lettuce she was planting, but had not noticed that she was sitting smack dab on top of a much-irritated ant bed. She was covered with hundreds of biting and stinging red ants! The stings were so nasty she felt there was no alternative but to shed her clothing and try to get rid of them. That was not enough, so she ran to the creek, jumped in, and attempted to wash the biting devils off.

Raising gardens was a rich tradition throughout Appalachia, but it was always a challenging endeavor. The first summer after their marriage, with great difficulty, Zelbert had taken a mule, plowed out a twenty-by-thirty-foot plot for a garden, and planted it. Plants soon came up, and attractive veggies of all sorts began to appear. Unfortunately, they were also attractive to deer, raccoons, skunks, crows, squirrels, insects, and anything else that had an affinity for eating.

Another setback was Zelbert's ill-conceived idea of using fish for fertilizer like the "Indians" did. He used this excuse for setting out a trot line in the Chucky River to catch fish and was gone for two days. That trip paid off with a couple of hundred pounds of fish. Enough to eat for a while and plenty to fertilize the garden. The big stinky downside was that the fish smell attracted all sorts of new critters, including buzzards and the neighbor's dogs from a mile away! But a herd of wild hogs invaded and completely obliterated the garden plot. Their first year's harvest was a dozen or so radishes and some early lettuce.

In those days, all mountain folks raised gardens. Most mountain homes were small and surrounded by pens of livestock and corn stalks. Even the 90-year-old widows would have a few tomato plants by their back doors. Also, people saved their favorite seeds and traded them back and forth. Some plant varieties had been passed down for hundreds of years, even back to when their ancestors came to the Appalachian Mountains from Scotland and Ireland. Without produce from gardens, a pig, a cow, and fish and game from the wild, many would have starved to death.

However, in their second year of gardening, Ocie Mae was determined to overcome nature and all its evils. First, she doused all the ant hills with coal oil and lit them on fire in a failed attempt to burn the little $%&* out of existence. She then made a mental note to ask Preacher Kester why, in tarnation, had God made ants and other bugs that attacked her garden?

However, Zelbert took the greater beating from the garden. Ocie demanded in no uncertain terms that he build a critter-proof fence around their garden spot. So, dutifully and reluctantly, he sat about the onerous task. The former owner had left a pile of ten-foot-long posts piled behind the smokehouse. There were enough to enclose a thirty-by-fifty-foot garden plot so he expanded the size. He used a post-hole digger from the shed to dig the holes. That took a month because the soil was hard and rocky. With unrelenting "tutoring" from Ocie, he enclosed the garden, sides, and top with chicken wire that would keep most animals and birds out, although it did nothing to discourage snakes and hungry bugs.

Then he rested until it was time to weed, harvest, and help Ocie can food. It was December when Ocie reminded Zelbert that the garden ground was full of big dirt clods and needed a "good tilling." In March, he still hadn't tilled it, and Ocie carefully outlined what would happen to his more charmed "domestic life" if he didn't get on the stick. Zelbert promised that within a week, it would be done. Being one who didn't particularly care for manual labor, Zelbert had a plan.

They went to bed four days later and magically woke up to an aggressively tilled garden. Zelbert had sprinkled some seed corn all over the garden space, and the wild hogs had come in during the night and rooted up the dirt as well as any flat lander's motorized tractor could. They just needed to take some rakes, level it out, and toss a dozen buckets or so of rocks over the hillside.

By the time this was finished, it was almost planting season again, and they needed fresh seed. This time, they agreed they would only plant "tried and true stuff." In those days, seeds were carefully gathered and dried for the next year's crop, with extras often shared with friends and neighbors. So, they visited their neighbors, asking for advice and seeds, if they didn't mind. As you can imagine, everyone had their favorites. Some varieties were raised by their ancestors for as long as their people could remember. Always looking for something new or unique, other seed varieties were brought in by relatives who'd traveled to different states or were ordered in by the Bulls Gap Feed Store.

Their second year's garden turned out great, except for a few casualties due to drought, planting a bit too early, an amazing array of insects, a large variety of crazy diseases, hand blisters from hoeing, weeding, lugging water from the creek, harvesting, digging a root cellar, canning, drying, shucking, an early killing freeze, and a bunch of other common gardening "pleasures."

And, by the way, Zelbert and Ocie Mae lived happily ever after...after they spent a wheelbarrow full of money on some ant poison.

For those interested in old-time gardening, below are some of the seed varieties that were popular. Most are heirlooms and still available online if you search for them.

Ocie Mae's Grandma said that the "Appalachian Trinity" of any garden was a combination of beans, corn, and taters. She'd plant them all in the same row.

Actually, there are probably more different kinds of beans originating in Appalachia than anywhere else in the entire nation. Some favorites are creasy beans, fodder beans, butter beans, string beans, Kentucky Wonders, Lazy Wife Greasy, Big Johns, Eagle Fork Big Reds, Thickety Greasy, Cades Cove Stick Bean, Goose Beans, Turkey Craw beans, and a hundred more. Legend has it that Goose Beans were discovered in the craw of a Wild Goose and Turkey Craw beads from the craw of a wild turkey, but I have my doubts. Nevertheless, much crazier stuff has happened in Appalachia. Zelbert said that Ocie Mae's mom "didn't know beans about beans" and that Brown Speckled Greasy Beans from Western North Carolina were the best. By the way, greasy beans are not greasy but have smooth, shiny skin. My wife's favorite pole bean is Rattlesnake. It seems to suffer the least from hot weather and diseases.

Aunt Berthy Hughett took issue with everyone and claimed that the most versatile bean known to mankind (and women, too) was the Tennessee Cornfield Bean. Historically, this variety was planted in cornfields and allowed to climb the corn stalks, rather than having to erect bean poles. She always planted by the signs that Mother Nature provided via the moon. She also raised "arsh taters" and turnips and "holed them up" in the ground and "kivered 'em" with straw for the winter.

Nathan Gulley and Sherry Carter (probably a shirttail cousin of the famous Carter family from the adjoining county) strongly argued about the best corn varieties. While both agreed that corn was the cornerstone of any garden, Nathan claimed that Jimmy Red corn was better than "anything in the known world." That's probably true when it comes to the tiny world he knew. This red dent corn was by far the most popular for making moonshine, but it also produces excellent cornbread. It's good grilled or boiled. Miz Carter argued that extra-sweet corn was best to grow in any garden and, if one wanted red kernels, they should raise Bloody Butcher. Of course, Sherry didn't make likker, at least that anyone knew of.

Addie Hughett (my Mamaw) recommended Candy Roaster Squash: This type of winter squash has a long, curved, tapered shape and resembles a banana. They can weigh from fifteen to sixty pounds each and store really well. Appalachians rarely ate pumpkin pies but used squash instead. It's thought this variety may have been raised by the prehistoric Cherokee Indians. Mamaw also recommended two types of tomatoes, Beefsteak and Cherokee Purple. Interestingly, the traditional Beefsteak is dark red, and the inside almost resembles rare beef, while the Kentucky Beefsteak variety is a deep yellow color. All have been passed down for generations. Mamaw also raised Plum Granny Queen Ann's Pocket Melons, golf-ball-sized melons that are pretty to look at and very aromatic. They were used in the early days instead of perfume or air fresheners, similar to citrus-smelling "horse apples" from the Osage Orange tree. We grow pocket melons in our garden. Although they are not very tasty, they are pretty, and a bowlful sits on the kitchen counter, making our kitchen smell nice all summer.

Rufus Cobb was new to the hills from the flatlands and wanted to take his neighbors' recommendations seriously. He'd heard that one would "reap what they sowed" and realized he wasn't sowing anything. He was embarrassed when told that sowing didn't mean sewing buttons on shirts or making clothes. With help, he got started by planting "no-fail" Cherry Belle Radishes, Southern Giant Curled Mustard, and Purple Top Turnips. Early Fortune variety cucumbers were recommended to him, but most people were doubtful he could pull them off because they required more prep work...like soaking the seeds overnight before planting.

Widder Wood said she always had a big patch of "walking" onions and would share a bulb or two with anyone who wanted some. In no time, they'd multiply into many onions. Bryant Gulley preferred Ramps (Allium tricoccum) because they "wuz free and growed wild like God intended." Few people agreed with Bryant after eating a ramp and insisted that the Devil himself (or perhaps herself) had created ramps. Bryant also claimed that "annuals" meant you got disappointed once a year. Widder Wood accused him of being "lazier than a suck-egg dog," and Bryant responded that he didn't think work would necessarily hurt anyone badly, but he wasn't taking any chances.

Crazy Daisey, the local melon expert, recommended that Zelbert and Ocie Mae consider raising the Bradford Family or Moon and Stars varieties of watermelons. However, given the steepness of their property, they'd have to anchor the melons with "stobs of wood" to prevent them from rolling out of the field. Because of this, she recommended a favorite of the Hughett clan, the Banana Melon, which is shaped like a torpedo. There are two kinds of banana melons: one tastes like watermelon, and the other tastes like cantaloupe. You won't find these in the stores because they don't store or ship well, but the flavors are better.

Miz Kitty Ledbedder recommended two kinds of okra, Cow Horn and Alabama Red. The author eats the latter straight off of the stalk and makes a meal of them while in the garden.

In the old days, there was no refrigeration, so the mountain folks had to use other ways to preserve and store food. In addition to fruit and vegetable cellars, they canned, dried, dehydrated, pickled, and made "leather britches." The britches were called "shucky beans" and were made from whole green beans, which were broken into pieces, strung up, and dried. Usually, they were run through with a needle and thread and hung in long strands behind a wood stove or on a sheet of newspaper in the sun to dry. When properly dried and cooked, they are delicious.

Preacher Hughett and Brother Robert Vann of the Mountain Valley Church always attempted to set a good example for the backsliders and raised twice as large a garden as they needed. These were for sharing with their neighbors and the needy. It was a long-standing tradition in Appalachia to share their harvest, as well as plants and seeds, particularly with those who were economically less well off or ill. Papaw once loaned his cow to a neighbor who had a baby and no milk.

Old times are no longer here, but it is hoped that my writings can keep a few of the customs alive.

Now, you all go play in the dirt, but watch out for the stinging ants!

THE WAMPUS CAT STARTED IT ALL

If you're faint of heart, this story may not be for you. In the old days (and even today), many Appalachian mountain people butchered their own meat. Frankly, this was a healthy practice because the meat they ate was devoid of antibiotics, growth hormones, dyes, pesticides, and who knows what else goes into the raising and preparation of today's grocery store products to keep them from spoiling.

Most homesteads raised chickens, a few hogs, and a cow or two. Hog-killing in the fall was both hard work and a festive time with lots of food and neighbors helping. In the stories of Zelbert and Ocie Mae Nicodemus, they depended heavily on pork from the hogs they raised and wild game and fish that were free for harvesting from the Appalachian forests. Deer, wild turkeys, raccoons, and many other animals were a potential source of protein.

Ocie Mae talked with her closest neighbor, Miz Kitty, Squint Ledbedder's wife, about how food was traditionally preserved in the hills, and Kitty's interest in the process was high.

Southern country hams were a favorite because they required no refrigeration. Also, who doesn't like ham? As a returning soldier, Squint brought Miz Kitty back from France after the war as a very practical "war trophy." Of course, France was a mess after the war, and Kitty jumped at the chance to marry someone from a stable country. However, "stable" is a relative term, and the hill people of Appalachia surprised her. Her name was actually Catherine Dorleac Fabienne, and she was fairly well educated. She quickly came to love living in the mountains of East Tennessee. Life was not easy, but nor was it in post-war France, where her parents had lost both their home and lives in the bombings of their town.

Miz Kitty was fascinated when the Nicodemuses slaughtered a hog, rendered the fat, and made all sorts of cuts of meat, bacon, pork chops, souse meat, chitins, etc. Zelbert may have been naïve about some things, but he was a master at bringing in game and fish from the forests. It was amazing how good a tracker he was, sometimes trailing a deer all day through the fields and woods. He was the best in the area.

It was no secret that Ocie's daddy expected more of Zelbert and was always pressuring him to get a "real job." Of course, a "real job" was always different for Zelbert than what his father-in-law figured.

Once, while watching Zelbert skillfully skin a squirrel, Miz Kitty said, "Zelbert, that's a beautiful animal. Why don't you learn taxidermy?" Zelbert wasn't intrigued by the idea because he hated taxes of any kind, especially the type the government was always trying to levy against moonshiners. Uncle Nathan spent more than 15 years in the Brushy Mountain State Penitentiary in Petros, Tennessee, and his only mistake was making high-quality alcohol used to improve the lives of his friends and neighbors and not paying taxes on it.

Kitty explained that taxidermy had nothing to do with taxes but was stuffing and preserving animals, so they looked real. She went on to explain that, in France, taxidermy was serious business, with special attention paid to making dead animals look much like they did in life. In fact, a Frenchman, Louis Dufresne of the Muséum National d'Histoire Naturelle in Paris, wrote extensively about the art as early as 1803. She even had a magazine article on the process that she translated for Zelbert. She read an advertisement to Zelbert that said, "Learn taxidermy! It's both fun and profitable. Make good money mounting and preserving fish, birds, and all kinds of animals. Make lamps, mirrors, and ashtrays! They sell easily and people will love you!"

Zelbert was hooked on the idea and found the topic fascinating. He spent many evenings thinking about pursuing a career in taxidermy. Being a great hunter, he would have no problem collecting "specimens," and the rest seemed simple enough. He knew all about shapes, sizes, and what the animals should look like.

However, the idea took serious hold of him once when hunting wild turkeys in the deep woods about eight miles from Bulls Gap. It had gotten late, and he was walking home on a pitch-black trail, and he couldn't see anything but the moon and trees. He heard the crashing of a falling branch and saw something he'd never seen before. It was a huge animal. It wasn't a deer because it was walking on its hind legs. He was close enough to tell that it wasn't a bear.

The animal had dropped down gracefully from a tree, stood before him, and stared. Zelbert also just stood there, terrified and frozen in place. He could smell the animal's breath, and he later explained that it smelled like something dead. It appeared to be part cat and part human, with glowing green eyes and large paws featuring long claws. The eyes terrified him. Whatever it was, it stared at him a bit longer, snarled, then turned around and slowly crept back into the deep woods, making eerie cries that sent chills up his back.

Rattled, Zelbert picked up the pace and hurried home as fast as he could in the dark. He made a mental note that someday he'd buy a flashlight like some of the city folk had but gave the thought up when he realized that he could never afford the never-ending need for batteries.

His father-in-law, Old Man Sutterfield, and Uncle Bryant Gulley were at his house when he arrived.

Seeing his white face, they asked what had happened. When he explained what he'd seen, they laughed and smelled his breath to see what he'd been drinking. He hadn't touched alcohol, so they surmised he must have had a fit or seizure or was going crazy.

However, Zelbert was steadfast in what he'd seen and wasn't known to be a drinkin' man. And, while he was a bit odd in his personality, he wasn't deranged.

Uncle Bryant, who was very knowledgeable about Appalachia, had everyone sit down and explained what Zelbert had just seen. He was sure Zelbert had seen a Wampus Cat, a fearsome beast that haunts the Appalachian woods. According to Native Americans, the Wampus Cat was once a Cherokee woman cursed by the spirits for sneaking and spying on a tribal ceremony reserved only for men. As punishment, she was transformed into a half-woman, half-cat creature and was forever banished to roam the wilderness. Some claimed that the Wampus Cat could shapeshift and take on the form of either a huge catlike creature or a beautiful woman. Zelbert declared that what he saw was far from beautiful and had to have weighed 500 or 600 pounds. Glowing green eyes were also sometimes reported by those who claimed to have seen Wampus Cats. Being a very secretive animal/humanoid, not many people had actually seen a Wampus Cat. Still, many believed in them and claimed to have heard them make noises in the woods.

People frequently saw bears, panthers, and wild boars in and around the Smoky Mountains. There have also been dozens of eyewitness reports by people who claim they've seen Bigfoot, headless monsters, or Wampus Cats walking through the mountains. Many claimed the Wampus had an odor like a cross between a sick dog and a skunk. They have reportedly been seen throughout Tennessee, Virginia, North Carolina, Kentucky, and West Virginia.

From that day forward, Zelbert wanted to get rich and famous by shooting a Wampus Cat, taxiderming its body, and charging people money to look at it. He became obsessed with the desire to be a taxidermist and thought about it day and night. He quizzed Miz Kitty some more and learned that taxidermy was a "dying art." (no pun intended). He also learned that Theodore Roosevelt had been a taxidermist. By the time Roosevelt was in his mid-twenties, he'd donated more than 600 preserved bird skins and animals to the Smithsonian. He later even went so far as to put together the *Roosevelt Museum of Natural History*. That later evolved into what is now the *American Museum of Natural History* in New York City.

Zelbert started saving up sawdust, old rags, and sand to use as stuffing in the animals after he skinned them and tanned their hides.

Ocie Mae's jealous sister, Wanda Mae, made fun of Zelbert and loudly told everyone how sickening it was for anyone to want to stuff dead animals and put them on display. She called him "creepy." He countered that maybe someday he'd taxidermize Wanda Mae herself and put her on display, but only charge people a penny to see her. In contrast, he'd charge a dollar for each peek at the Wampus Cat. Wanda Mae never backed away from a challenge and, with a sneer, countered, "Hit's not yore fault that you turned out the way ye are; bless yore sick and depraved heart."

That made Zelbert madder than a rattlesnake in a forest fire, and he said, "Wanda Mae, as I live and breathe air, iffen you wuz a man, I'd knock the snot bubbles right outta you." This went on for a few minutes until Ocie Mae talked them down.

Nevertheless, through it all, Zelbert stuck to his guns and proclaimed taxidermy to be a serious business, insisting that it required special skills to make a dead animal look much like it did in life. And he was just the man to do it!

There were, however, a few problems to overcome. For example, Roosevelt and others used arsenic to tan the skins. Unfortunately, that stuff was dangerous and regulated, and the cost didn't fit his budget. So, he improvised and soaked rat poison in alcohol as a tanning agent and preservative.

When he told the boys at the Jay Bird Country Store in Morristown about his plans to become a taxidermist, they were excited and lined up projects for him to take on. Jake knew where a big bass was hiding in Mays' Pond that he'd bring to him for mounting. Zelbert had some camouflage paint left over from painting his neighbor's tractor and would use it to color the fish.

Delroy said he'd shot a whitetail deer that he was sure would be a state record and that it sported several "drop tangs" that would make a "danged good mount for hangin' in the store." Pinkie asked, "What the heck is a "drop tang?" Delroy carefully explained, "It's them thar antlers what hangs down by their face, you idgit!'

Not wanting to be outdone, Pinkie told the boys he had a buck deer head in his barn with 23 points...on each side!

Uncle Andrew allowed that he had a favorite fighting cock that had never lost a fight and, although it didn't have many feathers left, he was a great rooster, and he wanted to preserve the memory and put him on the mantle above his fireplace.

Jake suggested to Zelbert that he might want to taxidermize Sooner, his favorite coonhound. After all, Roy Rogers had taxidermied his horse, Trigger. That was a good idea and was agreed to by all. Then they started arguing as to whether or not Rogers had taxidermied his wife, Dale Evans. To get the conversation back on track, Delroy claimed a veterinarian in Knoxville was also a taxidermist. People joked that he had a sign on his clinic that said, "Either way, you'll get your pet back."

There was another part of the learning curve that Zelbert had yet to master. Although he could easily harvest animals for taxidermy with his rifle, he needed more practice actually mounting them before going after the Wampus Cat. He would do this so as to fully master the art of taxidermy before mounting a Wampus Cat because they were very, very rare, and he might only get one chance to collect one.

Not one to overlook detail, Zelbert "barked" and taxidermied a squirrel as a starter project, and it turned out pretty good. Barking a squirrel is where you shoot the bark just beneath their head, and the flying bark knocks them out, leaving the skin undamaged.

Finally, he felt that he was ready to capture a Wampus Cat, but it didn't prove easy. He carried a net and a gun with him as he went into the mountains. Tired and after a week of relentless pursuit, he sat down under a big popular tree and pulled out his lunch and ate. Just as he finished, a huge Wampus Cat emerged from the bushes and charged him. He threw the net over it, cocked his gun, and was prepared to shoot when something strange and totally unexpected happened. The Wampus fixed his piercing gaze and glowing eyes on him, instantly causing him to have whole-body paralysis. He couldn't move! All he could do was just lay on the ground and quiver.

In that time of helplessness, Zelbert realized that the rare creature was not just an animal, but also a being with its own life, struggles, and desires. Scared and frozen in the Wampus Cat's stare, Zelbert pleaded for mercy and understanding. He also realized that capturing and killing a Wampus Cat for taxidermy would not bring him the fulfillment he sought. The Wampus Cat, sensing Zelbert's change of heart, slowly turned away and disappeared into the forest. Zelbert watched it go, feeling a mix of relief...and the paralysis gradually went away.

By morning, he was still wobbly but able to make his way back home. On the long walk home, he experienced a total change of heart and decided to dedicate his life to protecting and preserving creatures of the wild, rather than hunting them for taxidermy. He'd continue hunting for food, but nothing beyond that. In the end, Zelbert realized that taxidermy wasn't his calling after all...and that perhaps he should take up helping Ocie Mae make quilts instead.

After he arrived home from the hunting trip, he flopped on the floor and took a long nap. While he was in a deep slumber, Ocie Mae emptied out his food pouch and saw an empty moonshine jar.

OCIE MAE TAKES UP FLINTSNAPPIN'

In an earlier story in the saga of Ocie Mae and Zelbert Nicodemus, Zelbert was challenged by his father-in-law to "Git a dang job, or I'll shoot yore sorry a$$!" Since then, both he and Ocie had racked their brains three ways from Sunday, trying to think of ways to make money without moving to Morristown and working in the sock factory. Neither ever cared much for socks and shoes pinched their toes. Working in a factory didn't appeal to them anyway.

Zelbert grew up with eleven brothers and sisters in a two-room shack near Bulls Gap, Tennessee and never knew what it was like to sleep alone until he got married. The honeymoon days were educational and a lot of fun but lasted only a few weeks before he and Ocie started fighting like a couple of boar hogs.

Most people have trouble finding Bulls Gap on the map, but it's a real place where my Hughett and Gulley kinfolks were raised. You'll have difficulty finding Bulls Gap on a map because of the way the map is folded: Bulls Gap always seems to be in the crease.

At any rate, Zelbert tried breaking into a specialized preaching niche, but his rattlesnakes got loose in his father-in-law's mountain cabin and he and his new wife had no choice but to move out. Ever the entrepreneur, he decided to pursue fame and fortune by becoming a famous taxidermist. While he was off to a good start with a squirrel he had "barked," the results of his attempt to become a taxidermist weren't very promising. On his first project, the squirrel was severely cross-eyed and looked more like a deformed rat, even more so since the hair had fallen off its tail. His second attempt was also off to a bad start when he found that his barn cat, Killer, had eaten the ears and nose off his "specimen." He was pretty sure he could repair it, but for the time being, he was discouraged.

The final straw to get rich with taxidermy ended with his failed attempt to collect a rare Wampus Cat specimen, which killed his spirit.

Given Zelbert's bad start at finding financial stability, Ocie Mae, his young bride, decided that maybe she'd have to become the breadwinner in their Appalachian home. Besides, at age 22, she was already experiencing the early onset of a midlife crisis and wanted to do something that would stimulate her self-esteem and bring in needed money to the homestead at the same time. Between helping Zelbert feed his hogs, tending a garden, canning, and skinning hides from Zelbert's 'coons for later sale in town, she was experiencing mood swings, not sleeping well, and, occasionally, would take a nip of Nathan Gulley's special recipe moonshine…the kind that was "doubled" to 180 proof or so. Nathan bragged that he "didn't make no mean likker" and his product gained a reputation for calming one's nerves…sometimes for several days. Ocie had no hobbies and hated quilting, unlike what the other women seemed to glom onto. And while the procedure for getting pregnant was very compelling, she really didn't want any rug rats at this point in her life. Besides, they couldn't afford a rug anyway, and sweeping a carpet with a broom would prove fruitless. Someday, when they got electricity to the cabin, she'd consider a few of the fancy things in life. In the meantime, she wanted to be engaged in something both challenging and potentially lucrative since Zelbert seemed to be only good at hunting, fishing, running around the hills, and always strutting around like he was some kind of stud. So far, Ocie wasn't overly impressed by his strutting, but he never bored her.

The way Ocie was moping around and acting, her momma thought she must be pregnant. Miz Kitty, her neighbor from the flatlands, suggested that she do something stimulating and challenging.

Ocie Mae thought about it for a while and got to thinking about what resources she had access to. Their cabin in the holler had lots of bushes and rocks surrounding it. The rocks were interesting because they were attractive colors of gray and variations of brown...and shiny when you broke them open. Miz Kitty, who could read and seemed to know everything, said they were "chert rocks."

It so happened that Bryant Gulley visited the homestead and noticed the outcropping of chert. He was known to be the last of a dying breed of rock chippers or flint knappers. In other words, he knew how to make arrowheads, spear points, and knives from common chert rocks. It was something an old Cherokee Indian man from Sevier County had taught him when he was a kid. Seeing that the couple was intrigued, he pulled a cobble from the hillside, picked up a small, round hammering stone, and, within a few minutes, gave Zelbert a chipped-out arrowhead he could put on an arrow and use to hunt with. He then chipped out a really sharp stone skinning knife in just a few more minutes. Bryant Gulley had many talents. Mountain people could be creative with their time.

He explained that chert, flint, obsidian, and certain other rocks can break like glass and produce edges sharper than those of a knife made of steel. The trick to making arrowheads was to control the angle at which you hit the chert to remove flakes to shape the rock. He called them "concrete fractures" (conchoidal). He then reminded Zelbert of the time that a covey of quail had flushed and flew up between him and the Sutterfield house, and he let loose with his shotgun, breaking little round holes in the neighbor's window glass. Bryant said that chert and flint rocks break on that same angle, and the chipping was predictable.

In his demonstration, he knocked out the rough shape of an arrowhead with the hammer stone, pulled a small piece of deer antler out of his pocket, and chipped some sharp edges. He handily sliced through a piece of leather with it to prove it was razor sharp. He also told them that, at one time, all of our ancestors made stone tools. If they hadn't done so, we would not have survived as a human race. He also said if the Russians were to take over the United States, like they were constantly threatening to, people would still be able to make effective self-defense weapons and fight them off by just using rocks and sticks like those found in the holler.

While wandering the hills hunting, Zelbert would sometimes stumble across the location of old Indian campsites and find arrowheads and skin scrapers. He always wondered what it was like to live back in those days, and wondered if couples had in-law troubles back then, too.

Since his attempt to become a snake-handling preacher had fallen through and a cat had disfigured his latest taxidermy project, Zelbert considered giving up mounting animals and becoming a "flintsnapper" like Uncle Bryant.

The problem came when Ocie Mae said she had decided to take up the flintsnapping and for him to "back off." At first, Zelbert complained because he thought his manhood was being undermined. Then Ocie explained:

"Zelbert, we got plenty of rocks and we got deer horns, just like the old guys did, only I hain't old and iffen you menfolk can do sumpthin, us womenfolk can do hit a whole dam sight better iffen we takes a mind to. I never took to makin' quilts and sech, and breaking rocks into sumthin useful is better than breaking your skull open wid a rock and findin they ain't nuthin in thar. Now, you leave me be so's I can buckle down on Bryant's snappin' lessons and git my angles right and make good concrete fractures."

In the interest of transparency, it should be mentioned that Zelbert and Ocie Mae Nicodemus began arguing at least once a week after the honeymoon period had passed. After the traditional break-in period of their marriage, their arguments were shorter but more fierce and mostly revolved around ways to make money to keep the homestead going. While the hams and coon meat were good eating, Ocie yearned to adopt some of the big city ways, such as better food, a new dress, and wearing shoes. She loved going barefoot and was raised that way, but people looked at her funny when she went to town. She didn't want to live high on the hog, but she was a grown woman now and wanted to keep up with how the world was going. Maybe someday she'd even buy one of the bras she saw advertised in the Sears catalog. A bright red one with frills and lace all over it. Heaven knows she needed one. She had her eyes on the Dolly Parton "Choo Choo Special."

Whenever Ocie Mae and Zelbert had disagreements, they tended to fall back on the old-timey Appalachian language ways they grew up with. At the risk of giving the reader a headache, here's an example of one of the battles involving Ocie Mae's desire to become a flintknapper.

"Zelbert, iffn you don't git a money-payin' job soon, my daddy's gonna foller up on his promise and shoot yore sorry butt. I know hit's a problem cause yore own daddy couldn't hole down a good job if it wuz tied up wif a rope. I unnerstand that you got off to a bad start in life, and sometimes I think you ain't wired right, but Lord help me, as I live and breathe, I'm gonna fix you!"

"Ocie, you says you's gonna fix me? Whut in tarnation does you mean by thet? You know dang well and good that they ain't no better hunter or fisher man in these blessed hills and I kin work a mule as good as the best yahoo around. Plus, me and my pet hog, Sweet Pea, can keep us in meat forever as long as HUMPphrey, our ole stud hog and Sweet Pea keep knocking out piggies. An' when they's gone, they'll always be more."

Ocie responded, "Zelbert, why come you don't git usens a cow so's we kin milk hit? And some carpet rugs thet we can put in the outhouse. Sittin' out there, my feet gits cold on the dirt floor. Honey, I know you tries hard, and I knows you have a hankering for more milk, too. And I'm sorry our old nanny goat dried up. You couldn't coax milk outta her if you'uz to poker in the butt wid a stick. And I know you tried to milk Sweet Pea and she dang near tooken yore leg off with her tuskers. You should'uv knowed that women folk don't like you messin around wid dem thangs ceptin when they's in the mood and Sweet Pea is like yore momma, she haint inna mood for nuthin but eatin and squealin all the time. Now you git along with your taxiderming that coonskin and let me snap out another arrahead. I plan on sellin' them things to touristers in Gatlinberg for big money."

Finally, Zelbert said, "You leave Sweet Pea outta this!" after which he gave up and stomped off to feed the chickens. Zelbert had learned in the first few weeks of marriage to recognize when he'd not win an argument with Ocie Mae. His only reply before heading out the door to tend the animals was to say. "Ocie, I hain't got but one nerve left, and you done gone and got on hit. I feel a mybrain headache acomin' on. You make my tongue git so twisted around my eye teeth that I cain't see what I'm saying."

The honeymoon was certainly over, but he had learned that, indeed, the man is the head of the household, but the woman is the neck, and she can turn the head any way she wants to. When Zelbert was courtin' Ocie, the boys down at the Jay Bird Store didn't tell him about the downsides of marrying a hard-headed woman. To her credit, he knew Ocie was level-headed because snuff dripped out of her lips equal on both sides. One can never have everything.

After the love spat, Ocie Mae took a bucket and started looking for more chert cobbles she could use to make arrowheads. When she eventually would become a master flintsnapper, she would sell them to people in town and make big money that Zelbert could only dream about.

Life would be good.

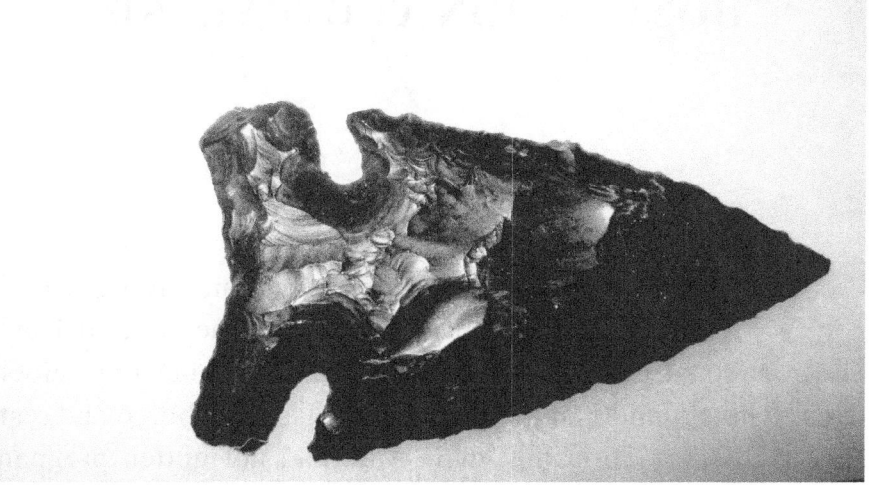

"Flintsnapped" Arrowhead

OCIE MAE AND ZELBERT HONEYMOON AT OPRYLAND

After being married for almost a year and living in their remote cabin in Panther Holler on the edge of Hawkins County in East Tennessee, Ocie Mae and Zelbert Nicodemus found that they were getting a little bored and restless in their relationship. Ocie Mae had not gotten pregnant like all the other women in the area, and they'd still not figured out how to scrape out a decent living from the hard dirt on the rocky hillsides. Also, they'd never had the time or money to realize their dream of taking a honeymoon like they'd heard the city folk did. Being young and adventurous, the time came when they decided to spice their life up by going on a genuine flatlander honeymoon.

From the get-go, Ocie Mae and Zelbert had some challenges in resolving conflicts in their marriage. They were two quite different people trying to become one as a married couple. It had gotten so bad at one point that there was some back and forth about whether their marriage would last, and that was stressful. They began their marriages as essentially two strangers with little in common other than a physical attraction and something else they just described as "I don't know what." Ocie had been living a hard life with a domineering hillbilly father and cowering mother, and she wanted to get away from that. Zelbert's life was one of relative bliss, with him wandering in the woods hunting and fishing and untethered by home rules. His dad had died, and he continued to raise pigs with his momma, but she began to insist that he start making a life of his own and get married like all the other guys in their area.

Then, he met Ocie at church. They just glanced at each other and instantly knew they had discovered love. When they made eye contact, they felt an unspeakable connection, something like they'd been searching for all their life. They couldn't explain it, but the feeling was overwhelming. So much so that they sometimes forgot to breathe and would have to pause and catch their breath.

Ocie's father did everything he could to scare Zelbert away from his daughter, but, like dogs in heat, he was unsuccessful at every turn. He finally gave in and reluctantly agreed to the wedding, mainly to avoid being embarrassed by an unwed and pregnant daughter. Life is complicated in all parts of the world, but it wouldn't be all that much different if one were in Appalachia, Argentina, or Africa.

When together, Ocie and Zelbert couldn't keep their hands off each other, even though they were always chaperoned. Feeling that they were in love, they dreamed and fantasized of uncovering the glorious pleasures of wedded bliss and carving out a life together. Being young, they also shared a craving for adventure and a different sort of excitement than raising hogs, chasing raccoons, and raising kids in the back hills.

But, as mentioned, they found that married life wasn't all roses and bliss as they'd envisioned. Preacher Jeff counseled them that the Devil was working on them and would break them up if he could. However, to date, Ocie and Zelbert had been pretty successful in working the kinks out...but both desired more. They'd seen less successful marriages end in divorce, alcoholism, or scandal.

According to Miz Kitty, Squint Ledbedder's French wife, their ability to get along as well as they did was due to Ocie's "inborn ability" to outthink Zelbert and smooth things over. Then she further clarified this by mentioning Zelbert's innate *"inability"* to come out on top of disagreements that required brains. In private, when talking with her mountaineer husband, Squint, Miz Kitty joked that Zelbert's "lower cognitive ability" may have been his greatest asset in resolving marital conflict. Unlike a lot of the mountain folk in her neighborhood, she had some education and read books about psychology stuff like this.

When Zelbert's friends asked why his marriage to such a headstrong woman as Ocie had worked out so well, he said, "My momma told me to jist take a walk when we wuz about to have a knock-down, drag-out fight. I won't lie to you, boys, I've done a Hell of a lot of walking since I got married!" Zelbert didn't use foul language hardly ever, but discovering the best way to deal with Ocie Mae was a puzzle he'd yet been able to solve.

Differences aside, both Ocie and Zelbert heartily agreed that a good honeymoon would be good for their marriage and give them a glimpse into what life outside the holler was like.

Zelbert envisioned going somewhere private where they could reconnect in a serious way and rekindle their passion. Offhand, he had in mind a remote and comfortable motel at Myrtle Beach, South Carolina. Ocie reminded him that it would be expensive, and they didn't have much money, plus there were sharks in the ocean there, and that made her nervous. Zelbert replied that she didn't have to get in the water, and she countered that she didn't want "to be left a widow and have to take care of the damned hogs and deal with his mother."

Ocie had heard good things about romantic honeymoon cabins in the woods near Gatlinburg in the Smokies. She talked of an ideal honeymoon that would be full of cuddles and snuggles, beautiful nature hikes, sunsets, and long conversations that would last all night until they fell asleep. She said, "Think about it, Zelbert, we'd be in a remote cabin and be close, just me and you together experiencing each other and the gorgeous wilderness!" But Zelbert reminded her that they already were living alone in a mountain cabin in beautiful, remote mountains, and that wasn't enough.

Ocie got his drift and countered with, "Well then, why don't we just take a tent and hike the Appalachian Trail and visit some historical sites and restaurants in towns along the way. That wouldn't cost much and would be an adventure where we'd be totally alone and having lots of alone time and fun." Zelbert reminded her that they could pitch a tent in the field beside their house and be just as isolated as in the Smokies. That suggestion didn't quite hit the mark with Zelbert, and he countered with, "Would it be romantic to wake up to a cold and dark campsite, with bugs, rain, and Wampus Cats running around in the woods?"

Ocie conceded his point and struggled to suggest another honeymoon destination. She remembered that Miz Kitty had once spent a weekend in Nashville and went to Grand Old Opry. That idea stuck. Both Ocie and Zelbert loved country music, and soon they were planning a honeymoon trip to Music City. Miz Kitty had a good memory and suggested how they might pull off such a trip on a tight budget. She and Squint had once stayed at Nashville's less-than-fancy but affordable Bozeman Motel. At that time, motel rooms cost anywhere from $6 to $50 a night, and she and Squint had splurged and budgeted $20 a night for lodging. To save on money, they ate twenty-cent cheeseburgers at the Red Barn and washed them down with fifteen-cent milkshakes. They also ate Janburgers at Jan's Fish and Chips for fifteen cents each. Jan's was on the corner of 17th and Jefferson Streets, but it was quite a walk to the Grand Old Opry. They also ate at Minnie Pearl's Roast Beef Restaurant on 2014 West End and got Moonshine Icees at the 7-Eleven on Gallatin Road. Armed with this information, Ocie was ready to plan their budget.

Then, reality hit. Ocie and Zelbert had only had $156.54 that could be used for the honeymoon. After crunching the numbers, it was obvious that they would not be staying in fancy motels and eating steak dinners. In fact, there was barely enough money to cover a few days in Nashville, not counting transportation costs to and from. And that was staying in a cheap motel and eating Janburgers.

However, being young and too naïve to believe that God somehow wouldn't provide for such a worthy cause, they continued to pursue their dream of a honeymoon in Nashville. To this end, they consulted with their relatives and friends for ideas.

Ole Man Sutterfield, Ocie Mae's grumpy daddy, strongly suggested that Ocie leave her "no-good-for-nothing husband and go to Nashville and find a man with talent, like a banjer player, and marry him." He liked banjo music. The boys on the porch at the Jay Bird Story had all sorts of sordid recommendations, most all of which could be summed up with the general concept of shacking up in a motel for a week in Bulls Gap and seriously working on conceiving a baby. In fact, they had several hare-brained theories about how to come up with twins. Bryant Gulley suggested buying a month's worth of his "young marrieds mood enhancer elixir" and essentially doing the same, "with no need of a stinkin' motel whar strangers sleep and carry on." Nathan Gulley advised that, in his experience, they were wasting their time when their minds could be relaxed more than they could imagine by obtaining a gallon or two of his special recipe and just relaxing somewhere…anywhere. All these suggestions caused both Ocie's and Zelbert's heads to ache. The actions suggested would be no more than temporary band-aids on their ailing marriage.

Interestingly, it was Aunt Berthy who suggested some avenues whereby they could be assured of a good chance at achieving their goals of exploring, relaxing, and enjoying each other's company in Nashville and reconnecting as a solid married couple. For those who have been reading my stories, you already know that Berthy was a paradox tucked away in the remote hills of Appalachia. Where she gained her knowledge, no one was sure, but most speculated that much of it came from the granny woman who mentored her in the use of crystals and spells to help influence life happenings. And her preacher daddy, John Harvey, also had an influence. The rest, she claimed to have obtained from reading the scriptures and personal inspiration. Aint Berthy was paradoxical by any measure.

Paradoxical means something or someone who is seemingly impossible or difficult to understand because of beliefs that appear to represent two opposite facts or characteristics. In Berthy's case, she was a devout Bible-thumping Christian woman who, for the most part, used the scriptures to guide her life's actions. On the other hand, she believed that crystals, incense, and ceremonies with candles had mystical powers and that the outcome of a melding of all these could give insight into human nature and affect relationships. Does this make sense? No, probably not, but it was what it was.

Ocie Mae spent an entire afternoon and late evening visiting with Berthy, discussing not only her desire to take a vacation honeymoon but also delving deep into the complicated question of how she and Zelbert could repair their marriage and make it strong again. (*Hang on, because this is a serious topic and could get long and crazy. I've attempted to understand Berthy's convictions over the years and still struggle with it.*)

Berthy explained that a spiritual relationship between a married couple and a carnal relationship are two paradoxical kinds of relationships. She went on to tell how a spiritual relationship is based on a connection between the souls or spirits of the spouses. It involves mutual love, trust, respect, and service to each other...and to God. A spiritual relationship would not be dependent on physical attraction or sexual intimacy, but rather on shared faith and values. She cited a few scriptures underlining how a spiritual relationship can help the spouses grow closer to God and to each other, and can bring them peace, joy, and fulfillment.

She went on to explain how the carnal aspect of a marriage is largely based on physical attraction and pleasure that's concerned more with gratification than the spiritual connection or emotional well-being of each other...but that, without the spiritual connection, carnal intimacy alone would only result in frustration, arguments, and emptiness. She cited this as the root cause of much of the philandering and alcoholism in the region.

Then, she emphasized that the spiritual and carnal tendencies of God's children are not mutually exclusive and that a healthy marriage should have a good balance of both carnal and spiritual aspects, with one fortifying the other.

Hearing deep thoughts like this from the old woman made Ocie's head spin and she said, "Berthy, skip all the mumbo-jumbo crap and help me!"

This is where Berthy put on another hat and brought out her candles and crystals. This time, she placed two red candles on the table alongside a red jasper stone that had a special significance and apparent mystical power to draw the couple together. Granny woman had told her that the red crystal, when used properly, could help couples grow in both their faith in God and enhance their intimacy, leading to a relationship with meaning and purpose, full of joy and fulfillment. However, for this to happen, the couple needed to communicate openly and honestly about all their needs and desires, both spiritual and carnal, and seek God's guidance and wisdom in helping to make their marriage strong against the forces of evil and boredom.

Ocie then confessed to Berthy that she sometimes had evil thoughts and once even wished that Zelbert would die and come back in the next life as a nasty lizard that would be stepped on by a horse and squooshed, but she had repented of that after Zelbert brought her some wild orchids he'd found in the woods. Sometimes, she had trouble controlling her thoughts.

Then, Ocie revealed that there was a time when she was walking at night and saw a couple passing by the church holding hands and cuddling each other, and she asked herself, "Why couldn't that be me?" Then she noticed her own shadow on the wall of the church and wondered if that was a sign and what it might mean. Berthy only replied that fate and action would only take a person so far, then it was up to the person to make things happen. The shadow was what "could be."

Before starting to work a spell that would help assure that their upcoming honeymoon would be successful, she explained that God and the power of the crystal, working together, could help heal their relationship and help them gain a relationship filled with love and happiness. Further, she emphasized that spells didn't take away a person's free will. She believed that it was harmful and unethical to use "unseen powers" to deliberately alter someone's will without their direct knowledge or consent. It was in this vein that she was known for casting spells that were intended to attract or influence a specific person to fall in love or enhance an existing relationship. In her experience, spells that were intended to restrict or control the free-will actions of another person seldom worked. Curses that were meant to cause harm or suffering were frowned on and started to conflict with the Bible's principle of "harm no one."

Alongside the candles and jasper, she laid out a piece of string and saturated it with jasmine and perfume. Then she tied the string tightly around both candles, one-quarter inch below the wick, and lit them. Then, she had Ocie think of Zelbert and recite the following phrase seven times: "If it's meant to be, let our souls melt together and our honeymoon be life-changing to our relationship."

Then Berthy explained the concept of the "twin flames" where each candle would burn down to the string, where the tops of the candles would melt together, and the two flames would become a single flame. This signified "soul connection," a concept that had nothing to do with cults but pure, connected love.

She then waved the red jasper crystal over the flame seven times, extinguishing it as it reached the string, and the merged flame appeared.

Berthy gave the red crystal to Ocie and admonished her to keep it in her possession from then on and to believe that it had the power to reduce her anxiety and open new doors in their relationship. In times of stress and need for special help, she was to clutch the crystal.

So, are you, as a reader, skeptical of some things that Berthy believed in? That's OK. One might explain all this as a mix of placebo and one's own intentions or being open-minded to the metaphysical properties of certain crystals. Ocie was a bit dubious about all the hocus pocus but wasn't going to knock it and would try to make it work for her. After all, people wore copper bracelets and believed they helped cure arthritis. Why not have vibrations from a crystal set in motion specific positive emotions, reminding her to refocus her energy? While it would be silly to think that crystals could heal broken bones, why couldn't they emotionally help, placebo or not? Who cares if crystals or copper bracelets are placebos, as long as they bring about a positive change for the better?

Berthy went on to explain that Jesus was able to cure people instantly with miracles. The Bible also provides examples of physical contact healing or aura interaction. In one instance, Christ made an ointment of spit and dirt and helped a blind man recover his sight. This suggests that performing a holy miracle to help someone may require them to exercise their will to believe. The spit and dirt Jesus used were just tools. Jesus didn't really need to use anything if the blind man had the faith to accept it.

Enough of this stuff, it's too heady for me to think about, but for my Aunt Berthy, it was real.

The day after leaving Berthy's cabin, Miz Kitty dropped by Panther Holler and told Ocie that Squint's cousin David and his wife Darlene owned a car and, coincidentally, would be passing though Nashville on their way to and from Memphis and would be willing to drop her and Zelbert off in the Music City for four days and pick them up on their way back to Mohawk. They actually lived in Bean Station but had a pickup and delivery to make in Mohawk. This coincidence brings up the topic of providence, or a manifestation of divine will, but that's a topic for another time. Either way, a door opened for Ocie and Zelbert to achieve their dream of honeymooning in Nashville.

So, with hardly any preplanning, Zelbert and Ocie Mae found themselves soon squirreled away in the cozy Bozeman Motel in Nashville and eating burgers at the Red Barn and shakes at Jan's Fish and Chips. From there, they walked to the Ryman Auditorium, where the Grand Ole Opry was broadcast from. Right away, they felt a bit uncomfortable when they realized that they didn't seem to fit in with some of the snooty city folks. They dressed differently, talked with a different accent, and stumbled in some of their reactions to the city. They were amazed by the sights and sounds of the big town. There were culture shocks such as dodging traffic, non-stop noise, sirens, people speaking foreign languages, and people who tried to exploit them. They saw women with outrageous makeup and scanty clothing on street corners and were blown away by the size of the William R. Snodgrass Building with its thirty-one floors.

Nevertheless, they loved country music and, growing up, had always secretly fantasized about running away from the hills, hitchhiking to Nashville, and somehow becoming famous and rich. The feeling of actually being there was exciting.

At the Ryman Auditorium, they carefully counted out their money and gained entrance to the vast room, which featured stained glass windows and seats reminiscent of long church pews. The auditorium was packed, and people were crammed in their seats as tight as sardines. They bought the cheaper tickets underneath the balcony and had to peer around support poles in order to see the stage, but this did not diminish their excitement.

And the show was marvelous! The stained-glass windows and benches made them feel like they were sitting in church. It was a sacred experience to actually be in the same room where so many great musicians had performed. East Tennessee had more than a dozen of its own who'd performed there. People such as Johnny Cash and June Carter Cash, who were raised just a few miles from Panther Holler. Other performers included Dolly Parton from Sevierville, Kenny Chesney from Knoxville, and Kelse Ballerini, who grew up in Knoxville. And Ashley Monroe and others. Then, of course, other East Tennesseans, like Ernie Ford, who was raised in Bristol, and "Stringbean" Akeman.

On a more positive note, another Grand Ole Opry and Hee Haw performer from Bulls Gap, Tennessee, frequently performed at the Ryman Auditorium. Archie Campbell was the hometown boy who made good in Nashville.

The night that Ocie Mae and Zelbert attended the Opry, along with a few other performers, they heard Jerry Lee Lewis's infamous performance that got him banned from Opryland for several years. He broke one of the rules by cursing and exceeding his allotted time limit. He is well known for the rock and roll songs, "Great Balls of Fire," "Johnny B. Good," and "A Whole Lotta Shakin' Going On."

Wowed by the performances in the great Ryman, Ocie and Zelbert returned to their motel room. The room was modest, but it had key amenities such as cable TV and a mini fridge. However, the main attraction was the "Magic Fingers" vibrating bed.

Zelbert's plan was to carry Ocie Mae over the threshold and make their way to the bed to christen the room. However, it didn't quite work out that way. Zelbert was so exhausted by the long program, the late hour, and the long walk back to the motel, he just lay down to rest a moment and fell asleep. Ocie Mae followed his example, and they woke up the next morning fully clothed and anxious to buy Janburgers and Breakfast Chips. That evening, they splurged and ate at Minnie Pearl's restaurant. An old couple was sitting beside them and heard them talking about their honeymoon. The couple paid for their meal, saying that someone did the same thing for them on their honeymoon at that same restaurant, and they wanted to keep the magic going.

After comparing notes over dinner and taking the brisk walk back to the motel, Zelbert and Ocie decided that there were more important things in life than the Grand Old Opry and cheeseburgers. They decided to just "camp out" in the motel rather than waste time in the noisy city. On their last night in the magic city, they were energetically talking about life, where they'd been, where they were at currently in their relationship, where they wanted to go, and how they might better achieve their life goals together. They then pulled out the stash of Uncle Bryant's "young marrieds mood enhancer elixir" and settled down and looked each other directly in the eyes as the evening comfortably wore on. Zelbert smelled the phantomlike whisper of her fragrance. He followed it, ever so slowly, letting his lips whisper across the edge of her ear and down the side of her neck. With a sigh, Ocie let her head drop back against his shoulder, and she said, "Zelbert, I don't know what makes me more tired, fighting against you or fighting for you."

He responded, "I'm not really worth either of those. I just love you. You turn my mind inside out and upside down. I love holding you and knowing that you care. "

Ever so slowly, Ocie grasped the red jasper crystal in her hand, and her gaze shifted to his mouth, and she said, "Kiss me," and the power of the unseen but felt spirit altered and defined their lives from that time forward. And the twin flames became one.

After a lazy morning the next day, David and Darlene picked them up, and they were back in their cozy and private Panther Holler home just in time for another sip of Uncle Bryant's amazing potion.

Honeymoon in Opryland

OCIE MAE GITS SIDEWAYS WITH THE PREACHER

My grandpa, Preacher Hughett, and Preacher Kester were friendly to each other, but there was a bit of tension regarding their styles. Unlike many, Papaw was a pure mountain preacher who preached from his heart and relied on divine inspiration. In a way, he had to. It wasn't known back in those days what dyslexia was, and he had to work hard to overcome it.

Unlike Papaw, Preacher Kester was a seminary-trained preacher who found getting his first job in the mountains a challenge, but he eventually adapted to the hellfire and brimstone style of preaching. Both ministers had quite a following. Papaw was Southern Baptist, and Preacher Kester was Pentecostal, both fine men and good preachers. You gotta remember that much of Appalachia was the polished buckle on the Bible Belt.

Papaw was mild and not one to get overly worked up and critical of sinners, but he certainly didn't tolerate their actions. His approach was one of gentle persuasion. Preacher Kester was more direct, like my great-great-grandpa, Preacher Stephen Hughett of Indian Valley in Floyd County, Virginia. Stephen was known for calling out apparent sinners in public. A 94-year-old guy I met once told me that when he was a young boy, Preacher Stephen stopped him in the road and told him he was going to Hell for wearing knickers (short pants), a new style at the time. That scared him.

Kester was like Stephen in several ways and frequently traveled around East Tennessee preaching "for the cause." Once, a new likker store was opening up in Newport, Tennessee, and he traveled there to meet with a dozen other preachers to protest the store opening by throwing fire and brimstone at all those coming there to buy likker. Whenever someone put their hands on the likker store door, Preacher Kester would say, "Brother, by puttin' yore hand on that door, yore opening a door right into the bowels of Hell! Repent while you can!" Some people took that message to heart, quickly withdrew their hand, and walked away, while the more brazen and thirsty souls just leered at the minister, pushed the door open, and traipsed on in. One ole boy was smarter than the rest and waited until someone else opened the door, grinned, and slipped through the door without touching the door or the handle, outsmarting the preachers. Some hillbillies are more intelligent than others.

Preacher Kester did have challenges from time to time. Some people said he wasn't the brightest possum in the holler, and he didn't know whether to wind his butt or scratch his watch. Once, he set up a gospel tent outside of Honaker, Virginia, when one of the ladies in the front row fell to her knees on the ground. The Preacher thought the good sister was overcome with the spirit and kneeling down to pray. He rushed to her side and asked, "Are you OK? Can I help?" Having forgotten to put on her hearing aids, the lady exclaimed loudly, "Yes, Preacher. My dad-blamed false teeth fell out, and they's lost in the damned grass."

Sorry, I digressed. As I was about to say, even though he married them up, Ocie Mae and Zelbert had a disagreement with Preacher Kester when he started pickin' on their Uncle Nathan.

Uncle Nathan made likker in a No Name Mountain cave near None O'yo Bidness Creek. Kester found out about it and organized a gaggle of preachers to try and shut him down. This riled more than a few locals because Nathan was a kind soul and known for not making "mean likker." He was just a mountaineer businessman trying to scrape out a living and Ocie Mae, Zelbert, and a dozen or so other upstanding people from the area who would never drink evil spirits, took offense and claimed that a little sip of Nathan's "fully organic" moonshine settled their stomachs and cured coughing. In the hills, there were a lot of unsettled stomachs and coughin', and Uncle Nathan took pride in providing a valuable public service.

Preacher Kester was a stubborn, pulpit-pounding and foot-stomping advocate for God. He didn't listen to Ocie Mae when she told him to "back off" his holy wagon and lay off Nathan. That didn't sit well, so Preacher Kester and some followers organized to harass Nathan at his cabin.

The Preacher's wife and Ocie Mae got into a simmering argument when the reverend's wife commented to Ocie, "Honey, I don't care what nobody says, when yore all gussied up, I think yore purty…in yore own way." Ocie didn't take such a backhanded compliment sitting down and responded, "Most people know that yore biscuit hain't done in the middle, but all usens can overlook that." The Preacher's wife replied, "I didn't mean to hurt your feelin's, darlin, but I'm shore yore still purdy in yore grandma's eyes." They didn't get in a fight, but Ocie was a large woman, and everything settled down when she said to the Preacher's wife, "Quit bein' ugly afore I whop you upside the head." Mountain people are extra civil until you tromp on their last nerve.

Not having many entertainment opportunities, various folks from the hollers gathered in front of Nathan's cabin to watch the show. Kester had enlisted the help of a couple of men with guitars, and he started preaching and singing "When the Roll is Called up

Yonder." Then he started swinging his hips and getting into "the zone" while a deacon passed a hat and took up a collection.

The Preacher then approached Nathan's door and yelled, "Nathan, I know yore in thar! This is Preacher Kester, and I'm speaking for the Lawd. I've been talking with some angels and you gotta quit makin and selling evil likker to my people." Nathan cracked the door, peered out, and said, "Preacher, I don't make no mean likker. I just make smooth stuff what's way better than them flatlander's wine they use in church house sacraments. Now, you and yore boys move along and leave me alone." After saying that, Nathan threw a fifty-dollar bill on the porch and said, "Put that in the collection plate and git the Hell outta here!" After which, he shot a 12-gauge shotgun into the air. Then, he gingerly placed six half-pint bottles of his "duck load" corn whiskey on the porch and said, "I'm afixin' to git mad but instead of whuppin you right here and now on the porch in front of God and everbody, I'm plumb wore out and goin' to bed. Y'all stay as long as you like," and he went back in the house.

Visibly startled, Preacher Kester turned tail and said to the crowd, "Nathan has done made an offering of fifty dolla to the Lawd. Now, I got to rush over to Zeb Barlow's house. He's got three starvin' youngins, and he just drapped on the floor at the county store with heart drapsy. Iffen I don't run over there and give him a blessin' I may end up tryin to raise the dead agin."

Uncle Nathan's duck load 'shine was different from his "goose load" likker. Both were old family recipes made from organically grown corn with a hint of the smell of German malted grain. People said they had a subtle sweetness that other likkers lacked. I asked a man what the difference was, and he told me, "Goose Load shine is 180 proof and hit kicks twict, jist like a cross-eyed mule. What that means is you has to swoller hit twict, onect on the way down and agin when hit tries to crawl back out. Duck Load is extry smooth and eases hits way into yore innards causing yore whole body to relax from the worries of the world and then hit starts to purifying yore blood. Nathan ain't like a lot of 'shiners and he distills all his likker twict resulting in medicine grade product." In truth, it actually was sorta medicinal because a little of it was used in cough syrup and other homemade elixirs mixed with wild herbs.

At first, the six bottles of 'shine just sat on the porch until an old granny woman shuffled forward and took two bottles and put 'em in her purse to help with her midwifing. Then there was a rush for the remaining bottles.

From that day on, Zelbert and Ocie Mae stayed shy of Preacher Kester and started attending Rev. J. E. Hughett's meetings at Mountain Valley Church.

Note: My Papaw, Rev. J. E. Hughett, was a mountain preacher in rural Greene County, Tennessee, and pastored the Mountain Valley Church that his daddy, John Harvey, had built. Rev. Stephen Hughett of Floyd County, Virginia, was real, but the old-time backsliders who knew him have passed on. My great-uncle Nathan was a lifelong moonshiner and, unfortunately, was forced to spend fifteen hard years in the Brushy Mountain State Prison in Petros, Tennessee, for evading likker taxes. He dug coal in the prison mine. Ocie Mae and Zelbert are made-up characters based on the personalities and lives of real people I knew. Preacher Kester is based on a real preacher I knew in Morristown.

Some have asked why I write a lot about preachers. There are several reasons: I'm descended from a long line of preachers: Baptist (regular, hard-shell & primitive), Pentecostal, and various flavors of Calvinists. In fact, the Hughetts fled Ireland in the late 1600s because of religious persecution. Also, over many years, my dad amassed over a thousand audio-taped sermons, "singin's," and interviews with preachers and mountaineers at backwoods church meetings and in their homes. As a boy, I accompanied my dad on many excursions and learned much about Appalachians. After My Dad died, I selected the best of these, obtained a grant from the Archives of Appalachia at East Tennessee State University, and transferred the audio recordings from reel-to-reel tapes to audio cassettes, donating them to their archives. The Harvey Lee Hughett Collection at ETSU comprises 120 tape recordings made between 1950 and 1977 of religious meetings at various Appalachian churches, homecomings, and interviews with rural individuals, including Reverend J. E. Hughett (my grandfather) and my great-uncle, Bryant Gulley (Mountain Medicine Man). The tapes may be reviewed for research by contacting the Archives of Appalachia. You can find out more by making an Internet search for the Harvey Lee Hughett Collection Archives of Appalachia, then click on Harvey Lee Hughett, Sr Archives Space Public Interface.

THE GREAT BULLS GAP MULE RACE

Whenever times appeared to be getting boring in Possum Holler, someone always came up with an idea for creating some excitement. Zelbert Nicodemus frequently got hare-brained ideas, and here's one that showed promise for kicking some fun into the Appalachian community…and making a little money at the same time.

Zelbert had been visiting with local moonshiner, Nathan Gulley, and together they concocted what they figured to be a surefire plan for getting filthy rich like the flatlanders who lived in Knoxville and Johnson City. Ocie Mae ran the idea by her daddy, and his response was, "That sorry, no-good for nuthin' excuse for a human man what you married is always gittin' in trubbel. You arta leave his butt and find someone what's got somethin' in his head other than rocks and moss. The only way that man could be dumber would be for him to be bigger…" And the rant went on. One could say that her father hadn't yet discovered Zelbert's good side, which, to be truthful, Ocie was having some trouble finding it herself, but life with him was never boring. Zelbert was funny, creative, and a great hunter and scrounger when it came to digging ginseng roots and chasing coons. However, making money to improve their lifestyle was a vague concept that always slipped out of his reach.

However, THIS TIME, his effort would be different! He wouldn't fail like he did with the taxidermy endeavor or trying to master the art of a snake-handling preacher. He and Nathan would partner up and sponsor the first mule race to ever come to Bulls Gap, Tennessee.

Of course, the first step in any planning project was to run the idea by Bryant Gulley, who claimed to know everything there ever was to know about anything. They counted on him for inspiration and ideas.

Bryant gave them a hardy greeting when they arrived at his hillside shack. "Come on in, my good frens, come right in. I wish you happiness and much joy on this wunnerful day. When the sun comed up this here morning, I said to myself, 'Self, hit's anuther splendid day in this hyar paradise. Sumthin' good is bound to happen." Then he paused and said, "I'll be right wid you boys as soon as I have my daily *starter and blowout* medicine. I notice that Nathan has done gone and brung me some more of that good base liquid for making my medicines. Hit's more organic than what others sells. Hain't got no additives. Jest pure Jimmy Red corn. I shore do thank'ye, Nathan. Sit down compadres!"

It should be mentioned that Bryant claimed to speak Spanish fluently and was always throwing out impressive foreign words like compadre, amigo, madre, hijo de maldito perro, and such. He taught Zelbert the phrase for hello in Spanish: "buenas dingas." Mexicans looked at him funny-like when he greeted them, but he figured that it just surprised them that he knew their lingo. He was always proud to say, "Usens up hyar on the mountain hain't dumb, ya'know. Ain't that right? Who'll gimme a halleluiah?"

At any rate, they sat down and waited for Bryant to finish his daily starter blowout ritual. This was generally all he had for breakfast, but today, he'd also feast on the ham that Zelbert brought with him.

Bryant was always a little suspicious of Zelbert because he'd named one of his pigs Cecil. Cecil was also Bryant's older brother's name, and he took it personally. Zelbert also had two pet possums, one named Clyde and the other Cecil. Having three Cecils in the same neighborhood sometimes caused confusion. Bryant didn't know about the possum, but that's for a future story.

As they met, they sat around a small table in front of the fireplace in Bryant's cabin. His wife brought out and served some herbal sassafras refreshment, topped off with liberal shots of Ratsbane and Ginseng elixirs. This helped settle their feast on the sugar-cured county ham that Zelbert had made up the year before. It had aged perfectly, and after they scraped the fuzz (mold) off, it was one of the best he'd ever made. The planning session was sure to be successful because Nathan brought along two fruit jars full of his special "mind enhancer" brew.

They explained to Bryant that they wanted to stage a big mule race and make lots of money and lucre in the process, maybe even enough to buy a tractor to replace the cantankerous mules that plowed the garden and dragged logs out of the woods. A tractor could do the same work and wouldn't be as stubborn as the mules. Zelbert and Nathan agreed they would share the use of the tractor. Nathan allowed that a tractor would increase the number of gallons of corn he could raise per acre. This was an entrepreneurial move as much as anything.

Bryant sat back in the chair, closed his eyes, and went into his "thinking and cogitatin' mode." After ten minutes, Zelbert thought Bryant might have gone to sleep or died, so he nudged him a bit. Bryant jerked his eyes open and immediately started talking energetically as if inspired. He loved words and talking, and the day's starter and blowout got him going in high gear. However, Zelbert and Nathan weren't prepared for the number of words he gave them that morning. They sat on the edges of their chairs and tried to stay awake.

Bryant began by saying, "I got long-eared weed mules running around all over my place, even unner my house. It's unpossible to git rid uv 'em, but we tries. I shoots 'em inna head and skins 'em, and my wife cooks 'em up." Then he went on about how good they tasted, how he seasoned them with his special herbs, and so on. Finally, Zelbert stepped in and said, "Bryant, we's a talkin' 'bout genuine horse mules… real mules, not your dad-nabbed long-eared rabbits."

Without so much as a pause, Bryant continued: "Firstest, you boys has gotta figger out what you wants to do.

Zelbert responded, "Whut in tarnation does thet mean? We's gonna have a danged mule race whar we races real mules, not yore stinkin' bunnies!" However, as Zelbert thought about it, a bunny race might be a great future project.

"OK, Zelbert, whar you gonna have this race at?"

"We haven't worked that out yit. We's counting on Widder Woods lettin' us use her pasture. Hit's flat as a flitter, and they's a passable road up to hit. And, besides, I used one of my mules to plow up her front yard so's she could raise corn thar. She owes me a favor."

"OK, whatcha gonna do iffen she says no or runs off with that flatlander from Morristown what keeps sniffin' around her."

"We got that all figged out. Nathan and I aim to dress up like haints and run him off the mountain the next time he shows up."

"Atter you gits a place to race nailed down, is they enough room to tie up a bunch of stubborn mules, chairs for people to sit on and a place for them to pee and sech. And will Widder Woods letcha use her spring to water a passle of poopin' mules?"

"Listen, Bryant, we come here for advice, not a lecture. Let's git on wid it!"

"I understand. When you gonna have this race? On a holiday, a weekend or whut? Sundays are out 'cause Preacher Kester will rail against hit and all you'll git will be a bunch of drunks and weirdos. And will you provide food and drinks, will you charge enterin' fees, have prizes, tickets, and what have ye? And how will you advertise? And where all will you send invites? And how are you gonna pay for all the stuff you need to set up a race?"

"Don't you worry none, Bryant. Me and Nathan is going to have a meetin' and work out all that little stuff."

"OK, since you are dead set on having a race, I have a few comments and ideas for ya. Will you allow donkeys to race, too? How long will the race be? A hunnert yards or a mile? Will you allow wimmen and out-of-town Yankees to race? What if someone gits kicked in the face or, worse, the crotch. What's yore plan? Will you allow bettin'? And Nathan's likker?"

"Bryant, we unnerstand and thank ye for yore advice but we's got to git going. They's lots to do. We're gonna cogitate about all that stuff you said, and me and Nathan has got to git our own mules ready to race. We have a plan whar she'll win, no matter who enters. We's been exercising her ever day to git'er in shape. And we 'bout got'er saddle broke since she's used to pullin' plows and draggin' logs."

It never occurred to Zelbert and Nathan that it was unethical to win the same race they sponsored, but this was just another little pesky detail that went over their heads. Over the next few weeks, Zelbert and Nathan continued to get Molly, their mule, into shape. They also scraped together a little money to buy flyers and ads in the area's newspapers. They got Widder Wood's permission, scared off her boyfriend, and did a bunch of other stuff in preparation for the race. It was going well. And better yet, there was a lot of excitement and interest.

The race was slated for Widder Wood's ten-acre pasture near Mohawk. It was one of the few relatively flat areas in that part of the county. Chairs were borrowed from a local church. The sisters in Preacher Kester's congregation set up a booth and sold cookies, ham sandwiches, and lemonade. Zelbert slaughtered one of his hogs and provided the ham on the condition that he got half the profits. Aunt Sarah was in charge of ticket sales and handing out the prizes.

They chose Squint Ledbetter to be in charge of security. Because Nathan's boys were selling moonshine from a tent in the nearby woods, they didn't want anyone to mess them up by getting hog-nosed drunk. People were scared of Squint because it was rumored that he had once killed a man. When asked about this, he replied, "Actually, I killed two, now git along afore I have to notch up a nuthern."

Horse and mule racing is a thrilling competition that has captivated people for centuries. The mesmerizing sounds of thundering hooves, the roar of the crowd's cheers, and the anticipation of all the glory their favorite mount could win. This was shaping up to be a great event!

People and mules started showing up on the day of the big race, and the enthusiasm really picked up. The mules were paraded around the racing area, and the jockeys mounted their mules and made their way to the starting line, a white line painted on the grass. The excitement continued to build as the mules made their way to the starting line. Ocie Mae and Mandy traded off as announcers and called out the names of the mules and their jockeys. The crowd cheered as each one was introduced.

There were ten contestants, nine men and one woman. Ocie highlighted each one as they stepped up to the starting line. They were:

- Lucky Strike (A mule who hoped to get lucky)
- Teeny Turner (A small but really frisky mule)
- Gluteus Maximus (Named for his most outstanding feature)
- Lollygagger (Lazy but fast to run away from work)

- Frisky No More (An inherited mule trait)
- Houdini (He could get out of anything)
- Derby (His motto, "Talk Derby to Me")
- Francis (Named in the dubious honor of the owner's mother-in-law)
- Molly (Zelbert and Nathan's entry). She was as fast as lightning when in the mood, but her body required a "mood enhancer." Zelbert had a surefire strategy planned to take care of that.
- Job (This mostly black mule was entered by a deacon from Preacher Kester's church and was described as an "overcomer." It was the most colorful mule because it had spots like its daddy, who may have been an Appaloosa. A cloth sign was carefully stitched and embroidered by the church ladies and affixed to each flank of Job: "First Epistle of John, Chapter 5: Verse 4". The sign made Nathan and Zelbert nervous, and, for the first time, they worried that their well-prepped mule might not win the race. They were confident when it came to beating any man or woman, but they had serious doubts about challenging God.

Then, the big moment came…and the race began.

Excitement was at a fever pitch when the starting gun went off and the mules leaped off the starting line. Their jockeys yelled and whipped their mules with leather straps. The crowd roared as the mules thundered down the track. The excitement increased as the mules rounded the bend and approached the end of the race. When they thundered across the finish line, the crowd of about a hundred people erupted into loud cheers. Then, the winning mule and rider got to take a victory lap around the makeshift track and in front of the crowd of whooping people.

And the trophy was awarded. Being short of money, the "trophy" was an ornate beer mug that Nathan's daddy had brought back from Germany after WWII.

But, as you might expect, not everything went well.

The mule Lucky Strike was not so lucky that day and got startled when Elroy's shotgun signaled the start. At first, he refused to run, but then he turned and ran the wrong way around the track. Needless to say, he didn't win.

Teeny Turner had an issue, too. She was carrying a speed-reducing weight load because the jockey weighed 312 pounds. Regular working mules can carry up to 350 pounds of live weight, but every pound is a disadvantage in a race. If you don't count the disqualifications, Teeny was panting heavily when she crossed the finish line dead last. There was concern she might have a heart attack, but after a bucket of grain, she got perky again, and for an additional bucket of grain, would have energetically trotted back out to the track.

Frisky also had a bad day. About halfway through the race, he reached his climax and lost his desire to run, and decided to veer off the track and search for some alone time and grass to eat. When his rider whacked him with the leather strap, he just sat down on the ground and watched the other mules race.

On the sidelines, there was some intrigue going on, too. One of the teenage boys tried to hold hands with Zeb Carpenter's daughter, and her father cold-cocked him with one blow of his fist. Squint stepped in and threw both of them across a barbed-wire fence.

One of the farmers was talking about how the feed stores were making a killin' by charging too much for hog chow, and Stella, the wife of the owner of the Bulls Gap Feed Store and Deli, overheard him and took issue. An argument ensued, and the woman said, "Luke, you don't know nuthin' 'bout farm animals and feed.

The feed store owner replied, "OK, Stella, you tell me how many toes does a pig have." Stella didn't hesitate to respond, "Luke, take off yore shoes and count 'em yoreself!

The sheriff, although he'd not been invited, did show up, and he promptly arrested Rufus Cobb. Rufus was blind in one eye and was smoking a nasty cigar that made his other eye water so badly that everything was blurry. It was irritating, but he'd paid five cents of good, hard-earned money for the cigar, and by heck, he was determined to smoke it 'til the bitter end. The problem came with the impaired vision, which caused him to stagger and bump into things. When he accidentally bumped into the sheriff, he was arrested for being drunk in public and hauled off to jail. This was unfortunate because Rufus was a known teetotaler and never touched alcohol. He was released after the race was over, but was not happy because he'd only smoked half the cigar.

Houdini's owner was so confident his mule was faster than Lollygagger that he bet $300 to Lolly's owner that he'd beat his mule. He won the bet and kept the money but had previously agreed to pay $100 of the money to the jockey that Lollygagger's owner had hired to ride for him.

Another jockey got so nervous before the race that he drank two half-pints of Nathan's "nerve relaxer" and fell asleep on a blanket near the racetrack. By the time the race started, he was late and missed the start. However, he saved face by saying, "Boys, I'll tell you right now that was some of the best sleep I've had since my wife went to visit her sister in Nashville."

However, the owner of Derby wasn't downbeat about losing the race. Like many Southerners, he took the loss in stride and put a positive spin on it. "Listen men, as I stan rite hyar and tell y'all this, my old Derby mule is the bestest mule of 'em all. He's an up-and-comer. He'd have won that race iffen he hadn't got out of the corral and eaten up my neighbor Regina's rose bushes. I wish she'd quit growing those thangs. Them flares has pizen in'em.

Howsomeever with all them briars stickin' em in the stomach, hit still took eight of the best mules this side of the Smoky Mountains to beat him. Derby's a fine racing mule. Iffen they waren't so all picky about who his momma was, I'd enter him in the Kentucky Derby. By the way, does any of you all want to buy a fine racing mule?"

Perhaps the most interesting thing to happen in the race was related to Molly; Zelbert, and Nathan's entry. Molly was nimble and very fast when she wanted to be. Zelbert found this out while plowing his cornfield one afternoon when they came across a rattlesnake. Molly went berserk like she'd been struck by twin lightning strikes and ran hell-bent for leather for two miles, dragging the plow the whole way, tearing up sod as she went, and stampeding and outrunning a herd of wild hogs.

As Zelbert lined up his mule on the starting line, Nathan approached Molly with a small wooden box with a hinged lid. It was left over from Zelbert's failed attempt to be a snake-handling preacher. All was going as planned as he opened the box. The rattler slithered out, rattling along the way. Molly went berserk, bucking and kicking, and accidentally killed the snake in the process, leaving Zelbert on the ground. Even with her delayed start, Molly then ran down the racetrack and easily outpaced all the other mules, but rather than make the turn in the track, she kept racing across the field, jumped a fence, and was found later in Grainger County cavorting with a mule by the name of Odie (short for Odysseus).

The most interesting entrant in the race was the mule Job and his mystery rider. In addition to selling refreshments to raise money to buy clothes and books for kids who wanted to go to school, the good sisters from the congregation had formed a close-knit racing crew made up of Job, a mule who was smarter than most men but just as stubborn, and a woman trainer who disliked the evils of alcohol. She frequently waded among the crowd and shouted the words of an anonymous poem from the prohibitionist Women's Christian Temperance Union: "Lips that Touch Liquor Shall Never Touch Mine!" Usually, being as undisciplined as many of the mules in the race, Nathan Gully didn't respond, but later said that she had drummed up more business for him than a hundred signs could have and briefly considered giving her a share of the day's profits.

Job's mystery jockey was obviously a female, given all the bulges in her costume. And she sported a costume. She wore all white, was barefoot, rode bareback, and had a set of wings flapping from her shoulders made of white turkey feathers. Even her hair had been sprinkled with flour to make it white. To add to the intrigue, she wore a Halloween mask with an angelic face. She said very few words. No one knew who she was.

The women's secret strategy was to not feed Job for twenty-four hours before the race, give him a juicy Granny Smith apple just before the race, and tie another one on a stick that the angel carried. It was a centuries-old trick, but it worked with Job. As the race started, they dangled a plump apple from a string and hung it in front of Job's eyes. The jockey steered by moving the apple. The theory was that the harder he ran, he'd not get closer to his favorite dessert. During the race, the apple would occasionally bounce off of Job's nose, the effect making him run even faster. Knowing mules were hardly different than men, they figured that an apple was better than the whip. However, it was widely known that mules differed from men in that the major things that motivated men were food and something else that evades my fragile mind, but food was one of them. By virtue of a chromosomal mix-up, food was about the only thing left in life to motivate mules.

With all the confusion and setbacks by the other racing mules, Job just sailed from start to finish without a hitch, not looking left or right, easily garnering first place. Unlike the other mules, he didn't try to veer off the track but just stayed focused on the dangling reward. Their strategy worked without a flaw, and they walked away with the winning trophy and a purse of $100.

A highly noticeable event was the post-race altercation between Zelbert (now the loser) and the jockey who rode Job to victory. The fight wasn't anything new to them as they'd done that dozens of times off the racetrack. Zelbert's companion friends guffawed and howled with laughter when the mystery jockey removed the mask, revealing the not-so-angelic face of Ocie Mae Nicodemus, Zelbert's usually beloved wife and help-mate, although the help-mate part was in serious dispute on trackside as they loudly argued the pros and cons of who should have won the race, how could she do such an underhanded thing to him, and so on.

However, all was not bad. After expenses and prizes were handed out, ticket sales for the race brought in an impressive $465, enough to buy a couple of new plows for the mules and store-bought dresses for their wives, who'd made them sleep on the floor during the prior month of race prepping. Also, Nathan's boys had sold several cases of "mood enhancer" for a tidy profit.

Life was pretty good, but they never staged another mule race.

Note from the Author: I more or less love mules, having grown up working them on the farm. They are a sterile hybrid created by breeding a donkey with a horse. My close friend, the late Dr. Gordon Woods of the University of Idaho, cloned the first equines in the world. I write about that and the connection with Dolly Parton in Volume 2 of Musing Appalachia, Wrestling with Life in the Flatlands, available from Amazon.com. Interestingly, the last I heard, one of Gordon's three cloned mules was racing professionally in California.

Mules are intelligent, tough as nails, sure-footed, and strong. They get a bad rap for being stubborn, but they're just being cautious. They will refuse to do something that makes them uncomfortable until they've had ample time to think about it. Studies show that mules are better than horses in cognitive intelligence. Another advantage of mules is that they don't require as much food as horses. Also, you gotta love Mules. They hate cats of any size and don't hesitate to attack them...even a cougar.

When I lived in Argentina, I met a horse rancher who had a herd of nearly 9,000 horses. He raised them exclusively for meat that was sold in France, Belgium, Italy, and a few other places. Early on, mule meat was considered a delicacy, too, but it may no longer be available because breeding mules is more expensive. While in South America, I occasionally ate horse meat. It's great meat. And it's better than beef. It's also cheaper and more sweet tasting. While you may say you're "hungry enough to eat a horse," it's illegal to consume horse or mule meat in the USA. That is, if you get caught.

FRANCES'S DINER IN HAZARD, KENTUCKY

When my wife, Sharl, and I lived in Kentucky, we liked to roam about the Hazard, Kentucky area. We loved it there. It had all we wanted. What we liked the most were the good, honest people (except the jerk at the gas station who gave me the wrong directions to Harlan County). Cool places to visit include the *Coal Miners' Museum* and the *Bobby Davis Museum*. They even had a weird *Mother Goose House*. We also enjoyed the beauty of the *Red River Gorge, the Natural Bridge, and Cumberland Falls.*

We especially loved eating at *France's Diner* on Combs Road. The food was totally authentic Appalachian, and, more importantly, back then, it was cheap. I've not been there in a while, but my mouth waters just thinking about it. By the way, they don't sponsor me, but if they were to give me a free meal, I'd jump at it.

On one trip to Hazard, I was eating a baloney sandwich, a side of fried banana peppers, and drinking a glass of strawberry Kool-Aid at France's Diner when a very buxom woman saw me and yelled, "There he is! It's him!" She rushed over to me and, with a screeching howl, grabbed me in a bear hug that pushed the air completely outta me. She was an impressive lady in about every way. In addition to being well-endowed, she wore a miniskirt with fishnet hose and pink-colored glasses, accompanied by inch-long, glittered eyelashes behind them. I was breathless!

Then she turned me loose when she realized she'd grabbed the wrong person. I like to think that I resemble Elvis on a bad day, and that was one of my better days. I thought that Sharyl would be impressed, but she was about to hit the hippie gal before she turned me loose.

That's just one of my fond memories of Hazard, Kentucky. If you visit Frances's Diner sometime, please tell me the food is still good. My suggestion would be to consider sitting with your back to the wall and your eyes on the door.

JEZEBEL AT THE
CHURCH POTUCK DINNER

Jezebel is frequently associated with idolatry and immorality in the Bible. Over the centuries, she has been depicted as a seductress, often described as a wicked and morally unrestrained woman who uses beauty, sex, and seduction to get what she wants from men. They are "Jezebels." For Jezebel sauce to show up at a hard-shell Baptist church potluck dinner caused a stir.

Knowing that my great-aunt Berthy was a touch crazy, sometimes people asked me what her momma was like. People don't remember much about my great-grandma Sallie Seals Hughett, except that her preacher husband was a very stern man and not given to foolishness. None.

Because he was a Primitive Baptist minister, he felt obligated to hand out extra heavy doses of discipline. My great-uncle Grant was the recipient of more than a few disciplinary sessions with a heavy leather belt. To add insult to injury, he'd have to pull his britches down in front of the other kids and take the lashes on his bare flesh. For the girls, he used willow tree branches to inflict pain, but didn't require them to bare their butts. Grant experienced both and said that he didn't prefer one over the other, but he observed that the belt seemed to raise the biggest welts while the willow switches stung the most. Aint Berthy was a slow learner when it came to discipline and got more than her fair share of whuppins. She was a curious girl and was always getting into some flavor of trouble.

Reverend John Harvey Hughett's wife, Sallie, had a keen sense of humor but had to hide some of her tricks to avoid chastisement from her husband. Her mischievous streak once got her into trouble with the entire congregation at Mountain Valley Baptist Church in Mohawk, Tennessee. I'm not aware that she was punished with a whipping at the time, but those weren't unheard of in the early days in the mountains. Along with her sewing and cooking skills, Sallie was known for her sweet demeanor...and she was a very pretty lady.

One Sunday, the church was hosting a potluck dinner along with the annual homecoming. Sallie remembered a recipe that her backslider aunt had once taught her and decided to prepare it for the enjoyment of the church members. Her aunt called it her "Sin-laden Jezebel Sauce." It was a spicy concoction of horseradish, peppers, mustard, and peach preserves and was known to pack a punch that was both immediate and subtle. It was the subtle part that got her into trouble because she added some moonshine and ginseng root powder to enhance the recipe's kick.

It was a fiery concoction, a rambunctious blend of sweet and spicy that could wake up the taste buds and cause them to scream if prepared too spicy. At the potluck, she proudly placed her dish on the table next to Mrs. Greenlee's deviled eggs and Ruby Johnson's baked ham. Rather than refer to it as Jezebel Sauce, she hand-scribbled a label calling it "Spicy Heavenly Mountain Delight Sauce, GUARANTEED to wake you up." Below this, she made a notation that it was best when used sparingly on all meats, biscuits, or over cream cheese with crackers.

As the congregation lined up to fill their plates, Bryant Gulley was the first to dive in with his usual enthusiasm for free, unlimited food. He spooned a generous helping of the sauce onto his plate, mistaking it for mild fruit preserves. He spread it thickly over a biscuit and took a huge bite. His reaction was immediate. His face turned bright red, his eyes got big, and he started fanning his mouth. "Lordy, have mercy on my soul!" he yelled, reaching for a glass of sweet tea.

Knowing what had happened, Sallie rushed over with a pitcher to refill his glass, "Bryant, that's real spicy sauce, and hit's got a lotta kick to hit," she said, trying to stifle her giggles.

Recovering, Bryant said, "Well, Miss Sallie, you shore know how to wake a man up! I think I'll try the deviled eggs from now on jist as soon as I catch my breath."

Others gathered around the table and put generous dollops of Sallie's sauce on their plates, unaware of the hidden twist. The first few bites were met with nods of approval and murmurs of delight. But then, the secret ingredients started manifesting themselves, and the heat soon began to burn.

As they shoveled the feast into their mouths, the responses were both exciting and varied. The immediate reaction was most often some version of "Hot as the very fires of Hell!" Rose Childers from Bulls Gap had to gulp down a quart of lemonade without putting the fruit jar down. Sister Martha was the first to react loudly. Her face turned red, she got bug-eyed, spit the concoction out, and without remembering that she was at church, exclaimed, "Damnation! What on the face of God's sweet, blessed earth is this #%^$? Then, coughing uncontrollably, she rushed off to get some ice water.

The kids were trying it out and having fun watching each other's reactions…followed by dares to take a second bite.

Noticing the commotion, the preacher came over. Priding himself on his tolerance for hot, spicy food, he took a generous helping. His eyes watered, and he broke into a sweat but refused to admit defeat. The entire church group watched in awe as he tried to maintain his composure, all while Sallie chuckled in the background. The preacher, sweating, admitted that it had more kick than a six-legged mule, and his voice was raspy and strained. Some were afraid he might pass out, but he soon got his breath back.

At that point, Sallie stepped in and admitted to everyone that the sauce was indeed extra spicy and that it was her aunt's special recipe for the family's Jezebel Sauce. She explained that the secret was to eat only a thin coating on the food because it was powerful stuff...and she remembered slipping up on the portion of pepper in the recipe. The cap came off the shaker and half the bottle of pepper fell in the mix. The pepper was one that her cousin had bought back for her after visiting the tourist attractions in Tijuana, Mexico. He called them *"Have a Hero"* peppers but she had never used them before. She tried to scrape much of it out but wasn't very successful.

People assured her that no lasting harm was done, but Preacher Hughett wasn't so kind. He said, "Sallie, hit wasn't funny to falsely label that stuff as *Heavenly* when hit was originally named after one of Satan's fallen angels."

Sallie said, "Oh, John, hit was just a bit of funning. Besides, hit's good stuff if you don't hog it down like peach jelly."

Afterward, several of the women asked for the recipe. Here it is, more or less.

Grandma Sallie's Version of Appalachian Jezebel Sauce (Warning: It can be hot)

Ingredients:
- 1 cup apple butter (5 oz)
- 1 cup peach preserves (5 oz)

- 1/4 to 1/3 cup prepared horseradish (Prepared horseradish is fresh horseradish that has been grated. You have to know that a little horseradish goes a long way. Don't overdo it, or you'll be kicked out of potlucks)
- 1 tablespoon yellow mustard powder
- 1/2 teaspoon black pepper
- 1 tablespoon honey or sorghum syrup
- 1 tablespoon of finely chopped sweet peppers
- 1/4 cup of Co-Cola, Dr. Pepper, or RC Cola (Moonshine would be optional)
- 1/4 teaspoon of powdered ginseng root (optional, available from Amazon)
- 1/2 to 1 teaspoon of finely chopped hot peppers or red pepper flakes of your choice (or more if you don't want people to eat seconds. At this point, you should flavor to taste. Note: I was going to add some of the hottest modern pepper varieties, but because of liability issues, I don't dare. That stuff will *light your fire,* but not in a good way. Don't dare use those!)

Instructions:

Mix well in a medium bowl until everything is thoroughly combined. Store in small mason jars or in airtight containers until ready to use. For the best flavor, allow the sauce to sit in the fridge for a day or so. Adjust the seasoning to taste to make it more or less spicy and vary the heat. Texans and borderline crazy people add Jalapeños. Use it as a glaze for any kind of meat or serve it on cream cheese and crackers.

If prepared correctly, this version of Jezebel Sauce will have the sweet and spicy profile you love, with a distinct Appalachian flair. That is, if you don't overdo the peppers.

Jezebel Sauce has been around for at least some time prior to the 1950s. It is especially popular in the southern United States. It evolved from the Southern tradition of combining sweet and spicy flavors.

Family Reunion Potluck Dinner (Photo by the author)

Great-Grandma Sallie was proud of her recipe's bold flavor and was not ashamed of it being named after the fiery and rebellious Jezebel. She was quoted as saying, "Jist a tiny, teensy dab of Jezebel goes a long way and will put some spice in yore life." She didn't dare compare the sauce to sin, but the comparison was obvious.

In addition to the peppers, family legend has it that the more subtle side effects of Grandma Sallie's Jezebel Sauce were due to the secret ingredients of moonshine and ginseng, and manifests itself in the number of children one has. If you ever wonder why Appalachian families tend to have lots of kids, now you know part of the reason why. Preserves have long been a staple in Southern cuisine, and certain recipes get passed down, including lesser-known delicacies that not everyone has had the opportunity to taste. One such recipe is Jezebel Sauce.

CRAZY HILLBILLY PREACHER STORIES

A mountain preacher said to Zelbert Nicodemus, "You gotta quit cussin', Zel, or the Lord's gonna strike you dead, and you won't go to Heaven! Zelbert's response was: "Dammit, Preacher. I ain't goin' to Hell! I repent too da*n fast!"

Knowing that religion can be a touchy subject to write about, I want to emphasize that the intent of the following stories is not to poke fun or make light of any religion or religious practice. I've found humor about everywhere I've been in my life, and sitting in front of pulpits, I've also seen some really funny stuff. The following stories are lighthearted and amusing tales related to preachers that I've either experienced or heard of from my kinfolks and friends. Remember, humor can be found even in unexpected places, including the world of taciturn preachers! And I'm told that laughter is good for the soul. I hope that's true. Otherwise, I'm a goner.

Other than being raised on the tarnished buckle of the Bible Belt and being around preacher families all my life, I have other sources for preacher stories. I had an unusual childhood. My granddaddy was a back-hills mountain preacher and pastored a church in the Mohawk area of Greene County, Tennessee. My great-grandaddy, Rev. John Harvey Hughett, was also a hard-shell Baptist, leaning heavily on the no-holds-barred, fire-and-brimstone type of preaching. His daddy and other kinfolks were also preachers, or almost so, from Floyd County, Virginia, back to Pennsylvania and Ireland in the 1700s. They came to America to avoid religious persecution. A few early Hughetts were Quakers, but I'm not sure what happened along the way to change that. Either way, from the time they arrived in the hills of Appalachia, the Hughetts have been stomping the head of Satan as Primitive Baptists or Pentecostal Holiness, etc. As in most families, there were a few backsliders who drank more than a little moonshine and occasionally got real crazy, but those stories are for another time.

Of course, where you have preachers, it goes without saying that the Devil stays busy firing up and inspiring the sinners. My kinfolks were not spared, but I will say that even the moonshiners, drunkards, and black sheep of the family were religious in their hearts. Religion was part of their heritage, and one can't escape that.

My daddy, Harvey Sr., spent a significant part of his life traveling through the hills of East Tennessee and surrounding states, recording old-timey preachings and singings on tape, interviewing elderly people, and visiting holler-bound relatives who lacked transportation out of the hills except when hitching rides from friends and neighbors. Dad would often take me with him on these trips to the back hills. As I got older, I kept notes on slips of paper of those experiences and funny things that happened. More than a few people have asked that I share some of the stories I picked up on these visits. I wrote about many of those in my books, Musing Appalachia (available on Amazon.com), but this is a brief summary of anecdotes too short for stories.

On our road trips, in addition to going to church, we'd sometimes get invited into homes or to help with chores, such as hog killin's or splitting firewood. At other times we'd stay over and go fishing, coon hunting, berry pickin', or whatever seemed to be a good thing to do at the time. When Daddy died, my brother and I were stuck with over a thousand reel-to-reel audio tapes of preachin's, sermons, and interviews with mountain people. Today, one hundred and twenty of these are part of the permanent collection in the *Archives of Appalachia* at East Tennessee State University. They've been digitized and are available to the public.

I liked accompanying Daddy when he traveled because we got to eat in interesting homes and try exciting foods, including baked possums and ramps. But I only tried those once.

In the beginning, I was hardly old enough to know what was going on. By the time he had finished his trips to the hills, I had grown up and moved away. Nevertheless, during my teen years, I was old enough to "look behind the pulpit" and get into trouble… but I did learn a lot of cool stuff. I write of some of that, and I hope others who know me have poor memories.

Occasionally, we visited Pentecostal Holiness churches where poisonous snakes were sometimes handled. My great-great-grandaddy was a Pentecostal preacher, as were a couple of other kin in Virginia, but I don't recall any Hughetts, including Preacher Stephen Hughett of Indian Valley, preaching with snakes or lye poison.

Like most of the Hughetts in the USA today, it's a pretty safe bet that anyone who spells their last name H-U-G-H-E-T-T is related to me somehow. However, for various and sundry reasons, a few changed the spelling to Hewitt, Hewett, etc. Some of these are attached to some pretty interesting stories, and not all of them were changed to escape the law.

One of my Facebook friends tickled me with his statement about snake-handling churches. Larry Sifford said, "We jist handle rubber snakes at our gatherin's 'cause we ain't built up enuff faith fer the real'ns." I still laugh about that, but there were no rubber snakes at the places my daddy took me. We witnessed actual, honest-to-goodness, poisonous rattlesnakes, copperheads, and coral snakes writhing around in the preacher's hands as they preached and danced around the pulpit.

So, let's skip the small talk and get started.

I remember one preacher who said something that caught everyone's attention, including a dumb kid like me. He said, "The Lord works in mysterious ways, jist like them possums in the woods." Everyone looked around with questions on their faces, "Possums? What do possums have to do with religion?"

The good preacher continued without a hitch by explaining, "The other evenin', after supper, I wuz walking in back of my house and prayin' about a problem when I seed a possum a dancin' and grinnin' at me. Hit was one of them little blue possums. He twirled, whirled, jumped up and down, and grinned at me with his big buggy eyes. Right away, I could see that the Lord was tryin' to give me a message." The preacher then walked to the side of the pulpit and, in a very soft voice, whispered to the congregation, "You see, the Lord was a'tryin' to tell me that we all should be joyful and shout praises and be happy, even when times are flat crazy in yore life." My daddy figured that the preacher had been drinking too much home-brew "cough medicine" that night.

Then he invited the congregation to meet at his private baptizing spot on the Chucky River, but this time, the baptisms would take place at night. The church didn't have a baptismal font, and the river provided easy access. So, they met by the water's edge that evening with lanterns supplemented by moonlight. Two repentant souls had agreed to be baptized and showed up in white clothes. He said, "Is all y'all ready to be warshed and cleansed uv yore sins?" Then they waded into the slow-moving, light brown water, and, one by one, he raised his right arm to the Heavens and proclaimed in a loud voice, "In the name of the Father God, I baptize you in this here holy water." Then, he dipped them under and held them until they were thoroughly soaked. Each came out of the water shouting, "Hallelujah! I'm borned again!" It was at that point that one of the old ladies whispered to her friend, "Didja see that? They went under all white and come out of the water brown. Do you thank they's really been warshed clean? I thank the preached needs to dip 'em again and wring' em out."

As an aside, I myself was baptized in the Nolichucky River near the bridge beyond Lowland where it crosses over into Bybee in Cocke County. And yes, the water was brown and the poison ivy on the riverbank left an extra impression.

Once, at a Mountain Valley Church homecoming potluck, the preacher invited the congregation members to bring special food with scriptural meanings. That was a creative idea and everyone had a good meal. Interestingly, the Devil's food cake was a big hit. The preacher took a slice of the aptly named cake and inadvertently said "Hit taste'es like a slice uv Heaven," until someone reminded him that it was "Devil's Food." He sputtered and spit it out.

One good woman brought "prayer-soaked cornbread." Another brought sugar-coated "Eden Apples" to signify Eve's temptation, but other than us kids, there were few takers. The Hot Cross Buns were a hit and disappeared rapidly. Other foods touted spices mentioned in the Bible, such as anise, cinnamon, dill, cumin, coriander, mustard, and salt. Each food with this spice was labeled with the appropriate scripture. Foods also showed up with the names of manna, Passover lamb, unleavened bread, grape juice, honey, and fish and loaves. One lady brought a cake she proudly labeled as "mammon," and it looked so delicious that everyone had to have a piece. If you know what mammon meant in the Bible, the desire to have some of this dish would underscore what NOT to partake of. This cake was avoided by those who knew the scriptures but greatly and immensely enjoyed by the unenlightened. Kinda like life, I guess.

Nathan Gulley showed up with a car trunk load of moonshine and offered free samples until the preacher ran him off. In his defense, he quoted one of his nearby competitors, Popcorn Sutton:

"Jesus turned water into wine. I turn water into moonshine." Nathan later returned without his hootch and asked if he could have two fried chickens and a Co-Cola. The suspicious ladies serving were curious whether he meant whole fried chickens or chickens cut into pieces.

Once, my daddy and I were attending a church meeting in Cosby, Tennessee. I can't remember the name, but it doesn't matter. This church meeting started off relatively similar to others, but ended with a surprise. I remember the preacher ambling up to the pulpit. People sat on hard pews, fanned themselves with complementary hand fans supplied by funeral homes, and waited for the sermon to start. It was common for preachers to use colorful expressions and analogies that interwove scripture with Appalachian wisdom and some humor, some of which could be taken two ways. Some uses I remember were not always acceptable in mixed company, especially in churches. However, you shouldn't underestimate the impact of shock by introducing the unpredictable.

The preacher took his coat off, cleared his throat, and began his sermon, "Brethren and Cistern, today's lesson comes from the Book of Genesis, the part whar Eve took a chomp out of the forbidden fruit. The problem was, upon taking a bite and getting Adam to do the same, they instantly knew they wuz naked as jay birds, and they was a scramble to find fig leaves to cover they selves up. The fact of the matter was that the apple didn't just giv 'em knowledge of good and bad; it also hit 'em over the head with lustful desires. Desires they'd not noticed before. Desires so good that, at first, they thought Satan was still trying to fool 'em." By then, the snake wuz gone, and they wuz on their own."

"Nevertheless, they wuz careful, but soon, Eve was hit with a bucket load of pride and started wantin' fancy clothes and sech, but Adam, being more practical, had a terrible hankering for cornbread with cracklins in it. And bar-b-qued pork ribs with a healthy side of fried okra. His newly transformed body also had a craving for moonshine, but he didn't know at the time that the Lord restricted that for medicinal uses. The Bible don't tell us much about hit, and Eve didn't know how to cook, much less make country cornbread. And cast-iron skillets hadn't been invented yet. Nor had moonshine, but that was a temptation that would come later. The garden was full of all kinds of fruit but not a single okra tree. And they blew that beautiful garden all away with jist one bite of one stinkin' apple. Actually, if you thank about hit, iffen they hadn't a fallen, we'd not have cornbread and country ham today... and you and me wouldn't have been borned."

The preacher then closed his Bible, jumped down from the pulpit, and headed straight for the church potluck in the parking lot. The aroma of fried chicken and lemonade filled the air, and the congregation took off after him, laughing. After they ate, the sermon began to sink in, and people were more receptive to the message. Preachers were pretty smart about getting congregations to listen.

Looking at my notes, at a tent revival in Russell County, Virginia, a preacher stated that the Roman Empire was strong for five hundred years until they started allowing divorce, and that that was the real cause of the fall of the Roman Empire. I had a history course in college once, and the professor never mentioned that, but these days, you can't trust some college teachers who were once hippies.

In addition to old-fashioned sex, frequent topics of sermons included drugs and likker. Sometimes, the sermons against sex were so candid that I suspect that more than a few babies had birthdays nine months afterward. While attending a Pentecostal church in Hazard, Kentucky, a preacher proclaimed that caffeine was the gateway to all other drugs and that everyone should quit drinking Co-cola and coffee. We never stuck around for the following week's meeting, but I suspect attendance was down.

We saw speaking in tongues, passing out from the Spirit entering people's bodies, exorcisms, etc., but those are sensitive topics, and I don't want to get struck by lightning for bringing them up. Am I superstitious or just practical? Yes!

A preacher over in Blowing Rock, North Carolina, told of how he went to a woman's home to find out why she was having problems with evil spirits, and he saw a statue of a Chinese dragon sitting on the fireplace mantle. He mentioned that the statue was not a dragon but actually a depiction of Satan, and that was the cause of all her ailments. Hearing this, she started crying and wailing because it was a gift from her deceased husband, who'd bought it for her in Korea while in the Army. The preacher said that he had to repeat verses from the Bible to calm her down, then exorcize an evil spirit out of the statue so she could get some relief.

Another preacher, this time in a very small town on the Tennessee/Georgia state border, once said that a preacher he knew taught that dinosaur bones were fabrications planted by Satan-worshipping scientists who had been brainwashed to put them in the ground to lead people away from God. However, he himself believed that dinosaurs were real and were created by God 14,000 years ago. He also claimed that the dinosaurs went extinct because they were too big to fit on Noah's Ark. That made sense to me at the time, especially when he said that many dinosaur bones had been found where there were once large bodies of water and buried under silt and mud, proving they died in the flood. He also said that all animals were herbivores before the Fall of Man, when death became possible. He cited lions and lambs getting along in the Garden of Eden. For proof, he explained that the remains of a species of ancient crocodiles had been found that had teeth adapted for eating vegetation, which clearly proved that crocodiles used to be vegetarian. I suspect that included lions, too. I'm not sure where he got these ideas, but they were interesting, to say the least, and maybe he was onto something? Some of this stuff you can't make up. They didn't homeschool much in those days, but that preacher would have been a humdinger of a science teacher!

When we lived in Blacksburg, Virginia, an interesting event happened at a small church in Shawsville. A preacher had been abruptly "let go" by the church elders for "undisclosed indiscretions." It doesn't take much imagination to figure out what that probably means. At any rate, the preacher was very well-liked, and the congregation was outraged. Prayer circles were held for the preacher "to bring him back to the Lord." The thinking was that he had to have been blindsided and unfairly tricked by Satan, something that could happen to anyone, and, after all, what good was repentance if you couldn't use it? The prayers fizzled out later when it became known precisely what the indiscretions were and who they were with.

Here's something I've witnessed, but I suspect that it's a rare occurrence. A few people liked to "get drunk on the spirit." They'd stumble around acting drunk, singing hymns and hugging trees, but strangely, they hadn't drunk a drop of alcohol. They'd mumble strange words, repeat scriptures, and you'd swear they were drunk. Then, at some point, they'd abruptly straighten up, sober as all get-out, and start preaching with a voice as loud and clear as a bell, obviously not drunk. I only saw this twice, and both times it creeped me out. But, then again, maybe I needed to drink in more of the right Spirit? Uncle Nathan had some "spirits" that he claimed to have the same effect, but one didn't snap out of the after-effects for a long time.

That reminds me of a teetotaler friend in Dandridge, Tennessee. He wasn't a preacher, but he'd had a stroke and could no longer walk a straight line. The last time I talked with Wade, he said, "Harvey, I'm about ready to drink a quart of moonshine to see if it'll straighten me up from stumbling and wobbling around."

Time for one of my favorite preacher jokes: A drunk man stumbled onto an old-fashioned baptism down at a wide spot in Lick Creek. Knowing that the man was in desperate need of being saved, the preacher dragged him into the water and forcefully dunked him. Gasping for air, when the drunk came up out of the water, the preacher asked, "Have you found Jesus?"

The man replied, "No!" so the preacher dunked him again.

The man came back up. Once again, the preacher asked, "Have you found Jesus yet?"

The drunk man replied, "Not yet!"

He gets dunked again.

For a third time, the preacher asked, "Have you found Jesus?"

The drunk replied, "Are you shore he fell in here? 'Cause I cain't see nobody down thar!"

Of course, some preachers will go to great lengths to catch the congregation's attention and break up a dull moment. I heard of a preacher who once abruptly stopped in the middle of his sermon, leaped up on a chair, then jumped onto the back of a deacon and rode him around. Of course, this was carefully planned with the deacon before the meeting, but people talked about those few unusual seconds in the meeting for years. And the topic of the sermon? *Taming Satan.* I forget how he made the sermon's title coincide with riding the deacon, but I'm sure it made sense.

Some churches organized *Hell House* events around Halloween. These were interactive experiences designed to depict the consequences of sinful choices. Participants would walk through scenes portraying drug abuse, abortion, suicide, and other moral issues. The goal was to scare attendees into making better life choices. One attendee remarked, "That sartinally skeered the Hell outta me!"

A few preachers prepared sermons on the theme of Judgment Day. For this, they'd sometimes dress volunteers as angels, spouse abusers, or even the Devil. The church was loosely organized into a courtroom. Attendees witnessed a mock trial where their eternal fate was decided. Although some sermons bordered on the bizarre, the objectives were to remind people of the importance of spiritual matters and encourage them to avoid sinning ways.

Once, at a church in Rhea Town (an old neighborhood in Morristown), the preacher held a "silent worship service." For 30 minutes, there wasn't a single spoken word, no sermon, no prayer, nothing. Imagine a service with no spoken words, sermons, hymns, or announcements; and nothing but silence. This was intended to promote personal reflection, contemplation, meditation, and prayer. It certainly was a technique that served the purpose of fostering introspection and worshiping differently. At the end, the preacher broke the silence with a short Sermon about Judgment Day. However, those thirty minutes seemed like hours! However, one man said "it seemed like Hell" to him as he contemplated his sins.

Mountain preachers weren't crazy but rather creative and cagy in their approach to getting people to interact with God. Over in Newport, Tennessee, there once was a meeting where prayer stations were set up around the church. Each station focused on a different aspect of prayer. For example: thanksgiving, repentance, forgiveness, and other topics. Congregation members would move from one station to another with differing prayer experiences. Both silent and vocal prayers were acceptable, so it got pretty noisy. I remember one woman praying in a loud voice that everyone could hear, "Oh Lord, bless my husband that he'll quit drinkin' evil likker and runnin' around with that floozy over at Del Rio." The husband wasn't in attendance. Everyone speculated that he was visiting someone over at Del Rio.

I can't vouch for the authenticity of any story where I wasn't in attendance. I heard some from Papaw, or second or third hand from others, mostly sober people. A few stories probably originated as folk tales but evolved into a form of reality. I won't go into detail on the following stories because there's not enough room here to do so, and people are already complaining that my stories are too long. My response to them is, "That's probably true if you're reading my stuff on a cell phone or have forgotten how to read from an actual book, or suffer from ADHD, OCD, or whatever the ailment of the day is." If you fall into this latter category, I wish that I could take you to a snake-handling church meeting and see if that might fix whatever ails you. Perspective helps in life...as well as humor.

Many of you know that my Papaw was a mountain preacher at Mountain Valley Church near Mohawk. This is a very old church, not to be confused with the newer Mt Valley Baptist Church at Bulls Gap. My great-grandpa built the church and preached there until Papaw took over. I have many fond memories of homecomings and attending services there. I write about Papaw and this church frequently. Papaw and his family lived up the holler about an eighth mile behind the church.

These stories are meant to entertain and highlight the colorful characters that populate the world of hillbilly preachers. Whether it's snake handling or preaching against loose wimmen, the moments of unpredictability of things that happen in what usually are solemn church meetings stick in our memory. One can learn a lot about mountain society by what they preach against...or for.

Of course, only a minuscule number of hillbillies handle snakes in church, but it's so far from the usual church practice that the topic is fascinating. This unique tradition is mainly limited to a few fervent (some say *flat-ass crazy*) preachers in rural Appalachia. They believe that their faith can protect them from snakebites. Given that scenario, I'm relatively faithless. I trust God, but I don't trust snakes. "Faith without works is dead." I have *faith* that snakes will bite me, and that my *work* is to stay the heck away from them!

On one of our travels, we heard stories about an old mountain preacher who had a church somewhere in the Smoky Mountains above Sevierville and who was especially interesting. People claimed that he was a stern man who had once raised a man from the dead. He didn't do snakes, but people who'd heard of him said everyone went away from his meetings edified and absolutely scared of even thinking about sinning. My dad and I spent a couple of years searching for this preacher, but we never found him. Sometimes, the stories about him got pretty wild, so I doubt he was real, but perhaps the stories started with real preachers and were exaggerated. Someone said there was a ballad about him, but I couldn't find the words for such on the Interweb. We were told that his preachin's were so wild that the humble wooden church walls would literally shake when he got wound up, along with the single light bulb dangling from the ceiling on a wire. And, reportedly, more than a couple of times, he kicked Satan out of one of his meetings.

Hellfire sermons were common in many backwoods churches in those days and, in some places, still are. Unlike many people today, back then, people were hungry for something to shake them up, and brimstone sermons certainly would shake the faithful to their souls and cause them to search for salvation from the woes of the harsh world. For a few, it was entertainment.

Even as a kid, I felt the energy of meetings and often got into the groove, especially when the preachers would do "the stomp." This was when the reverend would catch everyone by surprise in the middle of a whisper-quiet part of the sermon and suddenly stomp the floor loudly with his shoes and start preachin' repentance at the top of his voice. When I say, "top of his voice," I really mean "screaming" the word of the Lord as loud as humanly possible. This, coupled with the stomping, would wake the dead, including the old guys on the back row attempting to sober up from the previous hard night of hard drinkin' or coon huntin'.

The stomp" symbolized stomping the serpent head of Satan and getting rid of evil. If the "stomp" were to catch you by surprise, you could quickly get rid of the contents of your kidneys, or worse! Old-time Hellfire preachin's were never boring.

The stomp has roots in Genesis 3:15 and references Adam and Eve's fall into sin when God declared, "I will put enmity between you and the woman, and between your offspring and hers; he will crush your head, and you will strike his heel." I remember one preacher from over in Cocke County, sweat dripping down his brow, preaching the perils of temptation and the importance of resisting sin. He waved his Bible like a battle flag, shouting, "All you all listen. We gotta stomp out the Devil like a cockroach in a butter dish!" Try visualizing that.

Many preachers wore suits and ties, like my Papaw, but a few wore patched overalls and boots. Some tent preachers wore colorful sequined suits (like Preacher Zebedee Hughett of Virginia). Either way, behind the pulpit, their voices thundered like lightning, and everyone took careful note. A few people even openly repented at the end of the meeting. At a tent revival in Pulaski, Virginia, I remember a preacher saying, "If you don't accept God and repent, the Lord's gonna come down and knock the snot right outta ya!" I wish we'd gotten that on tape, but it slipped by us.

Of course, the challenge of any preacher in addressing a group of listeners is to capture their attention, engage them, and inspire change, whether it's to stop womanizing or to increase their tithe. To this end, ministers everywhere are trying to prepare and deliver engaging sermons.

Old-time preachers were certainly interesting and engaging. You can count on them preaching from their hearts about their faith journeys and struggles, and doing so with much passion. Most successful preachers could paint extraordinarily vivid mental pictures using parables, allegories, and real-life experiences to capture listeners' imaginations and emotions.

Mountain preachers varied the tone, volume, and pace of their sermons and interjected dramatic pauses. The better preachers were masters at appealing to emotions such as fear, love, hope, and conviction. Gestures, eye contact, stepping into the congregation, raising hands and looking heavenward, and soliciting affirmations were important. "Who'll give me an amen on that?" Those timeless techniques continue to inspire effective preaching to this day.

Unconventional church services capture one's attention and evoke curiosity, leading congregants to learn more about their origins, beliefs, and place in the world. Old-time Appalachian preachers were masters at this.

Another spin in a worship service was at a small Church near Christiansburg, Virginia. It was referred to as a "reverse offering." Instead of passing a plate and collecting tithes and offerings, congregation members were encouraged to take a few dollars out of the plate as it was passed around and use the money to bless the lives of someone else.

Services to heal the sick were popular. Healing prayers were given to people who would come forward and seek healing for physical, emotional or spiritual wounds. Often, laying on of hands and anointing with oils were used.

I once attended a meeting at the Powerhouse Church near my home in Morristown, and it got too wild to describe here. I will only say that it was totally unforgettable, and the music was terrific. You'll have some idea if you've seen the movie *The Blues Brothers* with John Belushi.

At a church at Cades Cove in the Smokies, the preacher invited people on a "worshiping nature walk" in the woods to explore and thank God for His wonderful creation. It was unfortunate that God's creation of chiggers and mosquitoes interfered with the evening's message.

A preacher at a revival in Knoxville once started his sermon by saying, "The best years of my life were spent in the arms of a woman that wasn't my wife!" The congregation and the preacher's wife were shocked! But then he added, "And that woman was my mother!" The congregation started laughing, and the sermon that followed was carefully listened to.

Inserting jokes into sermons was always welcomed. There's the story of the little boy who was feeling sick. The preacher had just been preaching about how God took a rib from Adam and created Eve. After church, Little Jimmie felt nauseous and said his side hurt, so he lay down on the long wooden pew. The preacher asked him if he was OK, and Jimmie answered, "I think I'm going to have a wife."

However, one of the best jokes I remember goes as follows. The preacher started his sermon by announcing, "This Sunday, we're going to be studying the importance of honesty." That seemed to be an appropriate topic, and people were ready. Then the pastor said, "In the New Testament, we read a lot about honesty, but before I begin, I'd like everyone who has read the Seventeenth Chapter of Mark to raise their hands.

About half of the congregation raised their hands!

PLUMGRANNIES

My Mamaw used to tend my brother and me when we were just little devils after Momma had reached the end of her rope. Of course, grandmas everywhere have a way with kids, even if it requires cookies or switchin's. My brother and I preferred the cookies and worked hard at being good. Once, my brother John picked some golf ball-sized melons from a vine in Mamaw's garden, and we attempted to eat them. They weren't very good, so we hid the remains under some cucumber plants, where Mamaw found them. Rather than spank us (that time), she laughed and said no damage was done because no one liked to eat plumgrannies, and they couldn't keep up with them because they grew so fast. Then she gave us a small basket of them and let us throw them at the chickens. The chickens were safe because they were behind chicken wire, and when the melons hit the wire, the chickens would scramble to eat them as they exploded. We only threw the soft, ripe ones that Mamaw picked for us. The green ones wouldn't blow apart on impact with the wire.

I asked her why she raised them if she didn't eat them. She replied that she loved the aroma. She let us smell the ripe ones she kept in her kitchen. She explained that the seeds had been passed down by ancestors who'd moved to Appalachia from Ireland hundreds of years earlier. Legend had it that Queen Anne of England used to carry them in her pocket to counteract "body smell." Mamaw loved the smell, but unlike Queen Anne, she said she didn't carry any with her.

The plants look like cucumber vines and are easy to grow. They flourish on a trellis or fence or sprawled on the ground. We save the seeds each year, and they always germinate and grow fine. They can be picked green and will ripen to a bright yellow or orange after a while. The older they are, the more aromatic.

My Aint Berthy also raised plumgrannies. I asked her if she carried any in her pocket to kill body smells, and I got a strict lesson on manners. Berthy said that, like Mamaw, she also liked the aroma but was attracted more to their association with their mystical properties that allowed her to communicate with the good spirits. She also explained that they symbolized the concept of aging gracefully. They become sweeter as they ripen, eventually maturing into their full potential over time. Even though plumgrannies wrinkle with age, like people, they gain even more inner beauty and grace.

She also alluded that the plumgranny might have been the forbidden fruit that tempted Eve in the Garden of Eden and, to some people, symbolized desire and temptation. I wasn't old enough at the time to understand where she was going with that, but these days, I wonder if the association could have been for their beauty and temptation as a forbidden indulgence. I admit that upon seeing my first plumgranny, I had a longing and hidden desire to partake of the forbidden fruit. But as mentioned earlier, Mamaw intervened and had us sacrifice our desires to the chickens.

I'm not sure how the symbolism of plumgrannies might relate to sensual stuff, but it does seem to fit as a powerful symbol for the maturing and transient nature of life. And their relatively short shelf life probably fits in there somewhere, like perhaps beauty not lasting forever, life is fleeting, or some such garbage as that. I had a college class on that kind of stuff once, and a pointy-headed professor had us read some poems by Pablo Neruda, who that got into that kind of smooshy, crazy stuff. He won a Nobel Prize for writing about Sex and Fruit. Mamaw would have ripped his lips off if she'd gotten ahold of him, and Aint Berthy would have cast a hex on him that he'd have not gotten over in his lifetime.

Plumgrannies (Grown by the author)

I digress; Plum Granny melons are also known as Queen Anne's Pocket melons. They develop into striking orange and yellow colors and are primarily grown for their decorative appeal and aroma. Some say they're edible, and others say no. We raise them but don't eat them. The ones we have are bland-tasting, and some claim the seeds are bad for you. Nevertheless, they always remind me of Mamaw and the fragrance of her kitchen, and I love those memories.

Come Springtime, you should plant some plumgrannies.

ZELBERT NICODEMUS MUSES APPALACHIA

Warning: If you weren't exposed to old-timey Appalachian dialect, the following may be tedious reading. For the rest of you, it may bring back memories of simpler times.

Mr. Harvey has gone fishin' and has ast me to write up sumpthin for all y'all while he's gone. He says iffen I does gud, mebbe I can tak hiz place writin' stuff someday. Of course, he high-tailed it out of the Tennessee hill country and went to a fancy university wif bunches of pinko perfessers, and all that purty well messed him up 'cause he don't talk as gud as he used to. Howsomeever, he still prefers to hang around these parts and write up stories up for crazy people to read. He mus be doing purty gud 'cause he's got a pickup truck and all. Hit's a 1963 Shiverla. I got a truck too but hit's sittin on cinder blocks rite now 'till I can scrape up enuf money to buy new tares. These roads up hyar is Hell on tares. The guvment wants to tax our likker but they don't want to fix our roads.

Mr. Harvey said I could be a famous riter iffen I learned to read a little better. My wif, Ocie Mae, has been tryin' to larn me to be read gooder. She started me out reading the Bible about a year ago and looky! Here I is! I got halfway through Genesis afore I figgered I had enuff book larnin' to git started on ritin. I figger I can go to the university later. But when I goes, I aims to go to the Univesty of Kentucky.

I oncst had a gurlfren from Hazard and she wuz good lookin and all that, but her daddy had another yahoo picked out fur her and he backed up his desare wif a shotgun. I ain't dumb so I come home again. I took her on a fancy date to France's Café over to Hazard and we had fine meal too. That wuz the bes $8.59 cents I ever spent…sorta. It wooda been better iffen her daddy hadn'a changed her mind on me. She had a butt two ax handles wide and her mind was sharp a Buck knife. Oh well, that's lif hyar in the hills! I thinks Ocie Mae is better, anyhow.

Ever since I married Ocie Mae, we's as happy as if we had good sense and between raisin' hawgs and coonskin huntin', we does right fine but we hain't havin' much luck follerin' the advice of God to Adam to multiply and replanish the earth. We hain't got no kids atter almost two years of genuine efforts. It ain't for tryin' like the blazes though, we give it a run ever chance we git. Onst, we hit it twenny times in twenny-four hours. That's our record but we keeps tryin' to break hit. They says around hayr that me and Ocie has looks of grim determination on our faces. I ain't shore whut that means but I'm hit means, "Happy but tard." We even went so far as to try Aunt Berthy's hexes n' crystals n' such but she says our "stars ain't linin' up" and I shud go back to readin' the Bible 'cause them boys back in those days had lots of kids.

When I pointd out to Ocie that them Bible people also had lots of wifes and concubines, she threatened to remove a couple of my treasured body parts wif a dull piece of glass. She has a gud way wif words, that woman. She then carefully pointed out that if I even wuz thankin about steppin' out on her, we'd have a serious "Come to Jesus" meetin', only I'd be the one meetin' him…or the devil. I think mabbe she should write stories.

I almost had a chance of marryin' a mousy woman whose main purpose in life was to belittle her man. Lucky fur me, Preacher Kester got married to that woman but thay hain't got no kids neither. I figger that's why hiz sermons on wimmen is so….I caint thank of a good wurd hyar so I'll come back to this later. At least no word whut won't git me in trubble.

I found the scriptures real interestin' what wif snakes, Satan, lions and lambs and sech and nobody had to worry 'bout wearin' no fancy clothes and stuff, but they couldn't have no kids neither until Eve got snookered by the evil snake. Ocie Mae says, kids or no kids, if I start gittin' evil-like and messin' around wif snakes and forbidden fruits like Preacher Kester rails about, she'll kick my sorry a$$ outta the house and feed me to Sweet Pea, my prize hawg. Ocie Mae don't put up wif no foolishness from nobody. I love Sweet Pea and wouldn't puter through that.

I guess them kids'll come along when they wants to. I'm doin' all I know how. I got plenny of frens over to Bulls Gap what iz always offerin' to step in and help Ocie Mae jump-start some babies, but Ocie Mae claims she'd end up killin' em iffen they comed around the hous and she'd haf to go to jail and I'd haf to do my own cookin' and that's goin' over the line fur me.

Bryant Gulley has fourteen-plus-one kids that call him daddy and he kindly offered to hep Ocie Mae out but she kicked him outta the cabin and explained to him how she'd fix'em so he never have no kids in the future iffen he cum around the place again. Fur shore, they says he's smart 'n all but Bryant didn't have enuff sense to know what kind of trubble was in sometimes. Him and his brudder, Nathan, is the same in that respect only Nathan gits caught.

Around these hayr parts, Ole Man Gulley really is an endless bunch of knowledge, but when it comes to wimmen, his head quits working. It don't help none that hiz thankin' is usually messed up by a half gallon fruit jar uv Nathan's white lightening.

When me and Mr. Harvey wuz growin' up, people said we talked funny, but I never took no stock n that 'cause it was everbuddy else frum the flatlands what used strange wurds. Mr. Harvey writes about that kind of stuff in his books, Musing Appalachia. I ain't shore whut "musing" means but I thank hit means "lovin." I gotta recomember to butter up Ocie Mae by sayin' stuff lik, "Ocie, I was out sloppin' Sweet Pea and got to musin' on you. I thank I needs a break. You have anythin' cooked up?"

You can buy hiz books on Amazon but I thank I told you that alreddy and I hope you do buyem' 'cause, iffen they makes enuff money, he's gonna buy him a new fishin' rod. One of them newfangled kinds what has a handle on hit and a winder thang. When he ain't usin' hit, I aim to borrow hit.

In the meantime, I'm gonna muse some stuff about thangs I 'member frum the ole days. I'll warm up by tellin y'all more stuff about Nathan Gulley…stuff what I remember that hit me funny. Nathan iz a brudder to Bryant. My wife says fur me to "hush my mouth right now" afore I git in trubble, 'cause I might hurt somebody's feelin's, but that never stopped Mr. Harvey when he writes. Buy hiz books! He needs a new fishing rod ever' since he lost his ole one when Cooter's granpa chased him off his fishin' pond. Hit was a good place to fish 'cause the carp wuz two-foot long and as feisty as Preacher Kester's wif. Hit didn't help none that he ripped hiz only pair of bib overhawls on the bob ware fence gittin' outta there! Cooter's papaw is a right stingy man, and none uv us sees eye-to-eye wif him on nuthin. I'm guessing we's gonna has to go toe-to-toe wid'em afore hits over.

Hayr in Mohawk, Tennessii, we lives real near whar D Boone cilled a bar. And over to Morristown, Davy Crockett's daddy's tavern still stands. And we lives next to the 'Chucky River and close to where John Jack Sevier the fighter of Indans lived. I thank he was a big-shot guverner too. And lots of riflemen come frum hyar who fought at the battle of King's Mountain. Our boys always loved a gud fight. Davy Crockett's folks was massacred by the Indans. And the son of the famous gun-makin' fambly, the Beans, found his wife with somebody else's baby after he'd been away to war a long time, so Bean cut off the baby's ears to make hit different frum the rest of the kids. Judge Andrew Jackson got aholt of Bean and he was tried, convicted, and soon excaped. Frens David and Darlene livs at Bean Station but they sez the town's named fur pioneer settler, Billy Bean and not thet baby whut got his years cut off...maybe.

Us folks aroun' hyar has Scotch-Irish blood and we luv a gud fight and sum uv us fit on both sides of the Civil War. Politics and wimmen wuz always gret reasons for a gud fight when they wadn't no wars to fight. Neighbors starin' at our wimmen or trespassin' on our land wuz gud reasons too. You know, that "eye for an eye" stuff. That's in the Bible, too. Mebbe I shoulda kept readin and larnin other practikal stuff I could use aroun hyar. Cum to thank 'bout hit, they had tons of babies back in them days too and mebbe I could pick up a few gud tips.

As you can see, they's plenty to rite about around these parts. Why, jist las week, the sheriff come out hyar and got in gun fight with some Georgia moonshiners what was hornin' in on Nathan's bizness, and he emptied his revolver gun at'em without touchin' them but one of the bullets did travel all the way to Mountain Valley Church and knocked out the light bulb over the pulpit. Sum of us figgers that was a warnin' of some kind frum God for Preacher Kester to straighten up and start livin' all the stuff he's prachin', but I ain't shore. That's my story.

Yeah, they's no end of stuff to writ about 'round hyar. Doncha you worry none 'bout that. That's what Mr. Harvey says. Says he could write forever and only repeat hisself a few dozen times.

Onest my momma and daddy got hitched, it didn't take em long to bred me good, 'cause I wuz raised in East Tennessee whar crazy stuff happens all the time. Most people hyar seems purty normal, 'cepting Preacher Kester and his woman. They's always smilin' and shaking hands and saying "Whatcha know? How ya gittin on?" And so on. I think they's too friendly with strangers, and that just ain't normal. You know what I mean? I guess I should cut em sum slack 'cause the Preacher heps Nathan's likker sales the more he preaches agin hit. Nathan is all into growin' his customer base if he's gonna be able to feed his fambly. His wife says she's gonna cut his "customer base" clean off iffen he don't watch his step wif the wimmin. And she'll do hit, too! She's got a temper like a hot-dipped rattlesnake when riled up.

Some thangs Nathan sez leaves me widout words to say. Per zample, Mr. Harvey's granpa, Preacher Hughett, was visiting over to hiz place and Nathan puts hiz hand out to Reverend Hughett and said, "Howdy, Preacher, how 'n the Hell are ye?" The good preacher didn't know whut to say to that, and I 'spect he's still wonderin'. I mean, tell me, iffen you wuz a preacher man, how would you answer that question? "How in Heaven are ye" sartenly wooden't fly aroun' hyar. Nathan shoulda been a preacher, he's gud at words and don't mix'em up when he's sober. Nathan knowed the preacher's wif and I thank he wuz right in whut he said.

Nathan wasn't all the way dumb though. He always kept a fiv' dolla bill in hiz pocketbook so's he could buy more of Uncle Bryant's special "herb medicine" when he runs out. 'Said hit was fur his arthritis and whatnot, and that hit kept him from gittin' ornry. His wife didn't much mind 'cause she had arthritis too and sneaks into his bottle when he's sleepin' off the medicine. They makes a good couple when they's both sleepin. Aint Berthy says they'd have had more than 14 kids iffen they didn't sleep so much.

People likes to tell of the story of when Mr. Gulley onest went into a store in Knoxville, and he had his pet toad frog a sittin' on his shoulder so hit could also see the big city sights. When he went to pay for a plug of Crippled Mule chawin' 'bakker, the clerk asked him, "Hey, where did you get that thing?" And the toad frog answered, "Cocke County, Tennessee. They's people like him all over the place down there."

Nathan and hiz woman had quite a passle of kids. Oncst, when hiz wife went into labor, Berthy, the best granny woman in the holler, came to help deliver the young'un. Hit wuz uv a nighttime, and they didn't have no 'lectricity, so she asked Nathan to hold the coal oil lantern up where she could see what was a goin' on.

Hit wudn't long afore a baby girl wuz brung squalling into the world. Then, Berthy said, "Wait, there, Nathan! Hold yore horses. Don't you git in no big hurry, I thank they's anothern' in there a tryin' to git out." And shore 'nuff, a 'nother baby come squirtin' out. This'en was a boy baby and squalling like a stuck hog. But Berthy kept on sayin', "Keep on a holdin' that lantern higher!" Then, within minutes, a third baby came into the world of Appalachia.

Puzzled, Nathan scratched hiz head and asked Berthy, "Do you thank hits the lantern light whats atractin' 'em?" The next day, when thangs had calmed down, he asked his wife if all that babying stuff hurt? She answered, "Hit's like pushing a watermelon through a garden hose. You shud try hit sometime, you idgit!"

Another time, a flatlander was hiking the hills and come across Nathan with his wrinkled face and toothless mouth, just a strokin' hiz beard, meditatin', and takin' hit easy in hiz rockin' chair on hiz front porch and a watchin' the buzzard birds fly around. And he was balder than a peeled egg.

The city guy said to Nathan, "Mister, I can't help but notice how happy and relaxed you look. What's your secret for a long, happy life?"

Nathan is reported to have answered, "I smokes three packs uv cigarettes a day. I chaws Red Coon tobaccer when I ain't smokin'. I also dranks a country-gallon of organic moonshine each and ever week, 'cept at Christmastime when us boys hyar in the hills ups the ante. I eats lots of hog fat and I never exercises."

"That's amazing," the man said. "How old are you?"

"Twenty-seven," Nathan said.

Now, I don't want you to get the wrong idea like the Yankees up North have about us people here in the highlands of Appalachia doing little or nuthin' except feuding and moonshining. The DamnYankees had spread the rumor that a stranger traveling in these mountains by himself was in danger of being struck by a bullet from almost any patch of trees that he passed, on the mere suspicion that he could be a revenue officer or a spy.

That's craziness, of course. However, I did hear the rumor about an undercover policeman snoopin' around. Nathan assured the flatlander that he was safe in the hills and that the rumors weren't true at all, and people "didn't need no police to bother' em." He said, "We hain't ashamed to set the record straight on ary a thang we do up hyar in the mountains. Yeah, we's pore, and it hain't no fun, but we don't ax nobody for no favors or handouts frum the guvment like flatlanders do. We stays way up hyar in these hollers and we minds our own bidness. When a stranger comes by, he's welcomed to the best stuff we've got, whatever hit might be; but iffen he sticks his nose in our business or threatens our way uv life or looks at our wimmen too long, he'll git his medicine real damned quick-like. Now, whut wuz hit you wuz a wantin', mister?"

"The discovered cop answered sheepishly, "I thank you for the information, Mr. Gulley, and I'd like to buy a gallon of your best medicine while I'm here. My arthritis has been acting up lately."

By the way, he failed to tell the police feller that if he drinks too much out of that fruit jar, "his tongue'll git twisted around his eye teeth and he won't be able to see what he's sayin'."

Now, you'all be careful. They's a fool killer runnin' loose somewhere out here.

THE HIDDEN CABIN ON ROCKY TOP MOUNTAIN

My name is Sonny. In 1958, I turned fourteen years old and attended a wedding celebration of a relative in a mountain cabin a few miles from the town of Del Rio in Cocke County, Tennessee. From the cabin, we had a great view of the imposing mountains that surrounded it. One of these was Rocky Top. This was before the country-western song made the mountain well-known. Rocky Top stands high and gets its name from a rocky outcropping at the peak. It's one of the steeper sub-peaks in the region and is associated with Thunderhead Mountain, which overlooks Cades Cove. The mountain has a colorful history that includes logging, hunting, moonshining, and stories of people who ventured into the area but never returned. It's heavily wooded, with spectacular views of the Great Smoky Mountains. Because of the rugged terrain and thick underbrush, there were no developed trails to the summit, although there were a few footpaths and animal trails. The hike is challenging. That may be different today. I've not been there for years.

The wedding took place in a picturesque clearing behind a house that Uncle Jimmie Gulley was borrowing from his boss at Bulls Gap. Jimmie was getting hitched to a cute gal from Mosheim. The bride and groom were dressed in their best church clothes and appeared to be a forever couple.

By Appalachian standards, the food was amazingly good. There were three tables with platters of fried chicken, sugar-cured country ham, and bowls of savory chicken and dumplings. The aroma of cast-iron skillet cornbread, red-eye gravy, and freshly baked cathead biscuits filled the air. Then there were side dishes of collard greens, leather britches, and fried crookneck squash. Desserts were peach stack cake with lots of layers and filling, sweet 'tater pies, and blackberry cobbler. All this, along with pickled okra, beets, and sweet pickles, gave the feast a special touch. Fresh-squeezed apple juice and sweet tea brought the meal together.

The peach stack cake was remarkable. The tradition originated in Appalachia and was especially popular for weddings. At one time, it signified the community of family and celebration. Like in the old days, Jimmie wanted each guest to bring a layer for the cake. These would then be assembled, and various fillings would be spread between the thin layers of the cake. Some cooks used apple butter or various preserves, but Jimmie loved peach jam, and that was the filling he got. Flavorings from ginger, cinnamon, and nutmeg enhanced the taste of the filling. The more layers that were contributed to the cake, the more popular the bride. The stack cake was more than just a dessert; it was a symbol of family unity and joint support for the wedding couple.

Uncle Carol brought his guitar and a banjo picker friend to provide lively background music. This was indeed a fitting Appalachian celebration for the bride and groom's marriage.

Guests filled their plates with generous portions, sat around in chairs, and reminisced about the good times, acknowledging that this was undoubtedly one of them. About a dozen teenagers were sitting on blankets on the lawn, busily eating and bragging about things they were proud of. Children played games while the adults shared stories and congratulated the newlyweds.

These were not well-off people, not even close. They were just regular people from the rural areas of the surrounding counties. Just everyday mountain folks having a great time with a celebration more extensive than many had ever experienced.

The bride wore a dress made by her Mamaw. It was beautiful, and no one could tell that it had been crafted from feed sack material. It was decorated with lace and embroidery. The groom wore a handmade suit, also made from locally sourced materials.

After my Papaw, Preacher J. E. Hughett, finished with the simple ceremony, the groom presented the bride with a hand-carved "love spoon," whose intent was to demonstrate his commitment and love. He was supposed to have hand-carved it himself, but the new generation was starting to lose the old ways, so he gave her a spoon that his grandfather had made for his wife before they were married. Jimmie did this because his grandmother made him do it because it was an old-time tradition going back to Ireland. Traditions are important in Appalachia. His momma gave him and his bride a double wedding ring quilt as a symbol of unity. Each piece of fabric had a family story associated with it, and his mother was busy describing the history of each quilt square to all who would listen.

There was no dancing or drinking of alcohol of any kind because Preacher Hughett was a Primitive Baptist minister, and such endeavors were considered precursors to temptation and sinning and weren't allowed. But with all the food, the games, the music, and the lively conversations, no one noticed. There was lots of laughter.

This celebration was unusual in another way, too. The family guests were invited to pitch tents, throw blankets on the lawn, and spend the night. Many of the attendees didn't own cars and depended on hitching rides, and late-night travel in the mountains was ill-advised. The elderly were bedded down in the house, as well as young mothers with nursing babies. The boys were camped on one side of the yard and the girls on the other.

Preacher Hughett guarded the camping area throughout the night to ensure propriety but only got a little sleep. It was a tough job. He said, "We don't want no babies with sore feet coming into this world." What he meant was a baby born six months after marriage rather than the traditional nine. When he heard this, Nathan Gulley commented, "Preacher, yore not lookin' at the sitiation wif complete eyes. Iffen we wuz to slip up and a few babies wuz to sneak into the world; we'd still be obeying the commandment of 'multiply and replenish the earth.' Now you go back to bed and git sum sleep. We'll make out jist fine." Of course, this just served to get Nathan a personalized one-on-one sermon that everyone could hear.

Lanterns were lit as the sun set over the mountains, casting a warm glow over the gathering. The sense of community and tradition was palpable, making the wedding a truly memorable event. Everyone would remember this wedding. All were filled with food and tired from the day's activities, and everyone went to sleep that night, content and happy.

About a dozen of the teenagers decided to get up early the next day and hike to the peak of Rocky Top to see if they could catch a glimpse of Mount LeConte, Clingmans Dome, and other mountains in the Smokies. They got up, ate a hasty breakfast, packed lunches for the all-day trek, and took off up a primitive trail leading away from the cabin.

As they pushed through the dense rhododendrons, they noticed that the air grew cooler. Some of the kids walked faster than the others, and they strung out along a narrow patch, zig zagging more or less up the mountain.

I stopped often to look at the plants, hoping to find a ginseng patch, so I was generally the last in line. But not exactly. My second cousin, Amy, also walked a bit slowly. She had a slight limp, and I wondered if she was OK, but I didn't say anything for fear of embarrassing her. She wore a plain dress, obviously made of Pillsbury sackcloth, because when she bent over, I could see the faint outline of the logo where it hadn't bleached out totally. I notice things like that.

I was a shy teen and pretty well scared of girls. She was also shy, but not as much as I was. She asked me, "Are you shore this deer trail is goin' the right way?" I told her I didn't have a clue and was just following the others, trusting they knew the way. Then, I said, "Hey, we're on an adventure, so I ain't worried. Nobody's gonna die. That only happens in the tall tales our folks tell us. Let's buck up and git on with it!"

Although the trail was narrow and bushes scraped against us, after three hours of hard climbing, we finally ended up on top of the peak, not far from the cliffs.

One cousin exclaimed (panting), "Hey! We finally made it! And look at that view, ain't that great?"

Amy said, "Amazing! We can see forever from up here. I'm glad that I came."

I pointed out what I thought had to be Clingman's Dome because it was the tallest mountain in the Smokies. Others exclaimed that another peak would be Mount LeConte because of its shape.

Amy said her legs felt like jelly, and she couldn't believe she'd made it all the way.

Then, we all sat on some rocks and ate the lunches we'd brought. There were biscuits, cornbread, a sack of pickles, slices of ham, and fried chicken. I'd brought a Boy Scout canteen along, and we passed it around, but it didn't go far. There were three pieces of pie, but they had gotten smashed on the hike up the mountain and now looked like jam with gobs of broken crust mixed in. We had a game to see who would get a mouthful because there were twelve of us and only three pieces of pie. A cousin gathered up a handful of gravel and had someone halve it. Then people guessed how many gravels were left in his hand. The three closest guesses each got a piece of pie. My luck was like always. I didn't win a piece, nor did Amy.

As a group, we walked around the top of the knob, looking for signs of another trail down the mountain, but there was just one other path. It seemed to be headed more directly in the direction of the cabin, but was smaller than the path we came up on. I thought it would add variety to the hike if we took the other trail, and I suggested that. It went down a ridge and appeared to be less steep. We voted, and nine kids chose to stick with the original trail they took up because they knew it was good. Amy, I, and another cousin voted to take the new trail down. We couldn't agree and were outvoted. We decided to split up, with a few of us taking the more adventurous trail. Just as we got ready to leave, the other cousin chickened out and joined the larger group. I asked Amy what she wanted to do. She hesitated, then said, "Whatever you do. I don't think you should hike alone."

Because it took us three hours to hike up the steep mountain, we figured that hiking down would be much quicker and, besides, it was a full five or six hours before it would be getting dark. That sealed it, Amy and I decided to hike down the new route. So, we took off down the ridgetop trail. It soon widened and fanned out, and we were proud of ourselves because it was easy downhill hiking along a ridgeline.

Then, we encountered a problem. At about what we figured to be one-third the way down the mountain, the path we were following split. One went along a new ridge to the left, while the other followed a different ridge to the right. Looking at the sun, I calculated that we should take the path along the ridge that led to the left. After about half a mile, the trail split again into two trails, each following a different ridge. We took a guess and again chose the one to the left. By now, we figured that we were about halfway down the mountain. After about a quarter of a mile, the trail stopped at a dead end on a small ledge. We guessed that if we skirted the ledge and got below it, we'd pick up the trail again and could continue on down the mountain.

However, after closer inspection, there was no trail below the ledge, so we side-hilled for a way, looking for an easier way down. We found a tiny deer trail that zig-zagged in the general direction we wanted to go. After about thirty minutes or so, the animal trail petered out, and we were perplexed. Amy was getting scared and held my hand as we traversed the slippery hillside on moss and dead leaves. We continued working our way downhill in a manner that had to lead to the bottom of the mountain and the road.

Then, we ran into yet another obstacle…a rhododendron thicket so thick we couldn't see more than six feet ahead. Our only option was to continue zig-zagging in a downward direction and pushing ourselves through the bushes. We were getting beaten up by limbs hitting us in the face and sawbriars cutting our legs.

By then, we estimated that we were about two-thirds the way down the mountain and had probably two and a half hours of light left.

It was at that point Amy yelled, "Sonny, looky! A cabin!" Indeed, it was a small log cabin. It was in the trees, about 12 feet by 12 feet, and had a door and a small window on one side. There was no trail to the cabin. The weathered wood blended seamlessly into the mountainside. The door was stuck, but it fell off the hinges with a shove. Inside, the air was musty. A tattered newspaper dated 1910 lay on a tiny table. Amy asked, "Why do you think anyone would live way back here in this place?" Her eyes were wide with curiosity.

"It could've been a miner or a moonshiner, I guess, or maybe a hermit or thief who wanted to hide from the world. You gotta have a big reason to come to a place like this."

Interestingly, the cabin appeared fully equipped, as if the owner was planning to return at any time. There were digging tools leaning against a wall, firewood stacked for the small wood stove, pans, dishes, and even canned goods still on the shelves. Winters had been rough on items that had frozen, and mice had eaten food that wasn't stored in tins. But everything was there, essentially untouched for probably 50 years.

We looked for treasure like gold or silver coins and found nothing. We did find an old single-barrel shotgun that had seriously rusted from the moisture over the years. And a tin box contained a stone object and some papers that were yellow and brittle with age.

The rock had strange inscriptions etched on it, but they didn't make any sense to us. We carefully laid the papers out on the table and attempted to decipher the blurred writing but were able to make out only a few words here and there. Whoever had lived there before appeared to have written about strange happenings and phenomena that couldn't be explained. Mention was made of flashing lights in the woods, eerie sounds, and the feeling of being watched by someone or something that appeared to be trying to stop him. The writer also mentioned ancient artifacts and something of value in a cave. The writing told of his belief in a possible treasure and (something illegible). The paper was accompanied by a crude map that was on the verge of crumbling into pieces. Symbols and lines led to an X, but the only word on the map that could be made out was "cave." They left the fragile papers on the table and examined the rock more closely. It had odd inscriptions and symbols but no words. All of this was a mystery, and Amy and I were starting to get the creeps.

We figured that whoever had lived there must have just been a crazy old hermit chasing some perceived treasure and felt that someone was trying to stop him. Then, he disappeared without a trace, leaving behind his hidden cabin and everything he owned. It didn't add up.

Then, we found another small piece of paper wadded up and stuck in the corner of the metal box. It ripped as we unfolded it. It was better preserved and read, "I found the entrance today. The symbols are there, and the spirits guided me to the cave. Tomorrow, I will take a lantern and go deeper into the cave to look for what is hidden there. I feel like evil spirits are watching me. I'm scared."

By all appearances, the old guy never returned. His cabin had been left undisturbed for half a century, and he obviously left with the intent of returning.

Amy and I had lost track of time, and it was getting late. We knew we had to leave quickly. But before we did, we shared a few timeless moments and a kiss that hinted at forever but was fleeting. We shut the door and continued our journey.

The trek down the mountain was fraught with uncertainty, and at one point, the eerie screams of a mountain lion echoed through the trees. However, we pressed on, driven by the hope of finding our way back to my uncle's cabin before darkness set in.

The air was starting to cool off, and the forest was quietening down. Amy said, "We have to hurry; it's getting dark. Be careful. The trail is really steep here."

Just as she said that my foot slipped on some loose leaves; I lost my balance and rolled down the slope, coming to an abrupt stop against a rhododendron bush. Amy yelled, "Sonny, are you OK?"

I told her that I thought that I'd be fine, but my ankle was killing me. It hurt to move it. Amy said, "What are we going to do? We're still close to the cabin. We could spend the night there if we have to."

I replied, "Are you crazy, Amy? Our folks would kill us, especially my Papaw. Remember, he's a preacher, and he'd never understand. We have to keep moving."

Amy said, "But your ankle is hurt and could be broken. What if you can't make it?"

I told Amy I'd rather die on the mountain than have my aunts speculate about me spending the night in a lonely mountain cabin with a cute girl. "Amy, help me get up, and I'll see if I can make it. We gotta hurry if we're going to make it back before dark." I winced, but I was able to stand. It wasn't easy, but there wasn't much of an alternative.

Then Amy whispered, "Did you hear that? I thought I heard a noise like someone or something walking in the woods and mumbling. Listen, do you hear it?"

I listened and said, "It's just the wind. Let's keep moving." I leaned on Amy for support and pushed through the pain. It was barely tolerable, but together, we were able to work our way through the underbrush and continue down the mountain, but we didn't get far before the hair on my back stood up as I was certain that I saw something big move in the trees behind us. I couldn't tell if it was real or my imagination. I had a strong feeling that we were being followed. I carried that feeling with me from that time on until we got off the mountain.

We came to a small stream and followed a game trail along its side and on down the mountain in the waning light until we reached a dirt road. We didn't recognize where we came out and weren't sure which way to go on the road, whether to go right or left. Falling back on my gut feeling, we started down the road to our right. We'd no more than gotten started when we heard the definite scream of a mountain lion. It was to our right, hidden in the underbrush, and sounded as if it were only forty or so yards away. It followed us for over a mile, making horrible and spine-chilling noises. We didn't have weapons, so we picked up rocks in case it leaped at us from the brush.

Then, a car approached with its headlights on, and the mountain lion quit making threatening noises. It was Uncle Jimmie. He took us back to the cabin, and we answered questions while we ate. Where he'd found us was four miles away from the cabin, and we were going the wrong way. Our parents were upset but happy that we'd not been seriously injured. The other kids had returned to the cabin three hours earlier, and all were in good spirits. Amy and I were scratched up, and I was limping, but we were both glad to be safe and away from the mountain. We got kidded a lot but took it in good stride. We never told anyone about kissing in the cabin.

Later on, after eating, Amy kept talking, "We must have wandered through the rhododendron thicket for hours. That cabin was sure well hidden. Do you think we should go back and look for it again? That old man was on to something and really went to a lot of trouble looking for whatever it was. Do you think we could find the cave based on what's on the map?"

After a few minutes of thinking it over, Amy continued, "I gotta tell you, Sonny, I was scared by the whole thing. Getting' lost, the scary noises we heard in the bushes, the cougar, and the confusing writing on the notes, plus the old man going to the cave and never returning. I don't want to go back. It's not that I'm overly superstitious or anything; I'm just practical. It's my nature."

I responded. "Yeah, I agree. It was almost like the mountain didn't want us to find that place. Amy, I'm sorry I talked you into taking the bad trail. I was careless."

In a moment of serious thought, Amy said, "Sonny, up on the mountain when you said that I was cute and we kissed, what were you thinking?"

Sonny responded, "Oh, I guess I just got caught up in the moment. You are pretty, and we're both adventurous, and we get along well together. You're not a crybaby when under pressure, like a lot of girls. Then it struck me that maybe we could date after getting off the mountain."

Amy thought about it a long while, then said, "Sonny, you're a brave guy…careless for absolute sure, but you have courage, and I like that. You didn't panic and pushed on to do the right thing, even after spraining your ankle. And you have good principles. You understand the importance of boundaries. While our feelings may be genuine, having boundaries is important. You respected your Papaw's teachings about boundaries and acted on those instead of what we both may have liked to have done."

Hidden Mountain Cabin

She continued, "I talked with my momma, and she said that we should remember that we're still young and careless and that we should be careful, that life is way more complicated than it might seem. Davy Crockett said once, 'Be sure you're right and then go ahead.' Momma also told me that second cousins getting married and having babies come with extra risks, such as increased chances for genetic disorders being inherited and passed on to the kids, for example, cystic fibrosis, birth defects, and such. She added, "The increased risk may be small, but it's real. I had a brother die of cystic fibrosis. That scares me as much as the panther on the mountain. I'll tell you what, let's kiss one more time and think about it for the next three months." With that, we returned to say farewell to the other wedding guests, packed up, and returned to our homes.

Some years later, Sonny and Amy married (but not to each other). Sonny had once returned to the mountain to look for the cabin. After three harrowing days of trying to retrace his steps down the mountain and crisscrossing the thick rhododendron, he never found the cabin or a cave, but he did hear the scream of a panther.

> *Note: The popular song, Rocky Top, has a fast and upbeat tempo and laments the loss of a simple way of life. It talks of a place where there are no telephone bills or smoggy smoke and thinks back on a love affair that once happened on Rocky Top with a woman "wild as a mink" and "sweet as a soda pop." The song's second verse tells of two strangers climbing Rocky Top, looking for a moonshine still...and never returning. The last verse speaks of a longing for a simple life and compares city life to being "trapped like a duck in a pen." Rocky Top was adopted as an official Tennessee state song in 1982.*

GRANDMA'S LESSON ON CUSSING
As related by Lee Jerome Lewis

It was a sunny Saturday morning, and Lee was buzzing with excitement. Today was the day he'd head to summer camp, a place filled with swimming, hiking, and all the adventures a twelve-year-old could dream of. He had packed his bags the night before, making sure he had his swim trunks, bug spray, and that one pair of socks with a mysterious hole that gave his big toe freedom.

However, the morning took an unexpected turn when he got into an argument with his brother. It started with a harmless spat over who could climb the tree in Grandma's yard fastest, but things quickly escalated. Before Lee knew it, he had cussed Timmy out loud enough for the neighbor's dog to start howling.

His grandma heard the commotion, but she didn't say a word. Instead, she went about her morning as usual, humming a tune from her youth and setting the table for breakfast. When it was time to eat, Lee noticed something peculiar: there was no plate set for him.

"Grandma," Lee asked, bewildered, "where's my breakfast?"

Grandma looked at him with a calm but stern expression. "Anyone who cusses like you did out there doesn't deserve to eat," she said simply and returned to her chores.

Lee's stomach grumbled louder than a hungry hound dog. But the worst was yet to come. When it was time to leave for camp, Grandma didn't give him a sack lunch either. Lee's heart sank as he imagined the long, foodless bus ride ahead.

As the bus pulled up to the house, Grandma walked Lee out. She had a quiet word with the bus driver and, to Lee's horror, instructed him to wait. The bus driver obliged, and Lee was told to go back into the house, blushing as the other kids on the bus snickered and whispered.

The bus drove away without him, and Grandma led a devastated Lee back inside the house. She opened the oven, revealing a delicious hot breakfast that made Lee's mouth water. He ate in silence, savoring every bite. Once he was done, Grandma sat him down for a lecture on the importance of words and the power they hold. She never raised her voice, nor did she spank him. Her disappointment spoke louder than any punishment could.

After breakfast, Grandma did something unexpected. She got into her old car...an event rarer than a solar eclipse...and drove Lee to camp herself. Lee was floored; Grandma hardly ever drove anywhere except to church and for occasional grocery runs.

When they finally arrived at camp, Lee gave Grandma a heartfelt hug. He had learned a valuable lesson. Words matter, and respect was not negotiable. As he waved goodbye and joined his fellow campers, he silently vowed to choose his words more wisely from that day forward. The story of how he almost missed camp due to his loose tongue became a lifelong memory and lesson. The moral of the tale was crystal clear: Think before you speak, especially in Grandma's house.

At camp, Lee got into a fistfight with a boy who made fun of his Hillbilly accent. He tackled the boy, pinned him to the ground, and said, "You @#$%^&*!!! Eat this," and then proceeded to sprinkle dirt into his mouth.

PREACHER JAMES JETHRO HUGHETT AND THE GOSPEL TENT

I first heard of Jethro when I read a classified advertisement in The Roanoke, *Virginia Times* newspaper in 1969.

"Wanted, Circus or Gospel Tent. Call JJ Hughett at (703) XXX XXXX." Curious, I called, and our friendship began. He explained that he was a minister and desired to buy a large tent in which to hold church revivals. I told him that I didn't have a tent for sale, but that both he and I spelled our last name in the unusual H-U-G-H-E-T-T way, and that I was confident that we were related. At that time, I was teaching at Virginia Tech and had an interest in genealogy, specifically tracing my family's origins. I learned that most Hughett ancestors in the USA, at one time or another, had lived in and passed through nearby Floyd County. My wife and I spent considerable time roaming the county looking for the gravesites of my relatives, and we found many.

Jethro invited us to visit with him and his wife the following week. He lived in a modest but comfortable home and promptly greeted us at the door. Immediately, I knew that we were related. He asked how I knew, and I said, "Because we both inherited the

Hughett ugly genes." At the time, I was in my mid-twenties and still awkward with my words, and he was in his forties.

He laughed, blew off the back-handed compliment, and invited us to sit a spell. While it is not debatable that Hughetts often had some homely-looking men, Hughett women that I know of frequently more than made up for it by being beautiful, in both looks and personality. Why the Hughett genes split up this way by the sexes, I can't explain, but at any rate, Jethro and I resembled each other with some minor differences. We established that our relationship was tied to a common ancestor, FIVE GENERATIONS BACK! In nearby Indian Valley.

Jethro had an interesting and unique face. I had trouble looking him in the eyes because his right eye would look straight at you, and the other just floated around. I'll guarandang-tee you that when faced with that, one has to look away. Being young and dumb in social graces (another Hughett man trait), I asked what had happened to his eye. He kept talking as if he'd not heard me and never answered that question. We chatted a bit more, and I asked him again, and he still ignored the question. I finally gave up and we moved on to another topic of conversation…the circus tent.

He explained that he pastored a small church and wanted to expand the congregation and get God's word to more people, and that a big gospel tent would be perfect. He could fold it up and move it from community to community for frequent revivals. He had the backing for a loan for enough money to buy a used tent and a few more chairs. He would use a pickup truck, trailer, and portable pulpit with a stage he already owned. He also had a sequined "preachin' suit" on layaway in Roanoke. With a big tent, he could be up and spreading God's word more broadly in no time.

About a year later, he called and invited my wife and me to a revival on the outskirts of Pulaski in his new tent. We assured him we'd be there and put it on our calendar.

It was an evening event with close to a hundred people in attendance, and it was impressive! He had a choir singing and a nice sound system that even passing cars could hear as they drove by on the rural community highway.

It turns out that Jethro was not a laid-back preacher but an old-time pulpit stomper who could make the tent shudder when he got on top of his game. I wasn't prepared for either the volume or variety of words that blessed the congregation that evening. At one point, he did "the stomp." It startled me when he stomped the wooden floor, making a loud sound that caused the portable pulpit to rattle and dust to rise. This was symbolic of stomping the serpent devil's influence out of our lives. He challenged the "old debbil" himself throughout the sermon and, as a finale, called a few members forward to be healed by the laying on of hands. Luckily, the offering plates were filled with enough money to make a good dent in paying off the tent and accessories. Obviously, he was in his element and glad that he'd repented his earlier indiscretions as a young man and was now leading other lost souls to the path of righteousness.

Then, he did something else that caught me off guard (I declare this is true). He held up two photographs, one of his wife and one of his daughter, and said that he felt something terrible would happen to them unless someone made an offering to the Lord on their behalf. Two old ladies on the front row eagerly opened their purses, pulled out fifty-dollar bills, and gave them to the preacher. He gave each of them a photograph, and the meeting continued with hallelujahs.

A few months later, I got another call from Jethro, wherein he invited me to a prayer meeting at his home. My father, Harvey Sr., was visiting us, and he and I were honored by the invitation.

When we showed up at his house, there was a circle of eight chairs in his small living room, all filled with women except for him, my dad, and me. The meeting started with a short sermon by

Preacher Jethro, followed by an invitation to all in attendance to share things they needed to pray for.

The first one to speak up was a lady in her forties who complained about her husband's drinking habit. From there, they went around the circle. The next lady explained that her married son had run off with a "cheap, hussy woman" from Christiansburg and was living in sin with her down in Shawsville. The next woman described how her husband came home drunk and beat her regularly, and she wanted God to do something about it. And they kept going around the circle until they came to my father. My daddy was a devout Hardshell Baptist who was raised attending the small Mountain Valley Church in Mohawk, Tennessee.

I still shake my head, but the following totally blindsided me. My father didn't hesitate to point his finger at me and said, "This is my son. He is a heathen, and he don't believe in the same God that we do. He tolerates churches what believes in baptism by sprinklin', woman preachers, and churches that accept queers into their congregation!"

> *Note: I do not belong to such a church as he described, and I don't know what got into him to say that. I try not to be critical, but it is true that I tolerate people and their right to believe what they want. This was always a point of contention between my father and me, and he obviously used that occasion to take a jab at me.*

Apparently, his assertion struck a sensitive nerve with everyone, and all (but me) quickly got down on their knees, folded their hands, and started earnestly praying for my soul...out loud! Simultaneously! And forcefully! I remained seated on my chair and watched in disbelief while this was happening. It was surreal. I remember thinking I'd give anything to have a videotape of that event because no one would ever believe me. It was apparent to me that each person tried to out-pray the person kneeling next to them, both in loudness and biting criticism of such a sinner as me. Forget the philanderers and the drunkards; their attention was focused on me.

After about ten minutes of praying, louder by the minute, each person essentially preaching a sermon of repentance targeted at me, they said "Amen," and without a goodbye, they put on their coats, and, one by one, everyone went home. The next day, my dad returned to East Tennessee, and I was glad to see him go. Preacher James Jethro Hughett cut off communication with me from that day forward.

Later, in comparing notes with my wife from our first meeting, while Jethro was ignoring my question about how his eye came to be the way it was, she was getting the "straight scoop" from his wife. She explained that back in Jethro's sinning days, his first wife had shot him in the eye with a .22 revolver, rendering the controlling muscles useless. She went on to describe how his wife had divorced him and, after he became a preacher, he once interrupted his sermon in a church service, pointed at her in the congregation, and proclaimed that God had told him that she was to be his wife. She took him at his word, and they were married. He was in his forties. My wife remembers her saying she was just over sixteen at the time of the inspired sermon. As I inferred before, he had a face that would stop an eight-day clock, and she was very attractive. I kept track of Jethro and learned that, probably because of the age difference, he died much earlier than she did. But I am pleased to tell you that their marriage was a happy one and, literally, "Made in Gospel Tent Heaven."

I once reminded my wife of the technique that Preacher Jethro had used to obtain a young wife, and my usually mild-mannered spouse told me that if I even seriously thought of doing such a thing remotely like that, she'd shoot me in the face, too, and then shoot me several times below the belt. My wife never lies, so I took her at her word.

Our perceived differences notwithstanding, I liked Jethro and remember putting fifteen dollars in the revival collection plate, a lot of money for my young family in the mid-sixties. The closing of that tent revival meeting was memorable, too. He said, "Thank you all, thank you, thank you everyone, and I thank you even more than you know. I look forward to someday meeting you on God's shining shore...and I hope that we all make it."

One can't make this stuff up. This story is true. I changed some names to keep kinfolks from getting irritated with me. And I'm not being critical of the folks who torched me. They were sincere, and I was...well, in the wrong place at the wrong time. That happens to me pretty often.

THE JAY BIRDS BOYS DEBATE CORNBREAD

It had been a slow week on the porch of the Jaybird Store near Morristown, Tennessee, and the four old geezers had about run out of stories about who had the best coon dog, what brand of knife held an edge the best, which wimmen in town were likely to be the kindest to their husbands, and so on. While they never agreed on any of this, they never tired of trying to come to some level of agreement.

The morning had been marching along pretty well until old lady Gooch entered the store to buy a pound of corn meal. As she was prancing away in a dress that was probably a hand-me-down from her considerably thinner stepdaughter, Delroy couldn't help himself but make a comment. He asked, "Boys, do you thank that woman can make good cornbread? I mean real good cornbread, like God intended hit to be made."

This caused the old guys to go quiet because they'd never contemplated that Ole Lady Gooch could even cook, let alone make good fixin's for meals.

Andrew said that his wife had heard that she put sugar in her cornbread recipe. That set off a firestorm of controversy because it was generally known among real Southerners that if you put sugar in cornbread, it becomes cake.

"Pinkie" Pinkston offered: "I caint believe that nobody would put sugar in cornbread except maybe a flatlander or a communist. And that includes Old Lady Gooch!"

Jake, generally known as the peacemaker among the old men said: "Listen, guys, some people puts moonshine in their coffee and others kiss their cows, so adding sugar ain't much of a stretch. My aunt went to Cincinnati, and she now makes hit wif sugar ever so often. She claims sugar makes hit more savory and brangs out the corn's natural flavor. A little sugar never hurt nobody, but cornbread with too much sugar flavor is usually a bad thang."

Pinkie couldn't resist and had to add: "I kin see whar addin' moonshine to coffee gives hit a good flavor, and that makes a lot of sense, and it even makes a little sense to add moonshine to cornbread as long as you don't cook the alkihol outta hit. Plus, hit makes even more sense that the natural flavor of corn-likker will add somethin' good to cornbread."

Delroy added: "Yeah, I kin go along with that as long as you cooks hit in a cast arn skillet and not one of them sissy Pyrex thangs they's selling in the store. Arn skillets give hit the right kind of flavor and the crust is thicker and tastier. If hit ain't got a good crust, hit ain't worth eatin'."

Andrew said, "Well, I agree with y'all on the sugar thang, but when you sop yore cornbread in pinto bean nectar, hit cain't be beat, but iffen hit had a sweet taste I thank I'd upheave hit. I gotta weak stomach when it comes to bad food. My momma says I git that frum my Scotch-Arsh blood. Besides, cornbread and beans will keep you warm thru the coldest mountain night. Doncha nobody know nuthin?"

Delroy: "Andrew, I eat some of yore woman's cornbread at the last church homecomin', and hit was so dry, hit would choke a stud mule. Hit took me a whole quart of sweet tea and a full stick uv butter afore I could choke hit down. I don't thank I could even have eat hit with a mess of collard greens."

Andrew: "Dry!? Heck, that's called texture, Son! And hit crumbles on purpose 'cause you's sposed to wet hit with a drizzle of sorghum syrup on hit. You do that, and you'll never go back to that Yankee cake they pass off as cornbread or that stuff yore wife cooks with the crusts like leather."

Jake: "Let's not start argufyin', boys. I thank we all can agree that no cornbread can be beat iffen hits et with a side dish of fried green tomaters."

Pinkie: "I didn't want to say nuthin, but eatin' fried green tomaters as a side dish is them playing like they's a vegetable."

Delroy: "They haint no side dish. We lived off 'maters a whole summer long onest when my daddy got laid off at the mill. We ate tomaters five ways frum Sunday, five days a week, except for times when we'd catch a coon or a squirrel to eat, then tomaters became side dishes."

Jake, again trying to restore order to the porch front: "Funny you should say that, Delroy. My Mamaw used to make a big batch of cornbread every Sunday, and the whole family would go over to her place, sit on the porch and eat and talk until the lightnin' bugs come out."

Andrew: "Yep, those were the best times in the world, wasn't they? Hit's funny how somethin' as simple as cornbread can bring back so many good memories. Our favorite recipes may be different, but the love and tradition behind them is the same. When you thank about hit, that's all that really matters, ain't it?"

Pinkie: "Now, listen heyr, fellers, we've strayed off the subject. Do you all thank that Ole Lady Gooch can make good cornbread?"

Jake: "I can't vouch for her cornbread cause I ain't never et none uv hers, but she brought the best pot of squirrel stew to the church potluck what I've ever et. Hit was so good, you'd cry and beg yore momma for a second helpin."

Andrew: "Jake, you mentioning squirrel got me to thankin,' I reckon y'all are furgettin' somethin' mighty important. The best woman cook is one who can make a meal outta nuthin'. My wife, bless her heart, once made a thanksgivin' feast outta two cans of beans, a handful of wild greens, and a squirrel that wandered into the backyard. Hit was so good that you coulda stuffed cornbread plumb full uv sugar, and nobody would've complained. Even Old Sooner, our hound dog whined for seconds. Hit wuz so tasty that he did tricks just to git another bite."

And you can guess how the rest of the day's conversations went....

> *NOTE: When the first settlers came to the United States, they found the Southern Native Americans raising corn or maize in fields. They used it in their foods in various ways. Many useful products could be made from corn, including alcohol (moonshine). Probably the reason that many Southerners prefer cornbread without sugar is that was the way their old kinfolks made it. Sugar was expensive and scarce in the early days, and they got used to eating it without sugar.*
>
> *My family raised corn on East Tennessee's steep hillsides and preferred that crop over raising tobacco. The latter brought in more money for the family, but it was highly labor-intensive, whereas corn was relatively easy to grow, harvest, process, and store. Cornmeal can be fashioned into ash cakes, hoecakes, and cornbread and baked in sizzling cast-iron skillets. No matter who you were, cornbread was accessible in the Americas.*
>
> *Differences in cornbread preferences are not too unlike preferences for religion or politics. There are various options to choose from, and personal tastes vary. However, you probably like the kind your momma or grandma made when it comes down to it.*

No one really knows who introduced sugar into the cornbread recipe, but Bristol native and Grand Ole Opry star, Tennessee Ernie Ford, said it wasn't right to put sugar in cornbread. And, if he said it, that's good enough for me.

THE CORNBREAD AND BEANS SHOWDOWN

If it weren't for cornbread and beans, my family may not have survived. There were times when we ate those for three meals a day. There was always a skillet of cornbread and a pot of beans on the stove. When hungry, we could count on 'em always being there. Whenever Daddy was able to tree a coon or grapple a catfish, it made for happy days in our mountain home near Bulls Gap, Tennessee. Money was almost non-existent, and food of any kind was hard to come by until Daddy got a job in town. However, even today, many decades later, I still love cornbread and beans.

Daddy loved his meals with wild ramps, but I never cared for any kind of onion. The scent of cornbread and beans makes any kitchen warm and inviting, but, to me, ramps are not for the faint-hearted. I once almost slipped up and dated a girl from Cosby, Tennessee, until she mentioned that she liked ramps. Sometimes, I got lucky. She was really nice, but I had to draw the line somewhere.

My Papaw, John Elbert Hughett, once organized a Cornbread and Bean Competition at Mountain Valley Church in Mohawk,

Tennessee. He was the preacher at the time and was looking for an activity that would improve fellowship and simultaneously fill the stomachs of the less fortunate, who were always invited to attend. We were poor, and some of us kids didn't own shoes, but some people were worse off.

For the big cookoff, contestants were invited to bring sample platters of their best or most creative recipes. Any kind of beans or peas could be used, but they had to be the main ingredients. The grand prize for each category was a 12" Lodge brand cast iron skillet made in South Pittsburg, Tennessee. The skillets were donated by an anonymous donor, probably a backslider who wanted to keep a low profile but still stay on the fringe of the preacher's good list.

The competition had dual criteria, the tastiest and the most creative. Cornbread and beans being what they are, about anything under the sun could be added. To keep from getting tired of eating the same thing every day, a lot of variations were experimented with in the hills.

To help assure fairness, the judges were Preacher Kester and Preacher Hughett, and their families were barred from entering the contest. In the event the judges couldn't agree, Bryant Gulley was to cast the deciding vote and make the final determination. He claimed to know all there was about the food in question. Some claimed that he indeed was "full of beans," but the jury was still out on the cornbread.

Local musicians were invited to provide music. Dancing or alcohol was not allowed. If someone wanted to sell local crafts, they were invited to do so. Games and contests were planned for the kids, including sack races, a pie-eating contest, and egg-toss games. A special attraction that year was to use extra-large goose eggs. The kids would toss quail eggs.

The Cornbread and Bean Showdown was much more than just a cooking competition; it was an outpouring of community spirit and Appalachian culture with the objective of fostering a festival of brotherhood and fun, with neighbors coming together to share their love of good food and tradition. It was something to look forward to in a lonely part of the country.

Anytime the church had an activity with free food, Nathan Gulley showed up and openly claimed to have repented of his moonshining. Traditionally, a few weeks later, he'd always be back on the mountain cooking mash and distilling "product" for sale to Yankees in Cincinnati. However, he claimed to have turned over a new leaf this year and was donating a thirty-gallon barrel full of his special Appalachian Yaupon Tea…NON-ALCOHOLIC! The sheriff sampled it first to make sure that it was as he described and announced that it not only appeared to be safe but was also tasty.

Nathan took delight in describing the tea to those who'd not tried it before. Yaupon tea has a unique and pleasant flavor profile that can vary depending on how the leaves are processed. Nathan's recipe was for roasted Yaupon leaves, which have a robust, nutty, slightly smoky taste with the aroma of roasted hickory nuts. It is less astringent than traditional black or green teas and is smooth and easy to drink. He added some honey to enhance the natural taste. Yaupon holly grows wild and contains caffeine. It's the only plant in the United States to have naturally occurring caffeine.

The competition was fierce that year, and everyone was eager to claim the glory that went along with winning the skillet. In the interest of not boring you, I'll skip the details of the judging and just hit a few highlights as I remember them.

As the cookoff began, the air was filled with the mouthwatering aroma of warm cornbread and simmering beans. Everyone eagerly dug into the array of dishes. The preachers made the rounds, sampling each dish with serious expressions, jotting down notes as they went. Uncle Bryant followed behind them and took big samples so as to assure fairness. He was momentarily sidetracked when he stopped to eat a half-dozen of Novella Dyer's famous deviled eggs.

My cousin Imogen Jarnigan had prepared cornbread infused with a blend of her secret herbs. Being a self-professed herb expert, Uncle Bryant quickly picked out the faint flavors of passion fruit, blackberries, and pokeweed. He complained that with those ingredients, it wasn't really cornbread but just a fancy fruitcake and ought to be disqualified. Then, he ate another two slices to make sure of his assessment. It contained another flavor he couldn't identify, and Imogene refused to tell him. She said if she told him that with his big mouth, it'd never be a secret again. Imogene and Bryant didn't always get along, and she gave him a one-two jab by also saying, "Bryant, yore nose is so long, iffen you wuz to turn yore head sideways, you'd knock half the people here down."

When Preacher Kester sampled Imogene's cornbread, he exclaimed loudly, "Praise the Lord! That's good stuff! Can I get a witness? Somebody, please say amen!" Preacher Hughett then stepped up, took a bite, and said, "Hallelujah! That's heavenly cornbread! Satan, get thee behind me and let me have some more!" Right away, Imogene seemed to have a winner.

Sharon Cobb entered a cornbread that was a tried-and-true family recipe that she claimed was "good enough to make a grown man cry." Usually, that may have been true, but this time, she had left out the moonshine and ginseng, rendering the recipe safe for mixed company. When Nathan Gulley sampled Sharon's cornbread, he exclaimed, "Well, I'll be dag nabbed! Her cornbread hain't no got kick a'tall to hit like last year. Hit ain't fit fur hogs without thet ole-timey kick. Sharon, you butter come see me. I got sum stuff you kin add to hit what'll make men bawl and scream like babies agin!"

Reverend Hughett disagreed with Nathan after eating a sample of Sharon's cornbread. He and Preacher Kester both agreed, saying, "The devil is a liar if he says this cornbread ain't top-notch."

Sharon wasn't ruffled by Nathan's remarks. She just winked at the judges and smiled, knowing that anything Bryant could say would give her a leg up over the other competition. She wasn't out to win a skillet but mostly to have some fun.

Miss Cleo, the spinster Sunday School teacher, was nervous but excited and had spent weeks perfecting her Pinto and Turkey Craw Bean Soup recipe, adding a touch of honey, some ground-up teaberry leaves, and a dash of cinnamon for a unique twist. She hoped it would stand out among the more traditional entries. Preacher Hughett said, smiling, "Miss Cleo, these beans are something real special." Miss Cleo blushed with pride when Preacher Kester agreed. Only the really old-timers raised Turkey Craw beans anymore, but her family always had.

However, the pièce de résistance and surprise piece of the whole competition was the old family recipe that great-aunt Berthy Dyer entered. She called it "Enchanted Hillbilly Caviar," and she'd never shared the recipe in public before. Preacher Kester exclaimed, "Tarnation, Berthy! That thars purdy stuff! I haint never seed nuthin' like hit afore. Hit's beautiful, what's hit taste like?" Then, the judges grabbed bowls and dug in with their spoons.

Preacher Hughett, always one to try anything, took a generous helping of Aunt Berthy's caviar. His eyes widened as he took his first bite, and a big grin spread across his face. "Well, bless my soul, and as sure as the Lord is my Shepherd, this is the best Hillbilly Caviar I done ever tasted!" Then he filled his bowl with seconds.

Word quickly spread about Aunt Berthy's dish, and soon everyone was clamoring for a taste. In no time, the big bowl was emptied.

Mrs. Greenlee, noticing the growing merriment surrounding Berthy's recipe and raising an eyebrow, asked with a knowing smile. "Berthy, did you put some uv yore special stuff in that caviar?" Aunt Berthy, never one to lie, chuckled and replied, "Just a big tablespoon full of my special elixir I makes frum the wild herbs I find in the holler behind my cabin. I tell you what, Mrs. Greenlee, I had no idea hit' ed cause such a ruckus! You'd think these people hadn't eaten good food afore."

After the judges announced that Imogene Jarnigan had won the cornbread competition and Berthy Dyer the bean competition, both received a new Lodge cast iron skillet and lots of attention. Immediately, there was a crowd of people surrounding them asking for their recipes.

Unfortunately, there are complainers in every group of people, and those who brought chili bean and pinto soup bean recipes were the most vocal. They wanted Berthy's Hillbilly Caviar recipe to be disqualified because they claimed it was just a no-cook, ready-in-minutes, eye-catchy "appetizer salad side dish" and not real food. But the judge's decree was final.

I may write up their recipes at another time. When wild herbs are involved in anything, you must be extra careful. While Yaupon, Ginseng, Goldenseal, Teaberry, and other wild plants were mentioned by Berthy, you must be positive in their identification when collecting and the amounts used.

Beans and cornbread have long been staples in Appalachian and hillbilly kitchens for practical and cultural reasons. They'll keep you alive because they're protein-rich and nutritious. Also, they are cheap and universally available. Actually, in the old days, we didn't have to buy 'em. We raised corn and ground the meal, and beans were always a big part of our garden. They're hardy, grow well in Appalachia, and can be stored.

When Armageddon hits, we'll be ready!

Notes on Southern Cornbread: When making cornbread and to give it variety, you can experiment with optional ingredients such as cheese, crumbled bacon or bacon grease, jalapeños, herbs (fresh thyme, rosemary, chives), wild ramps, garden greens, honey, jam, corn kernels, dried fruit, chopped nuts, seeds (flax, chia, sesame), pumpkin puree, or spices such as smoked paprika, cayenne pepper, cumin, or whatever you think will taste good and not make your guests sick…unless you want to cure a bunch of dinner-time moochers, then you can add whatever strikes your fantasy.

Adding some of your favorite foods to cornbread can be exciting. And, yes, some people have added moonshine to the recipe in hopes of a unique flavor, but too much will make the cornbread soggy, and it could catch fire. You should experiment first and keep the bottle away from your spouse. We don't recommend moonshine for cooking. It is best used for giving your spouse a back rub, but if you do that, you may totally forget to take the cornbread out of the oven. Creative cooking has its risks.

Also, the combination of Southern-style green beans, slow-cooked with bacon or ham hocks, goes great with the crumbly texture of cornbread. One of my favorite foods in the whole world is to sop up the "pot likker" with cornbread after eating the cooked turnip greens, collard greens, or mustard greens. Just add seasoning to taste, such as salt, pepper, and (especially!) a splash of white vinegar.

Other great Appalachian side dishes that go exceptionally well with cornbread include fried green tomatoes, potato salad, poke sallet, fried okra, corn pudding, sautéed spinach, sweet tater casserole, and, of course, coleslaw.

Cornbread pairs wonderfully with soups, stews, or as a side dish for a big meal. When I was growing up, often the side dishes were the main meal. It all depended on what food happened to be available at the time. For us, when we were lucky, main meals for supper usually consisted of country ham, chicken and dumplings, chili, pulled pork, fried chicken, macaroni and cheese, baked beans, beef stew, BBQ, catfish, snapping turtle, raccoon, squirrel, duck, marsh rabbit (aka muskrat), Canadian geese, cottontails, quail, and other assorted free foods acquired in the woods. I intentionally left possum out. I did so because I don't like the taste of the grease. I also didn't include skunk because meat procurement is tedious. But don't get me wrong, I've eaten skunk and would do so again…but only if you catch and prepare it.

As you can see, I'm hungry and got sidetracked by thoughts of my favorite foods. The following story may take your appetite away, but it's historically, totally true.

THEY HUNG AN ELEPHANT!

WARNING: This story describes the true story of the hanging of a circus elephant and may be too disturbing for some readers. I only share this so we may learn lessons from the past. I kinda wish I hadn't written about it. On the other hand, it's proof that truth is stranger than fiction.

On September 13, 1916, when my great-uncle Bryant Gulley was 34 years old, he said he went to Erwin, Tennessee to witness a historical event that probably never happened in the entire world before nor since. He'd heard about elephants and wanted to see if they were really as large as was claimed. He saw much more than he bargained for.

If you've ever lived in East Tennessee, you already know this place is crawling with crazy people and even crazier stories. If they're not totally true, they probably started out true. This one is true all the way through, but I wish that it weren't. It's just another example of truth being stranger than fiction.

What follows is the story of a ten-thousand-pound circus elephant known as "Big Mary" or "Murderous Mary," who was hanged from a gallows for murder.

Mary's story began in Kingsport. She was a key attraction of the Sparks World Famous Circus Show. The Spark's Circus was billed as the cleanest and most Sunday-school-like circus in the country. It boasted of having no gamblers, short-change artists, scams, or hoaxes. Mary was advertised to be the largest living land animal in the world in captivity. She'd always been gentle until she got to this Appalachian city.

As things tend to happen, a domino effect was set in motion. The problem arose when Mary's keeper suddenly left for another job, leaving the circus to find a last-minute substitute to care for Mary and the other animals.

Mary's new keeper was Walter Eldridge, nicknamed Red because of his rust-color hair. Only a few days earlier, Red had been hired on as an assistant elephant trainer to replace the original keeper. He was a drifter who had zero experience or training in handling elephants. Apparently, he was a hobo at the time of his hiring but had once been a bellhop in another state.

In any case, the requirement of the circus was that he just had to be able to ride on the elephant's back and handle an 'elephant stick' or goad. It's a tool with a sharp, pointed hook at one end, used by elephant handlers to guide and control the animals while riding. It was kinda like a fireplace poker.

So, right away, Red Eldridge found himself on the back of Big Mary, leading a parade down the main street of a city that prides itself as one of "Progress and Tradition." Mary was the star animal of the show, although there were four other elephants and numerous exotic animals.

There have been several accounts of Red Eldredge's demise. Many claim that he viciously prodded Mary behind the ear with the sharp hook after she veered off course and reached down to nibble on a pile of a watermelon rinds by the side of the road. Eldredge apparently had forgotten to feed Mary that morning, and she was both thirsty and hungry.

When Eldridge stabbed the elephant to get her back on course, Mary, not used to being mistreated, lost patience and did what any self-respecting 10,000-pound, hungry, and thirsty animal would have done. She grabbed Eldredge with her trunk, slammed him hard to the ground, and stepped on his head viciously, flattening it until it was unrecognizable. Calmly, with that obstacle out of the way, she continued nibbling on the watermelon rinds. Her self-preservation instincts had come into play.

Of course, the spectators were terrified and screaming, and they scattered in all directions away from the scene.

It's reported that a blacksmith then pulled a pistol, calculated where Mary's heart might be, and shot her. He unloaded six rounds of ammunition at her thick hide and jumped out of the way to keep from being crushed when she fell over. To his surprise, the elephant was unfazed. Oblivious to the bullets, she calmly just looked at him with curiosity and went back to eating the watermelon.

Coming out of shock at Red's violent demise, the panicked townspeople started yelling, "Kill the elephant! Kill her! She's a murderer!" People demanded that something be done with the murdering elephant, and the circus management was unsure what to do because nothing like this had ever happened before. They turned the matter over to the police. After reviewing the situation, it was determined that a murder indeed had been committed. There was some discussion about whether it had been self-defense or pre-meditated. Given the size of Mary, self-defense was ruled out. And, as far as the laws were understood, pre-meditated murder demanded a death sentence. Of course, there were no jails large enough to cage an elephant; essentially, she'd been caged all her life anyway. But justice had to be served, and she would need to suffer the same fate as other murderers in those times. It was hastily determined that she should hang by the neck until dead. Instead of an entertaining circus show of an elephant doing tricks, the big show was now to be a lynching.

The hanging of any living being is a distasteful task by any definition, but the question of how to hang an elephant borders on bad science fiction.

The circus owners, Charlie Sparks and his wife, "Miss Addy," reluctantly agreed, and it was decided to hang the elephant by the neck from a huge railcar-mounted industrial crane. On the next day, September 13, 1916, Murderous Mary was transported by train to Unicoi County, Tennessee, where a crowd of over 2,500 people (including children) gathered at the Clinchfield Railroad workshop. I hate to recount what happened next, but this is what occurred.

While my Uncle Bryant claimed to have been present at the hanging, he felt pity for Mary in the way things were handled. In retrospect, he thought that it was a hare-brained idea to begin with and was botched from the start...plus it was inhumane. To make things worse, as Mary was being led away, the other circus elephants trumpeted sorrowfully as if they knew something terrible was afoot.

When they got to the Erwin railyard, they put a chain around one of Mary's legs and tied it to a rail to keep her from running away. Then, they wrapped a chain around her neck. The heavy chain was attached to a 100-ton railcar-mounted derrick, the idea being to lift her by the neck and hang her until she died of strangulation, allowing justice to be served for the murder.

Unfortunately, no one thought of unhooking the chain from her leg, and as the derrick was put into action and as she was hoisted into the air, there was a gut-wrenching cracking noise. It was the sound of her bones and ligaments snapping under the strain. She had been raised no more than five feet when the chain around her neck snapped, and she dropped to the ground, further breaking her hip. After falling, Mary just sat there on her haunches, motionless.

Still alive, a stronger chain was put around her neck, and the industrial crane was powered up again and, this time, Mary was hoisted fifteen feet into the air, her thick legs thrashing, and her agonized shrieks and grunts audible over the laughs and cheers of those watching.

Uncle Bryant said that people held their breath for a long time while she hung there until a veterinarian declared her dead.

Bryant also recounted that the sound of the chain breaking and Mary's hip cracking sent a chill up his back and would haunt him until the day he died. And he was a toughened mountain man. Some people left in disgust because of what they were seeing.

A huge hole was excavated near the railroad shop, and Mary was quickly buried. The exact spot has been forgotten, and the grave was unmarked. It was not something the town of Erwin wanted to boast about. Asphalt now covers the old train yards. Some locals think that the site of the burial may be where the Unicoi County Public Library now sits.

As you might expect, then the finger-pointing started. Some blamed the Circus owners, others the railroad for being an accomplice, and others for Kingsport sending the problem to Erwin, and others blamed the Sparks for letting an untrained person tend to her. In any case, when the dust settled, it was the town of Erwin that had its reputation smeared the most.

The gruesome story about Mary was published in local newspapers, the *Knoxville Sentinel*, and then spread in the news media across the globe.

Of course, if anything like this were to happen today, the circus owners likely would be locked up and the jail key thrown away. Or hung by a vigilante crowd. The cruelty of Mary falling to the ground with a shattered hip and wailing in horrible pain is unfathomable and certainly would have repercussions in today's animal rights world.

In recent years, Erwin has made a strong effort to recover from that early, bizarre, and macabre image of their community.

Unable to escape the reality of what had happened, they initiated an event they call the *Erwin Elephant Revival* in Mary's honor. They auction off elephant statues painted by local artists. The money from this effort is donated to several charities, especially the *Elephant Sanctuary* in Hohenwald, a town south of Nashville. Hohenwald is also the location where Meriwether Lewis, a member of the Lewis and Clark Expedition, died. He's buried nearby.

Is this story really true? Did it happen for real? I'm sorry to say, yes. After reading this, it should be evident that truth actually can be stranger than any fiction you could think up.

INTERESTING AND CRAZY APPALACHIAN NAMES

Everyone knows that Southerners can get a little creative with their names. Sometimes by a lot! What are some of the most interesting first names that you've heard? What is yours? What about nicknames? Either way, all of us have had to endure names and (often) nicknames that were given to us by others. Some names are passed down for generations.

Many of the names we go by are timeless and loved by all. A lot of them are quintessentially Southern or Appalachian. Examples would be Georgia Mae, Fannie Mae, Elli Mae, Ethel Mae, Ida Mae, Daisy Mae, Edna-Ruth, Billy Bob, Gomer, Zeke, Betty-Lou, Ruby-Jo, Bobby-Joe, Billie-Jean, Peggy-Sue, Levi, Hattie, Inez, Imogene, Zoe, Lulu, Jed, Angel, Elmira, RJ, JR, JD, TJ, CJ, BJ, and, of course, Elvis (the Pelvis).

Also, some names are shortened or pronounced differently from how they are spelled. A few examples are Berthy (Bertha), Sairy (Sara), Shermy (Sherman), Dottie (Dorothy), Mandy (Amanda), Zeb (Zebedee), Az (Azariah), Cas (Charles), Bubba (brother), and the list goes on.

Of course, a few names are pretty strange to flatlanders who live in the cities…but they still carry meaning for us and our loved ones. Zoah-Rosilla, Leander-Enoch, Narcissus-Priscilla, Lavinia, Uranah, Sophronia, Jabella, Drusilla, and perhaps Othel and Fredonia.

Often, there are interesting stories associated with nicknames such as Booger, Red Dog, Bunny, Littlun', Popcorn, Chochi, Skipper, Skeeter, Sissy, Bitsy, Scooter, Guppy, Frog, Toad, Mutt, Stubb, Dink, Pinkie, Stormy, Hot Lips, and on and on.

Some cute, intimate nicknames are reserved for our closest friends, lovers, or spouses. Due to their implied meanings, these may only make sense to the people involved. Although I suspect that the list is long, I'll just mention a few: Pookie, Button, Trixie, Cookie, Cuddles, Dumpling, Love, Sugar Lips, Cupcake, Puddin', Hun-Bun, Hotsie, Sassy, Punkin', Tootsie, Tiger, Snookums, Frisk (Frisky), and a ton of others I won't print.

SOUTHERN YAUPON TEA: THE FIRST JOLT DRINK

Yaupon Tea is one that you should consider trying, and it may grow wild near you. It is known by several names, including Carolina Tea, Indian Tea, and Apalachine Tea. It has a unique flavor and offers a "kick" from caffeine, but without the jolt effects often associated with caffeine. Compared with coffee, it contains a third less caffeine and is smoother and gentler. It's rich in antioxidants, which are believed to help reduce inflammation and improve one's focus and memory. It also contains theobromine, a mood-enhancing drug. A few studies suggest that yaupon tea may help protect against certain types of cancer.

This historically significant beverage is made from the leaves of the wild Yaupon Holly plant, and grows in Texas, Oklahoma, Louisiana, Arkansas, Mississippi, Alabama, Georgia, Florida, South Carolina, North Carolina, Virginia, and parts of Tennessee. Yaupon is the only native plant in the USA that contains naturally occurring caffeine.

It was widely used by early pioneers and many Southeastern tribes, including the Cherokee, Chickasaw, Creek (Muscogee), Choctaw, and others. Native Americans frequently consumed a strong version in religious ceremonies. In an extremely high concentration, it was known as the "Black Drink." Depending on the potency of the Black Drink, it could have euphoria-inducing properties or emetic results. Emetics, which induce vomiting, sweating, and urination, were believed to help purify the body and spirit by removing physical and spiritual impurities. And it contributed to the plant's scientific name (Ilex vomitoria). This potent version was used in purification rituals, council gatherings, and sometimes to get hyped before battle. However, in less radical preparations, it's a delightful tea with many positive advantages. As you might suspect, it was also a popular trade item in the early days.

Although a few claim to have added yaupon flavoring to moonshine, it's unknown just how safe (or unsafe) that might be because the "mood-enhancing" properties of yaupon could get mixed up with moonshine's "alcohol-induced antics." We don't recommend moonshine in any form.

Here's how to make yaupon tea:

Ingredients:
- Fresh or dried yaupon holly leaves (but not the berries)
- Water
- Sweetener, as desired

Instructions:
- If you have access to yaupon holly plants, you can harvest the leaves yourself. Or you can purchase dried yaupon leaves from online sources.

- If you have fresh leaves, let them air dry on a baking sheet for a few days. Alternatively, you can dry them in a low-heat oven (150-200°F) for a few hours, until they are crisp.

- Then you steep about a teaspoon of dried yaupon leaves for each cup of water in a teapot or infuser. Pour hot water (170-180°F) over the leaves and let them steep for 4-6 minutes, or adjust the time to suit your desired strength. Adjust the steeping time to your taste preference. Another method is to simmer the leaves in a pot of water for 5-10 minutes. The longer you simmer, the stronger the tea (Note: Don't make it as strong as Native Americans did, unless you're a fan of "having your system cleansed" or performing a war dance).

- Strain the tea into a cup and drink it plain. Alternatively, depending on one's preference, sweeteners or flavorings such as honey, mint, or lemon can be added.

Yaupon tea has a smooth, earthy flavor with a slight natural sweetness, making it a delightful and healthy beverage. It can be enjoyed either hot or cold. When I lived in Argentina, we drank Yerba Mate, which is another plant in the holly family. I found the taste similar to Yaupon. The aroma is also reminiscent of roasted grain or nuts. Interestingly, in South America, Yerba Mate is sometimes steeped in hot milk to create a refreshing cool-weather drink. It's an acquired taste, but I don't see why milk wouldn't work with yaupon.

Uncle Nathan always took delight in describing yaupon tea to those who'd not tried it before. The unique and pleasant flavor varies depending on how the leaves are processed. Nathan's recipe was for roasted yaupon leaves and had a robust, nutty, and slightly smoky taste with the aroma of roasted hickory nuts. It is less astringent than traditional black or green teas

Y'all be good now…and if you cain't be good…you know….

A NOISY, SPEED DATING FREE-FOR-ALL

Nearly every summer, a unique phenomenon impacts many parts of Appalachia and the Midwest...katydids and cicadas! Pointy-headed college professors may differ in their opinion, but as far as I'm concerned, they're more or less the same are thing, even though they look and sound different. Both are very loud and obnoxious.

Actually, katydids are usually green and look sorta like fancy grasshoppers or crickets, with wings that resemble leaves. Cicadas, on the other hand, are fatter and rounder and are usually black. I love the bulging, bright red eyes of the cicada, probably because you know they're looking at you. In some seasons, the eyes are black. I'm not positive why Mother Nature does that, but I'm pretty sure it has something to do with sex. The black-eyed ones don't hatch and court in a cluster-love-fest. I won't let my daughters use red eye shadow.

When in season, millions of these creatures will start crawling out of the ground or trees, singing their arousing mating songs and engaging in courtship. Interestingly, in addition to being amazingly prolific, cicadas are the loudest insects on earth, and when you get hundreds of thousands in your neighborhood singing together in a chorus, it's magical. However, the magic doesn't last long before the noise starts driving you crazy.

The cicada song is about 100 decibels. That's as loud as a lawnmower with a bad muffler and a little less noisy than a heavy metal rock concert, but not as irritating.

The katydids have a high-pitched, staccato-like "song" made up of halting clicks which sound like someone saying, "Ka-ty-did." All this ain't bad for ugly bugs that are only an inch long with a four-inch wingspan.

Their buzz is enchanting until you try to concentrate on anything else or sleep. Either way, you'll be amazed…and deafened. According to something I once read in the New York Times, if you could line all the cicadas up from a large hatch, they'd reach the moon and back more than 30 times! That's way more impressive than my ex-girlfriend's lipstick collection.

I've heard that, in some places, there may be more than a million cicadas per acre. I'm not good at math, but I think that's about 25 or 30 bugs per square foot. Last year's cicadas belonged to Brood X. They hatch in different broods. The timing of the emergence of Brood XIX will depend on the weather. These periodic insects emerge every 13 or 17 years. I'm not sure why they emerge in odd-numbered years, but I think it may be Biblical or have something to do with witchcraft.

I also heard that this year, two broods could emerge from the ground simultaneously. The last time this happened was in 1803, 221 years ago.

They don't sting or bite and are safe to handle. As kids, we spent many fun hours playing with them. We'd tie strings to a rear leg and let them fly around like a kite, or let our cat, Kitty Tom, play with them. They also make excellent fish bait, but fish soon engorge and fill up on them, and then they're not as good for bait. But it beats digging worms.

Some mountain folk claim that the date of the first Katydid chirp in summer corresponds with the frost day the following September, but we didn't remember to keep track, so don't put any stock in that.

My momma was an intelligent woman, and she'd tell me some pretty exciting bedtime stories. They weren't always pretty, but I always thought they were excellent. I once asked her how Katydids got their name, and she told me the following (more or less).

"Once, they wuz a beautiful mountain girl by the name of Katy from Cocke County, Tennessee. She left the hills for a week to visit a friend near Nashville. There, she met and fell in love with a handsome guitar player who was trying to git a spot on the Grand Ole Opry. After exchanging a few letters, the guitar player visited her house to meet her family. She was head-over-heels in love with him and intended to marry him. While visiting at her East Tennessee mountain home, the good-looking git-fiddle player fell in love with the pretty mountain girl's younger sister, who was also a good-looker, and she also had the advantage of knowing how to play a lively dulcimer. After just a couple of songs together, they started some serious courtin' and talked of a blissful lifetime of making beautiful music together and breaking into the big time at the Ryman Auditorium. The jilted sister got really pissed off, and she invited the couple on a hike in the woods, killed them, and hid their bodies in a cave. No one had seen any of this, and everyone up and down the holler refused to believe that anyone as cute and innocent looking as the pretty mountain girl could have done such an evil deed. Listen closely because this is where things got interesting. All this coincided with a rare hatch of Katydids, and they loudly proclaimed in an incriminating chorus…"Katy did it! Katy did it!" And that, my son, is where them bugs got their names. Now go to sleep, afore I tan yore hide!"

We didn't have air conditioning back then, and we'd leave the windows open, so the chatter of Katydid's story of love and jealousy is forever embedded in my mind.

My momma had some strange bedtime stories, but I always thought they were good. If you read my story in Volume 2 of Musing Appalachia, you'll understand. The story is entitled "Stuff My Momma Told Me." It's mostly about "birds and bees," lovey-dovey stuff, and the many downsides of getting married, but you'll love Momma's warped sense of humor.

Aunt Berthy always claimed that cicadas embodied magic and were connected to the millions of people who had died and whose spirits lived in the ground, coming up to warn mankind that they, too, would one day be buried and resurrected.

Different cultures interpret cicadas (or katydids, if you prefer) with transformation, rebirth, and immortality. Apparently, the Cherokee Indians didn't buy into the concept of cicadas being reborn spirits of past relatives (like some tribes believe the coyote to be). Many tribes viewed them as a delicious delicacy and one of Mother Nature's richest sources of protein and eagerly ate them roasted or boiled.

When I was in Africa, I ate large roasted locusts (similar insects) and they're actually quite tasty…that is, if you like Cheetos without sugar or orange dye. We removed the wings and legs because the former tended to stick to the roof of the mouth, and the latter pricked the palate. I suspect that eating insects is an acquired taste born out of a necessity to survive in harsh times…sorta like eating oysters or stewed okra. In any case, when the swarm is on, it's easy to quickly harvest enough to fatten up several hungry armies in no time. There are written accounts of the Cherokees digging up the young cicadas, taking off their legs, and frying them as a celebratory treat. I guess that makes sense if you had to wait 13 years or so for the next swarm. Others made pies or pickled them for later use. Actually, they did this with a variety of insects, including wasps, but cicadas and katydids were a plentiful gift from Heaven. Well, not really Heaven since they came from the ground, but a gift, nevertheless. If you've ever eaten ant larvae, you'll quickly appreciate eating the giant cicadas. Experts suggest that you eat the fresh ones while they are white, just emerging from the ground, and before their shell hardens.

Aren't you glad that you read this?

Cicada Speed Dater

MAMAW'S HILLBILLY CAVIAR

I'll share with you an old-time recipe for Mamaw's Enchanted Hillbilly Caviar. Uncle Nathan summed it up by saying that the dish was "...like a woman I met early on in my life. She wasn't much on looks, but she could cook better'n anybody you could ever share a table with, and she was downright tasty, so I married her!"

Whenever Mamaw was cooking, I could smell the food within a hundred feet of her cabin, when she cooked with wild ramps, two hundred feet. For breakfast, she always served sawmill gravy and cathead biscuits. But, for lunch, cornbread and beans were the staples. There was ALWAYS a pot of beans on the stove and cornbread waiting nearby. For special occasions, she'd sometimes make Hillbilly Caviar, a bean dish that was not only delicious but also colorful and healthy. It was a sure hit at any gathering.

Hillbilly Caviar has lots of variations. It's also known as Redneck Caviar and is a mixture of beans, corn, tangy vinaigrette (if desired), and various other ingredients, depending on how adventurous you want to be. It is delightful to eat and easy to make.

The recipe is simple. Two or three kinds of beans are typically used, and black-eyed peas are usually added. Black beans add lots of color, as well as robust flavor to the recipe. A variety of other ingredients are important, too, and yellow kernel corn adds nice color. Various bean varieties work well, such as Great Northern, Navy, and Butter Beans, among others. A platter of moist mixed cooked beans may be topped with a tangy dressing and served with cornbread. A homemade dressing recipe follows below, but Italian works in a pinch. If the beans come from a can and/or are pre-cooked, you don't need to cook them. A variation that Mamaw liked was a "wet version" that was more soupy. For this, the recipe was simmered, and a liquid of her preference was added. The "wet" version is my favorite for taste, but it doesn't look as pretty. The dry version is prettier and good with nachos. It's also tasty.

Pinto or "Soup Beans" are an indispensable staple in any country home and have a mild and slightly nutty flavor. And their texture is smooth and creamy. They're "OK" in Hillbilly Caviar, but more colorful beans that don't "cream up" are more delightful to look at…but they all taste good. Mamaw preferred Greasy Beans, Turkey Craw Beans, and Lazy Daisy Beans. These were always accompanied by Black-eyed Peas and, sometimes, Garbanzos.

Less common and "very Appalachian" are the Greasy Beans. They have a rich, earthy flavor with a hint of nuttiness. They are more flavorful than regular beans. They get their name from smooth, shiny pods that "appear greasy" but aren't.

Turkey Craw Beans are an heirloom variety with an interesting Appalachian history and are known for their speckled appearance and hearty flavor. Legend has it that, in 1802, a pioneer from Kentucky shot a wild turkey and found a few bean seeds in its gizzard (craw). Since then, the resultant bean has been popular in the mountainous regions of Tennessee, Virginia, and North Carolina.

Lazy Daisy Beans are uncommon but are easy to grow and have a delicious flavor. The seeds are white, pretty, and taste great.

Case Knife Beans are named for long, flat pods that resemble a Case knife. They are also an old Appalachian variety. Other popular heirlooms include Old Joe Clark Beans, Shelly Beans, Cornfield Beans, Gizzard Beans from Haywood County, NC, and the list goes on. More than 175 varieties of heirloom beans have been identified in Appalachia. If any of the beans mentioned sound interesting to you, most seeds can be ordered from Amazon or specialty online seed companies.

Most people don't know this, but moonshine can also be made from beans. That makes sense, given that all the beans are grown in Appalachia. Traditionally, corn is preferred, but bean-based moonshine is known for having a faint but attractive pea aroma and taste, making it unique. Uncle Nathan experimented with beans during a bad year but found that acquiring and processing corn was less labor-intensive and cheaper. Also, malt is needed to help with fermentation, which is an extra expense. Finally, the faint aftertaste of corn-based moonshine on one's palate is an acquired taste that has been honed over many centuries.

Depending on Mamaw's mood and what she could find in her kitchen cabinet, she would sometimes experiment with her recipe and add cinnamon, cloves, nutmeg, vanilla, star anise, ginger, cardamom, allspice, bay, orange peel, or wild herbs she'd pick from the woods. And veggies when the mood struck her. Of course, these sometimes made for a complex and unpredictable flavor. Mamaw was a teetotaler and never added moonshine. On the other hand, Uncle Nathan added copious amounts to his cornbread and beans but usually consumed it directly and separately from a fruit jar.

HILLBILLY CAVIAR RECIPE INGREDIENTS:

- 2 cans (15.25 ounces) of cooked, mixed beans, rinsed and drained
- 1 can (15.25 ounces) black-eyed peas, rinsed and drained
- 1 can (15.25 ounces) yellow corn, drained
- 2 bell peppers of different colors (orange, red, or yellow), chopped
- (You may add jalapeño peppers for some heat)
- 1 chopped red onion (and/or ramps if you're near crazy)
- Avocado if you want it to be creamy (optional)
- 1/8 cup of chopped fresh cilantro
- ¼ cup olive oil
- ¼ cup granulated sugar
- ½ cup white vinegar
- Salt and pepper to taste

Also, as options, you also may wish to add a cup of cherry tomatoes, halved, and perhaps diced celery, and/or some chopped parsley

HILLBILLY CAVIAR DRESSING

(your tastes may vary but dressing is not always added to the Caviar "soup.")

- 1/4 cup olive oil
- 3 tablespoons vinegar
- 1 tablespoon mustard

- 1 teaspoon dried oregano
- Salt and pepper to taste

Instructions:
- In a large bowl, combine the beans, black-eyed peas, cherry tomatoes, red bell pepper, green bell pepper, red onion, celery, parsley, etc.
- Mix and pour the dressing over the bean mixture and mix well.
- Cover the bowl and refrigerate for at least an hour to let the flavors meld together.
- If making the soupy kind, cook it until it just starts to bubble then simmer.
- Serve chilled or warm with a side dish and enjoy!

Hillbilly Caviar

Food Pairing: Cornbread pairs wonderfully with this dish, as well as other soups and stews. Hillbilly Caviar prepared this way can be served as a side dish for a big meal. When I was growing up, often the side dishes were the main meal. It all depended on what food happened to be available at the time.

Y'all be good now…and if you cain't be good…you know…

BEING SOUTHERN, SOUTHERNESS, AND APPALACHIA

I have to ask, do you like pan-fried chicken? Gravy with biscuits? Coleslaw? Peach cobbler? Pecan pie? Most Southerners like them.

What about chicken gizzards, collard greens, cornbread, and macaroni and cheese? Now, let's up the ante a little. Do you like your cornbread crumbled up in buttermilk when you eat it? What about pinto beans and cornbread for breakfast? How about grits without sugar? Black-eyed peas with hog jowl? Mustard greens? Turnip greens? Hush puppies? Country ham and redeye gravy? Sorghum molasses? Sweet taters? Fried green tomatoes? Fried catfish? Or a Moon Pie chased with an RC Cola with a pack of Tom's salted peanuts chucked in the bottle?

Okay, that's probably good. Now, what about cracklings, souse meat, head cheese, ham hocks, wild turkey, venison, quail, cow's tongue, and (Heaven forbid!) baloney and weenies? (If you only knew what went into the making of those).

Foods tend to distinguish cultures, and the Southern culture is chock-full of good foods, many of which even the flatlanders have adopted and regularly eat. But there's more.

Ernest Hemingway once said, "In order to write about life, you must live it." It bothers me that so many Appalachians get a bad rap for being raised where they were and eating what they sometimes do…a bad rap by people who were not raised there and didn't experience what it meant to be raised Appalachian.

Actually, being Southern and being Appalachian are different. Both have fought negative stereotypes for generations, but the people who were raised in the back hills of the protective mountains and hollers of Appalachia seem to have fared the worst.

One has to ask what does it mean to be a Southern Appalachian? And does it relate to food? What is "Southerness?" That's a seldom-used word, and I wish there were an equivalent word for "Appalachianess" but, if there is, I've not come across it. This is in spite of more than 600,000 books being written about Southern Identity, which often includes us folks and our food from the Appalachian territories.

We've endured being called Rednecks, Hillbillies, Crackers, White Trash and Bible Thumpers. Those are derogatory terms often associated with being backward, ignorant, uncultured, poor hygiene, hostile, conservative, bigots…or eating some pretty crazy stuff.

Of course, those uncomplimentary terms about Southerners largely originated with misguided generalities that were initiated by mostly Northerners and Hollywood. Admittedly, they evoke one's interest and imagination and make popular movies for the entertainment of non-Appalachians.

Okay, I admit that Appalachians and Southerners, in general, are extraordinarily colorful characters, and we come in all kinds of packages. People from other places come to our mountains for vacations, family, or work. More than a few, being human, don't like some of our food or the way we talk. For sure, not everyone is a fan of eating okra, catfish, redeye gravy, or an occasional raccoon. I love all that food, but concerning 'coon meat, let me tell you, don't knock it until you've tried it. A skilled cook can turn it into a gourmet meal. There's a store just a mile from my house that sells raccoon meat, small, medium, or large. The same goes for other less popular but relatively exotic backwoods and tasty meats such as squirrel, groundhog, and even skunk meat. Properly fixed, they all can be delicious. Heck, it's just meat! I've even eaten crow. Obviously, some meats are an acquired taste, such as possum, wild ducks, and Canadian geese. If you can make a Green Winged Teal or a Goldeneye duck taste yummy, you need an award of some kind...but, if you could do so, you would make my point: How different foods taste is mainly in the fixing...and what you were raised with.

People outside of Appalachia tend to denigrate and make light of customs they haven't experienced firsthand. I'm confident that someone, somewhere, knows how to make possum and duck taste delicious. Therefore, I'm not going to knock it until I get a chance to try it. However, if you were to drink enough moonshine before dinner as an apéritif, I'm pretty confident that it would aggressively stimulate your appetite and prepare your palate for whatever kind of food you might throw into your mouth.

When I was in Africa, street vendors near the docks were selling barbecued Norway Rats on sticks, similar to large sausages with legs. Not being acquainted with their hygiene practices, I refrained from trying it, but I was tempted because the aroma was great, and I was hungry. Properly prepared, I'm confident that you and I could come to love it. But not being from that area of the world, it would be easy for us to criticize and make fun of that custom. How's that different than eating some of the meats available in your area? What about oysters? Did you ever wonder who ate the first one? What about buttermilk? Chocolate gravy? White gravy spread over fresh ripe tomatoes? Smooshed banana mixed with peanut butter and mayonnaise in sandwiches? Boiled peanuts? Pickled pig's feet? I love it all, but I married into a family that makes fun of some of my food preferences. Partly, it's what your momma fixed as you were growing up. I've mostly learned to live with the fact that everyone in the world doesn't have the same taste for good food.

On the other hand, I steer clear of foods that smell funny or I've not been properly introduced to. For example, Casu Marzu is an Italian dish that never caught on in our country like Pizza did. It's made from sheep's milk that's left to rot and attract flies; the maggots digest the cheese and make it soft and creamy. Some of the more squeamish people remove the maggots before eating. OK, how does cornbread smothered in buttermilk sound to you now?

Then, there's Jellied Veal from Sweden, which is made of ground-up veal, gelatin, and seasonings. It's cooked and placed in a mold to gel, then sliced and served cold. Some people don't like the texture or appearance of the meat. Wait! That's hardly different from Appalachian head cheese or souse meat, another of my favorites. Hey, I ain't knocking until I've tried it! Yes, jellied veal from Sweden sounds great! Probably. In the meantime, I'm sticking with head cheese and souse.

I didn't start out with the intent of writing about food, but I love eating. Especially Appalachian Southern food. It's my favorite pastime. I see that it's about lunchtime. Will an RC Cola serve as an apéritif in a pinch?

HILLBILLY ELEGY, "Y'ALL, ARE THEY KILLING US SOFTLY?"

Has your accent or where you're from ever had an adverse effect on you in school, or in the workplace, getting a loan, etc.? The topic of discrimination against Appalachians because of where we were raised and how we talk goes beyond politics. I've experienced discrimination over the years, and it has always concerned me. Luckily, I was able to survive and beat out the bigots I ran across in life. I hope that we can promote understanding and empathy instead of bigotry.

A bigot is defined as someone who is obstinate and intolerant when it comes to their personal opinions and prejudices. They frequently treat members of a certain group with intolerance or non-acceptance. Appalachians, hillbillies, religious groups, and racial groups are often the target of bigotry. Bigots are found in all parts of society and can be found everywhere. If you've never had an encounter with them, you may be living in a cave.

The term "elegy" could be used metaphorically, symbolizing a sense of loss for Appalachian culture, including our language.

Most Appalachians dislike being called "hillbillies" because of the negative stigma frequently attached to our mountain dialects. Appalachians have been fighting prejudice and negative stereotypes since the early 1900s. These have been exaggerated and perpetuated in movies, TV, and comic strips. A few examples include Li'l Abner, Snuffy Smith, Gomer Pyle, Deliverance, and The Beverly Hillbillies. Unfortunately, these have tended to shape people's beliefs about Appalachians. Misconceptions portrayed in the media too often present roadblocks for rural Appalachians who venture into the cities for work or education.

After World War II, many thousands of Appalachians seeking higher-paying jobs and a higher living standard flocked to destinations such as Detroit, Chicago, Cleveland, Cincinnati, Pittsburgh, and other industrial towns.

In the cities, society told the Appalachians that they needed to change their speech habits to be more "normal." They were often undervalued because of their dialect. This led to a lack of self-confidence and "code-switching," which denotes switching one's speech pattern to match one's audience. For example, when I first attended college, I soon felt compelled to change my speech pattern to match the language pattern spoken by the professors and the students around me. However, when I returned to my home in Appalachia, I would instantly and subconsciously start speaking the mountain dialect again. Poor self-confidence often leads to code-switching.

After being the first Hughett in the genealogical line to graduate from high school (Bulls Gap, Tennessee, Class of 1940), my father escaped the poverty of the hills of rural Greene County, Tennessee, and joined the Army. Academically, he was a high-achieving student, but going to school in those days did not come easily for a family with only a mule for transportation. He wore tattered work clothes in any weather and had to walk or ride a bicycle to and from his mountain home to school. Sometimes, he would spend the week in town working for folks in exchange for room and board.

He became a mechanic and test pilot in the United States Army Air Corps (which was the precursor to the United States Air Force). He also learned the trade of a machinist there. The skills he learned in the military served him well all his life. Mountain people were undoubtedly not dumb; they just lacked training for better jobs. After a debilitating plane crash, Dad was given a medical discharge and invited to take a job at the Oak Ridge National Laboratory in Tennessee as a master machinist with the Manhattan Project.

At the time, the Oak Ridge bomb-making facility was not referred to as a nuclear lab. On paper, Dad worked for the Tennessee Eastman Corporation, a contractor for a highly secretive initiative that would later be associated with the Oak Ridge National Laboratory. If you want to know more about this, you should see the 2023 movie, "Oppenheimer." Also, *Honeymoon in Oak Ridge* by Filmmaker Joe Tripic is a good documentary. However, the documentary "*Oak Ridge: 75 Years of the Secret City*" is available on YouTube and is excellent. It is probably not an exaggeration to state that there is not a person on earth who has not been impacted by the nuclear research and development that took place at the lab.

The scenario of mountain boys joining the military was mainly for the men, but not entirely. My great-aunt Berthy's daughter, Nova, joined the WACs (Women's Army Corps) and served in a non-combatant position. For her, this was also a way to escape the hills. Once the Appalachians left the military, most had acquired practical training, fresh perspectives, and new aspirations. The dream of moving on in life and buying a car and house with running water, a flush toilet, a refrigerator, and so on became achievable goals now that they were armed with marketable skills. As mentioned, after WWII, there was a mass movement of people from the hill country to jobs in factories and homes in the flatlands. The first departure occurred when the Great Depression forced many families to leave rural areas. Life for many Appalachians was never the same after the wars.

I apologize for the above digression. It was important to lay the groundwork for the sticky topic of accents and linguistic racism against Appalachians. I will not say too much about it and then shut up. In this day and age of political correctness, I sometimes get into trouble with things I say. However, you will understand if you were raised in Appalachia.

At one point, the Oak Ridge National Laboratory went so far as to offer "Southern Accent Reduction" classes. However, after a short while, the plan was scrapped when many employees were offended by the training program. The six-week course claimed to help workers "be remembered for what you say and not how you say it." Ask yourself, if your employer today encouraged you to enroll in classes on how to speak with an accent that the management felt was "acceptable for you," how would you feel?

Various people have responded to my stories about Appalachia and our unique speech patterns and have given examples of discrimination because of the way we enunciate our words and formulate our sentences. What works in Appalachia does not always go over well in Cincinnati. I mention Cincinnati because, at one time, discrimination in this Ohio town was so bad against Appalachians moving there to work that the town felt compelled to enact an official city ordinance to try and calm things down. Discrimination is not always just about race or religion. Have you experienced linguistic racism?

I never noticed it much while growing up in East Tennessee, but experienced a little when I taught at the University of Kentucky and Virginia Tech. It was not much of an issue there, although faculty who were raised and educated in non-Southern areas tended to look down on those of us who had not yet learned to suppress the residuals of speech passed down to us Appalachians from Shakespeare's time. As I mentioned in my book, Musing Appalachia (Available from Amazon), it was an issue for me from time to time. I had to work harder than my peers to prove my worth in the professional academic world of higher education. Luckily, I prevailed, but I often wonder how many Appalachians acquiesced to the pressures of the "stuffed shirts" and suffered being passed over for promotions, raises, or tenure because of negative and erroneous "hillbilly" perceptions?

On the other hand, I have to remind myself that linguistic discrimination is probably not intentional. Many people are unaware that they have biases. They tend to make judgments about others without even realizing they are doing it. Either way, it is too easy for Southerners with noticeable accents to feel the demoralizing effects of discrimination in the workplace, at school, or in other places.

A highway patrolman once stopped me in a western state for speeding, and the officer said, "Hmm, Virginia plates. That makes total sense. I am surprised that you hillbillies can even drive a car." Of course, I was not in a position to argue with the policeman who was poised to write me a citation.

Are Appalachians a minority culture? Relatively speaking, yes. However, that is changing as we marry city-bred spouses or move outside the culture where we were raised.

So, what is linguistic racism? Most agree that linguistic racism occurs when discrimination is repeatedly used against people based on the use of their language, their accent, or the way they talk. If you think about it, people who speak Arabic, Chinese, Spanish, or some other foreign language and have a thick accent are sometimes perceived as inferior to those with whom we are more accustomed to dealing. Some may even be mocked and called derogatory names.

Do we subconsciously commit subtle acts of linguistic racism? Multidialectism is a social reality. British English and American English may be one example. Another might be the accent of people from rural Louisiana compared with the Cajun accent, or any Southern state compared with someone from New York. I believe that we should not denounce accents but accept them as a linguistic and cultural asset, rather than something to be modified and "fixed," as was the intent of the Oak Ridge program. Not everyone will agree with me on this, and there are valid exceptions where basic or critical communications are seriously hampered or present safety issues. Air traffic controllers or medical professionals might be examples.

In general, linguistic shame and guilt might be replaced with linguistic pride. Embracing and harnessing different languages and varieties of accents can be a win-win situation and may even lead to solidarity rather than emphasizing distinctions to the detriment of minoritized groups. I should not look down on you just because you have a different accent or use words that I am not used to hearing.

Therefore, let us celebrate the traditions and customs that make Appalachia unique and share them with others. We can enjoy the food, music, art, and festivals that reflect Appalachian culture and invite our friends and family to join us. We could even learn some quaint new Southern expressions, idioms, and slang and use them in our conversations.

If you have waded through my tirade this far, I will end with a true story. When my grandfather was a young boy living in rural Mohawk, Tennessee, his parents wanted him to get some schooling. Few previous Hughetts in our family tree had that chance. His family was too poor to buy shoes, and my great-grandmother did not have a decent pair of pants for him to wear outside of the homestead. So, she had him wear a hand-me-down dress from his older sister to school. The dress was nicely crafted of flour sack material but did not have a pattern, so she thought that it might work in their financial bind. After a few days of schooling, the kids made fun of his clothes and language skills. They mocked his pronunciation, questioned his intelligence, and his teachers doubted his abilities. That made him feel unwelcome and inferior.

I can understand the clothes thing of wearing a dress, but at that time, learning the proper use of language was a vital part of why kids went to school. At any rate, Papaw was greatly embarrassed and quit going to school. He never returned. He eventually learned to read when he married, and his wife taught him. Despite his lack of formal schooling, he became a successful minister and got a nice job in a furniture factory. However, he could have achieved much more if he had obtained an education early on.

Here is where I may ruffle a few feathers. In today's schools, quite a few students come from foreign countries. Most have accents, a poor grasp of proper English, and may need help trying to fit in. I hope that we do not belittle anyone trying to pursue the passion of an education, hoping to make a difference in their lives and the world. Our accents reflect our identity, our culture, and our journey. Be proud of your heritage and the accents…and be kind to others who tread a difficult or different path.

¡Hasta la próxima, y'all!

ACKNOWLEDGEMENTS

I'm deeply grateful to the people about whom I write. I changed some names and a few places in order to keep peace in the family. Appalachians are some of the craziest and most interesting people you could ever encounter. Humor and strange happenings are daily affairs. My stories have two purposes: to entertain and to inform the reader about backhills customs and people I grew up with.

I can't list them all here, but there are hundreds of mountain people who have touched my life and amplified my worldview. I acknowledge my great aunts and uncles, cousins, Mamaw and Papaw, Aunt Dorothy, my Daddy and Momma, Earl and Sherry Carter, Dr. Glenn Wilde, and Janet Conrad. Janet is Aint Berthy's granddaughter and has shared many memories with me. Others also have shared stories, photos, and advice that have helped fortify my love for the people of Appalachia.

Frankly, if you remember how many teats there are on a possum and their configuration, I'd be happy.

Made in the USA
Coppell, TX
18 January 2026

67578219R00177